IMAGES
of America

SOUTH HOLLAND

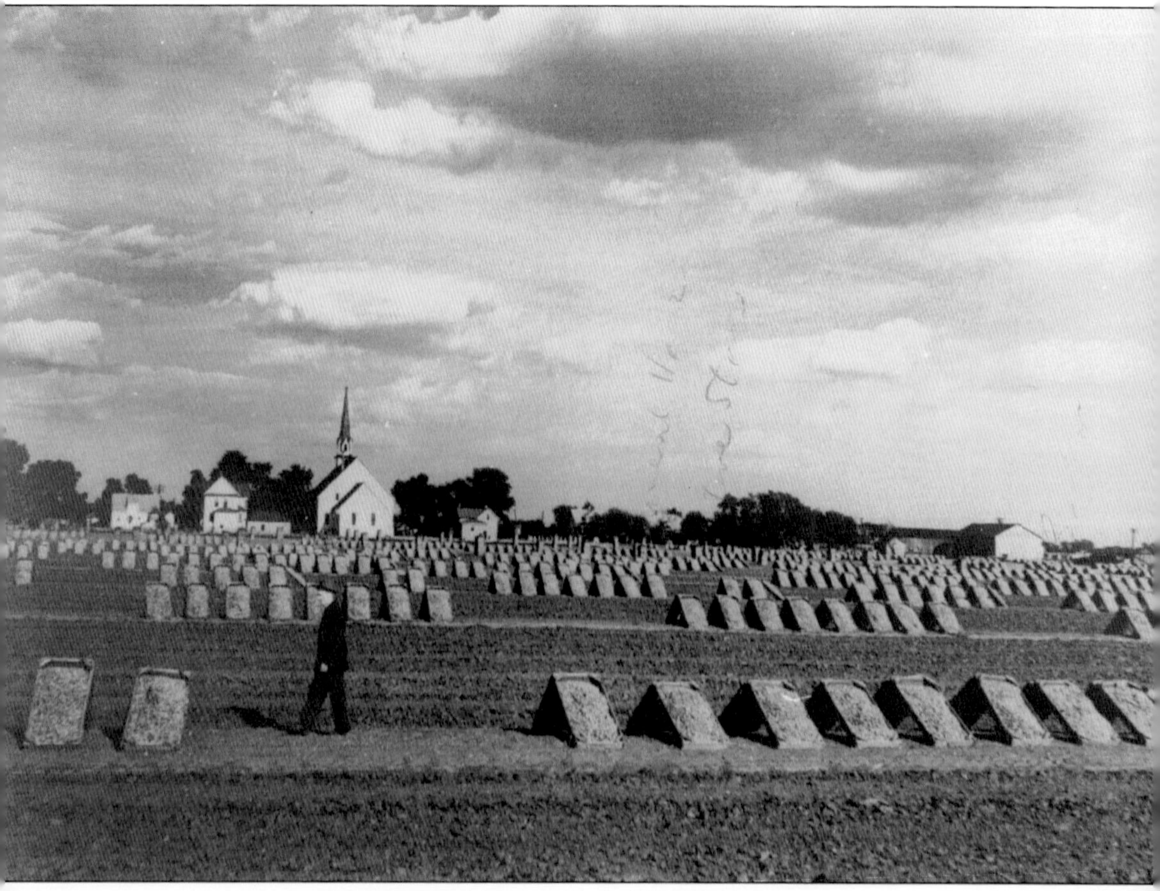

IMAGES
of America

SOUTH HOLLAND

Carrie Elizabeth Steinweg

ARCADIA
PUBLISHING

ISBN 978-0-7385-2334-7

Published by Arcadia Publishing
Charleston, South Carolina

Printed in the United States of America

Library of Congress Catalog Card Number: 2003103773

For all general information contact Arcadia Publishing at:
Telephone 843-853-2070
Fax 843-853-0044
E-Mail sales@arcadiapublishing.com
For customer service and orders:
Toll-Free 1-888-313-2665

Visit us on the Internet at www.arcadiapublishing.com

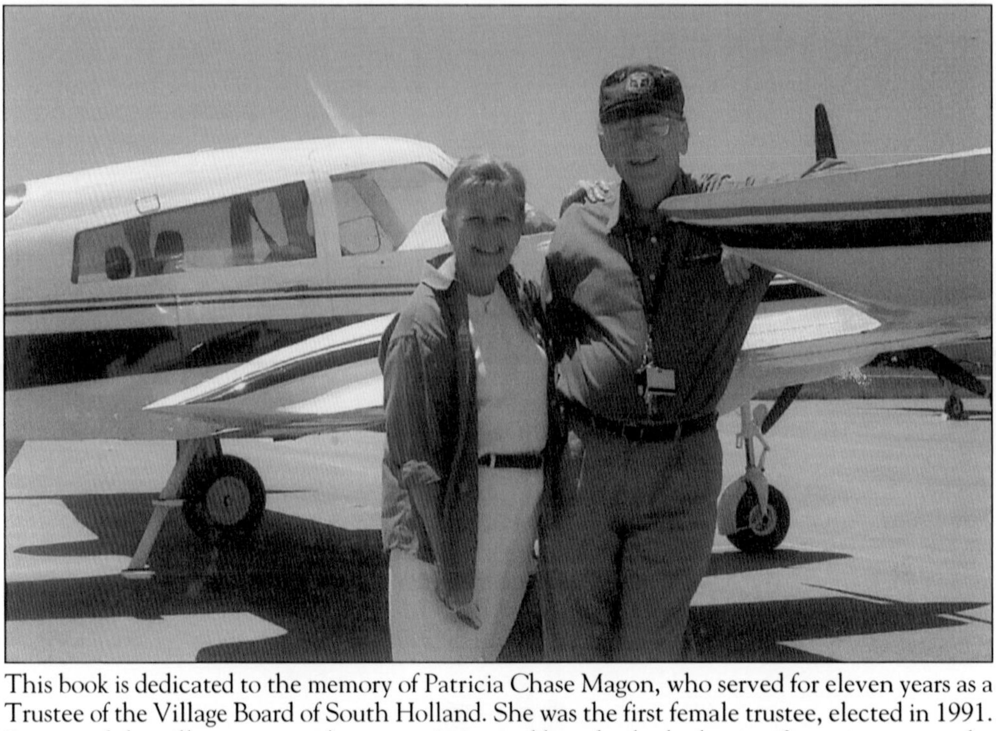

This book is dedicated to the memory of Patricia Chase Magon, who served for eleven years as a Trustee of the Village Board of South Holland. She was the first female trustee, elected in 1991. Pat served the village on countless committees and boards; she had a significant impact on the village and all those who knew her. She and her husband, John, and her four children all shared a love of aviation and became licensed pilots.

Contents

ACKNOWLEDGMENTS

This publication would not have been possible without the assistance of several individuals. Those who have worked with the South Holland Historical Society to preserve artifacts, photos, and documents have done a tremendous job. Thanks to their efforts, the proud history of this community can be shared with generations to come. Many thanks to Ed Smith, who was willing to spend time at the museum with me, allowing me to dig through old photographs and offering bits of history and wisdom along the way. Perhaps the person most responsible for the compilation of photos in this book is the late Dr. Carl Walvoord, whose hobby of collecting old photographs provided a visual history of South Holland in the early 1900s. In 1983 he donated his collection to the South Holland Historical Society. Many of the photographs in this book are from his collection.

Many others provided both photographs and memories that helped me in my completion of this book: Joan Summit, Administrative Assistant to Mayor Don DeGraff; Gary Lester, Principal of Thornwood High School; Harry and Alice Pals, Debbie Lameroux, Eric Kennedy, Jim Veld, Joan Van Baren, Luella Bader, Georgian Van Drunen, and Deputy Fire Chief Jim Altoff.

I should also acknowledge the role of Edna Ferber, whose 1924 Pulitzer Prize winning novel, *So Big*, made people outside of the area today known as South Holland aware of the intense pride of the Dutch immigrants who settled in the area and their contributions as hard working farmers and people of faith.

INTRODUCTION

In 1847, the first Dutch settlers made their way to what is now known as South Holland. The long journey often took up to eight weeks or longer in harsh conditions. Some of the families left comfortable homes overseas in search in search of religious freedom. Many family members were lost on these voyages to disease and were buried at sea.

Hendrik de Jong, his wife Geertje (De Vries) and their twelve children were the first to purchase land (at $1.25 an acre) in de Laage Prairie (Low Prairie), which also came to be known as Holland Bridge and finally South Holland in 1870.

Other families followed: the Killewingers, Scheuurwaters, Zobouts, and Paarlbergs. Antje Paarlberg is one of the best known of the early settlers. Having lost her husband at sea, she arrived in the United States with seven children to raise on her own. Her youngest, just an infant, died not long after her arrival in the U.S. The home built by her son, Pieter, still stands just off 170th Street and Paxton Avenue.

Those first settlers farmed the fertile soil around the Little Calumet River, harvesting a variety of vegetables and fruits. In the early days, many farmers would load up horse drawn wagons with their crops that would be taken to Chicago to be sold at the Water Street market. In the beginning, the trip would take three days.

Seeking an opportunity to freely follow their faith, fourteen families formed the Low Prairie Church, led by Rev. W.C. Wust, who traveled from Holland for the establishment of the church. The first building was constructed in 1848 on land donated by Hendrik de Jong. Several descendents of those original families still reside in the area and are still members of the church, today called First Reformed Church of South Holland. Services were still held in the Dutch language into the 1940s.

Several branches of that first church were later established in South Holland and as the community grew, churches of other faiths were introduced. However, the faith-centered values that were so desired by the early settlers continue to be prominent in the South Holland of the 21st century.

As the village grew, the livelihood of the community's men grew to include businessmen among the many farmers. They ran general stores, a butcher shop, a lumber company, a transportation company, and a paint store, as well as establishing businesses in other specialties. However, no industry was bigger in South Holland than that of the onion set.

Charles Waterman first developed the onion set industry in the 1890s. By 1913, he was contracting with about 60 farmers and shipping his onion sets throughout the country. By the late 1930s, there were 200 onion set farmers in South Holland and more yet by the early 1940s. South Holland was soon producing over half of the onion sets in the United States and earned the title, "Onion Capital of the World."

As the village's population grew and the Calumet Expressway was built, farmland evolved into housing subdivisions and the long legacy of farming began to fade away. By 1960, less than fifty farmers remained. Now in 2003, the farms that created this village are just a distant memory.

One of the institutions that has managed to stand the test of time is the South Holland Trust and Savings Bank, which is now located just across the street from its original location. Established in 1911, the bank was able to withstand the Great Depression and four bank robberies.

What started as a small enclave of Dutch immigrants, who preferred to remain separate from the rest of society, holding onto the ideals and beliefs that provided their strength and endurance, was not able to stop the wheels of modernization. South Holland today is somewhat like its neighboring communities in the suburban world. However, the town has been able to retain a bit of that close-knit and faith-centered feel that it has always been known for. With liquor establishments prohibited in the village, a Blue Law that restricts the operations of many businesses on Sundays, and the fact that South Holland has only single family dwellings continue the faith and family centered values that created South Holland. That these ideals continue to be realized in today's world is a testament to the determined and hard-working Dutch who built the village and their many descendants who have maintained that quality of life .

One

FARMING

"My father was one of the first onion farmers in South Holland. He farmed on the land from the river north to 147th along State Street. In those days it was all done by hand one row at a time."

—Harry Pals, grandson of Arie Pals, who settled in South Holland in 1864.

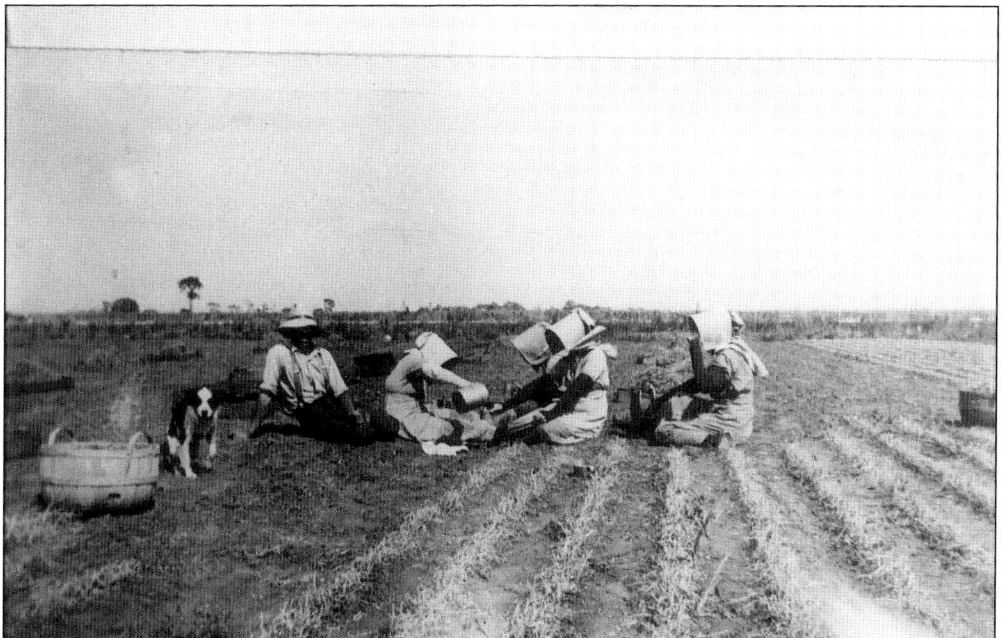

Some youngsters take a break from work during onion harvest. Breaks usually occurred at 9 a.m. and 3 p.m. during the 10-hour work day, which ran from 7 a.m. until 6 p.m. (Photo courtesy of South Holland Historical Society from the collection of Dr. Carl Walvoord.)

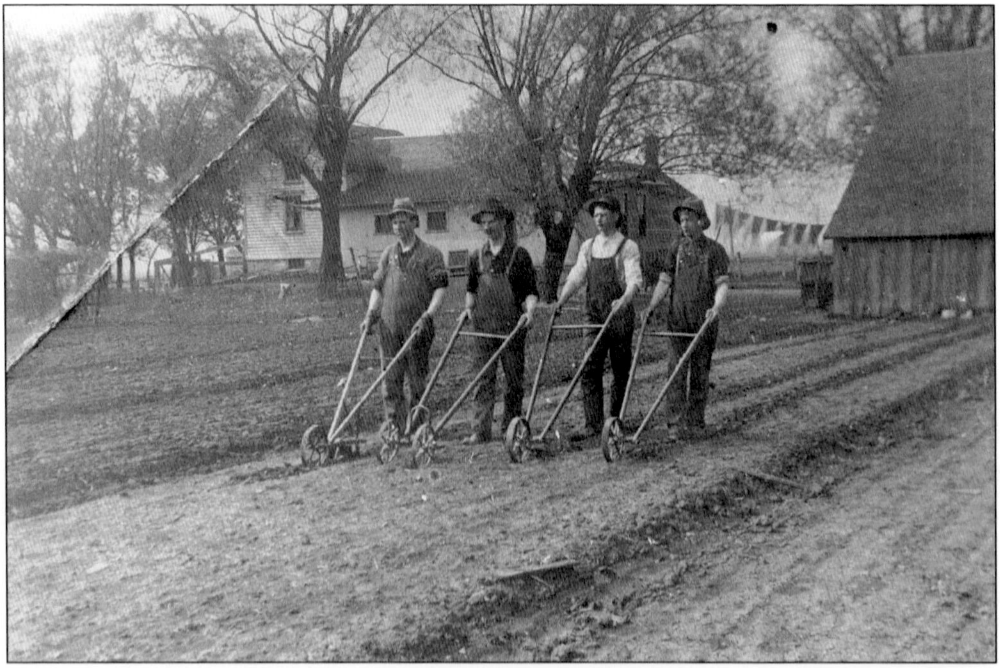

Using old hand cultivators on onion sets are John De Young, Henry K. De Young, John J. Van Der Aa, and Andrew Van Der Aa. The Van Der Aa brothers' parents were killed in a train accident. They then lived with Henry K. De Young. (Photo courtesy of South Holland Historical Society from the collection of Dr. Carl Walvoord.)

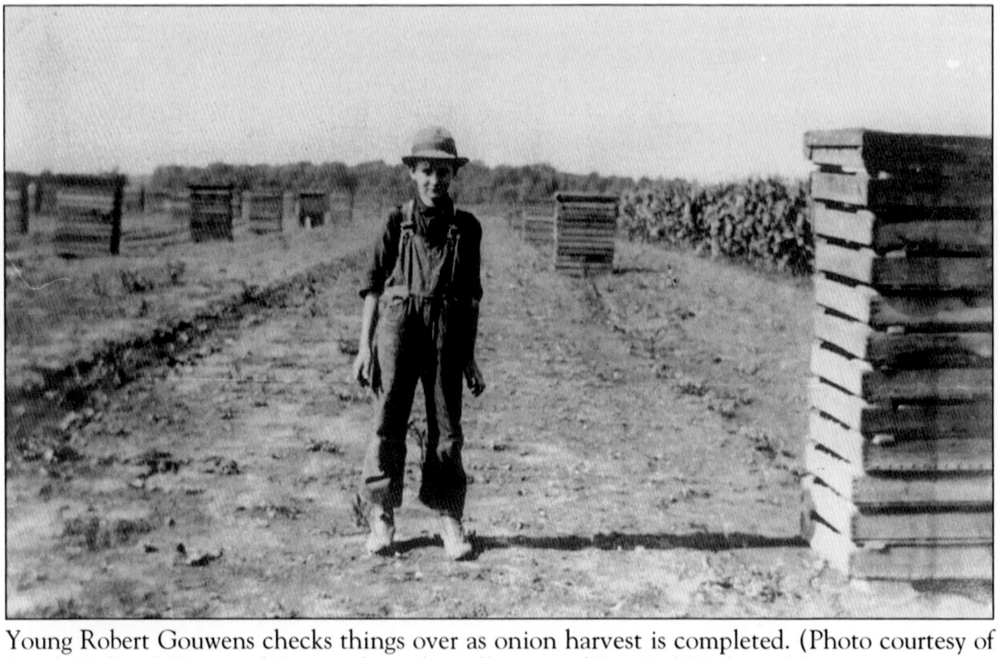

Young Robert Gouwens checks things over as onion harvest is completed. (Photo courtesy of South Holland Historical Society from the collection of Dr. Carl Walvoord.)

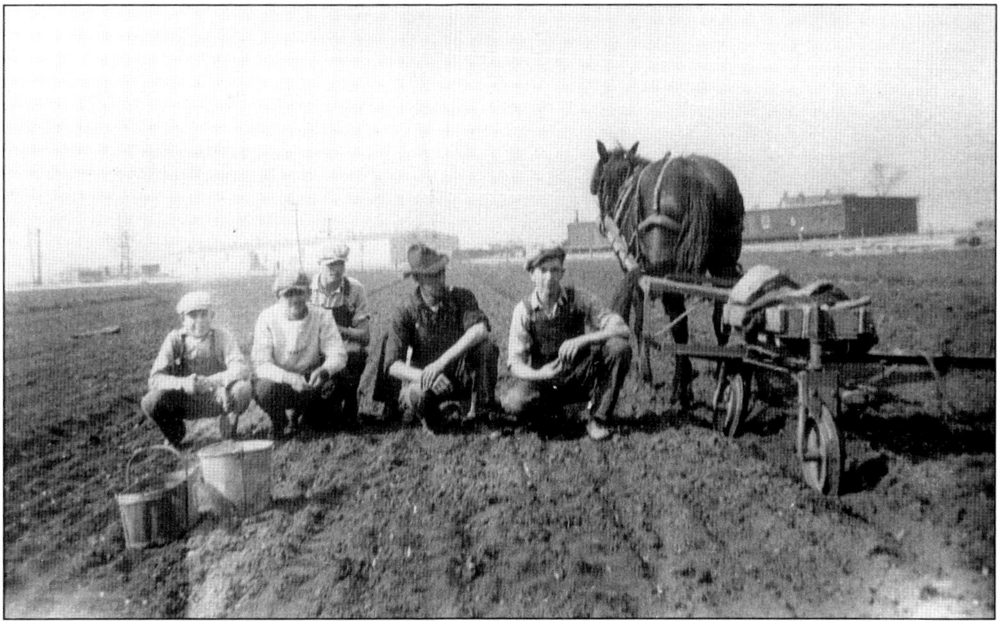

George Diepen, Anthony Dunker, John Muilenburg, John K. De Young, and Clarence W. De Young plant onion sets in this 1929 photo. (Photo courtesy of South Holland Historical Society from the collection of Dr. Carl Walvoord.)

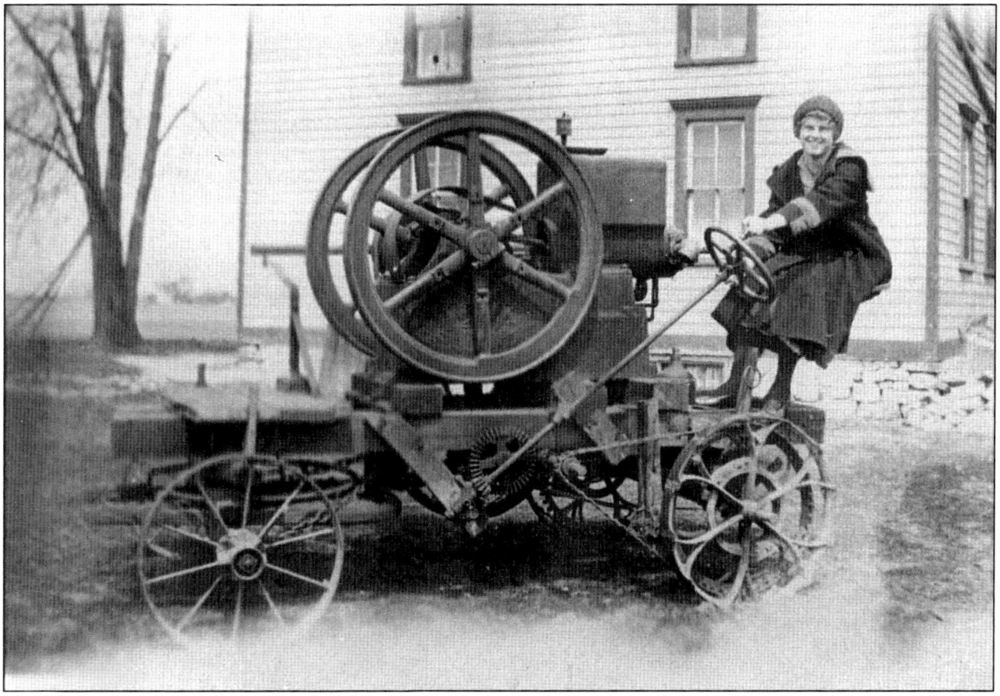

Jenny Anker at the controls of an old 15-horsepower Fairbanks-Morse gasoline corn stalk shredder, which had a water-cooled engine that was driven by a belt and started by spinning the fly wheel. It was used to shred corn stalks. (Photo courtesy of South Holland Historical Society from the collection of Dr. Carl Walvoord.)

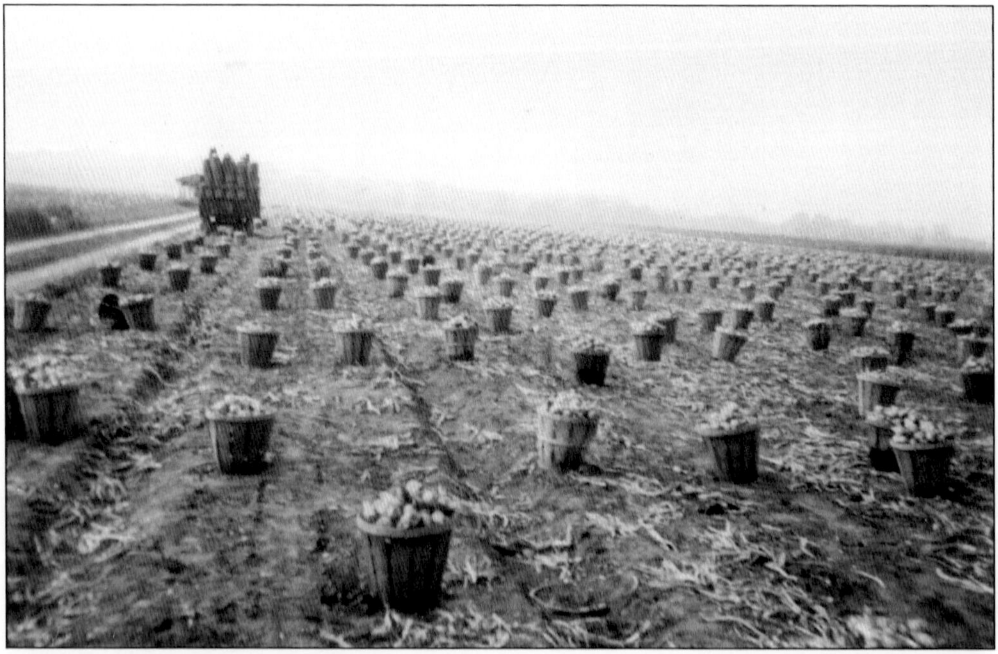

The back of this photograph reads, "A bumper crop of big onions on the farm of James De Graff. 625 – 50 lb. bags, 31,250 lbs. per acre." (Photo courtesy of South Holland Historical Society from the collection of Dr. Carl Walvoord.)

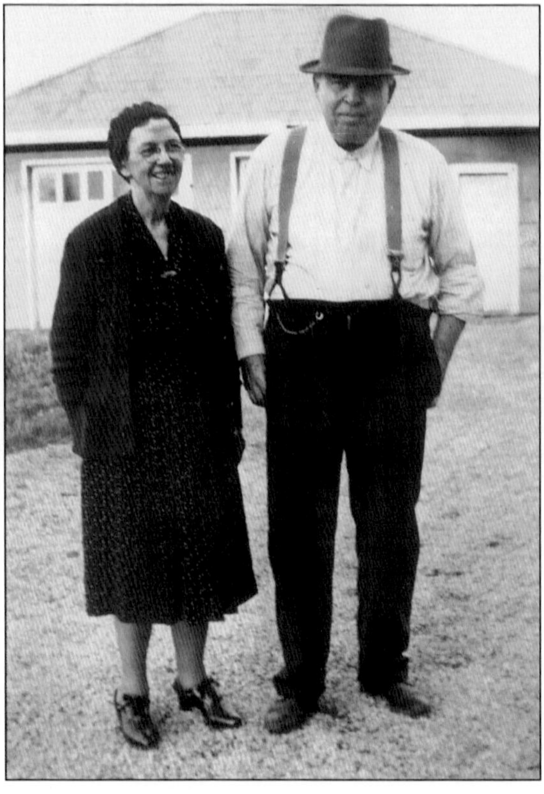

In 1856 Adriaan Van Baren, then 36 years old, came to the United States from the Netherlands. He settled in the Roseland area and his son, Gijsbert (Gise) and wife, Aaltje (Alice), later settled in South Holland and began growing and shipping onion sets. The couple had seven children—five sons and two daughters. All five boys continued working on the family farm. Pictured here are Gise and Alice Van Baren. (Photo courtesy of Joan Van Baren.)

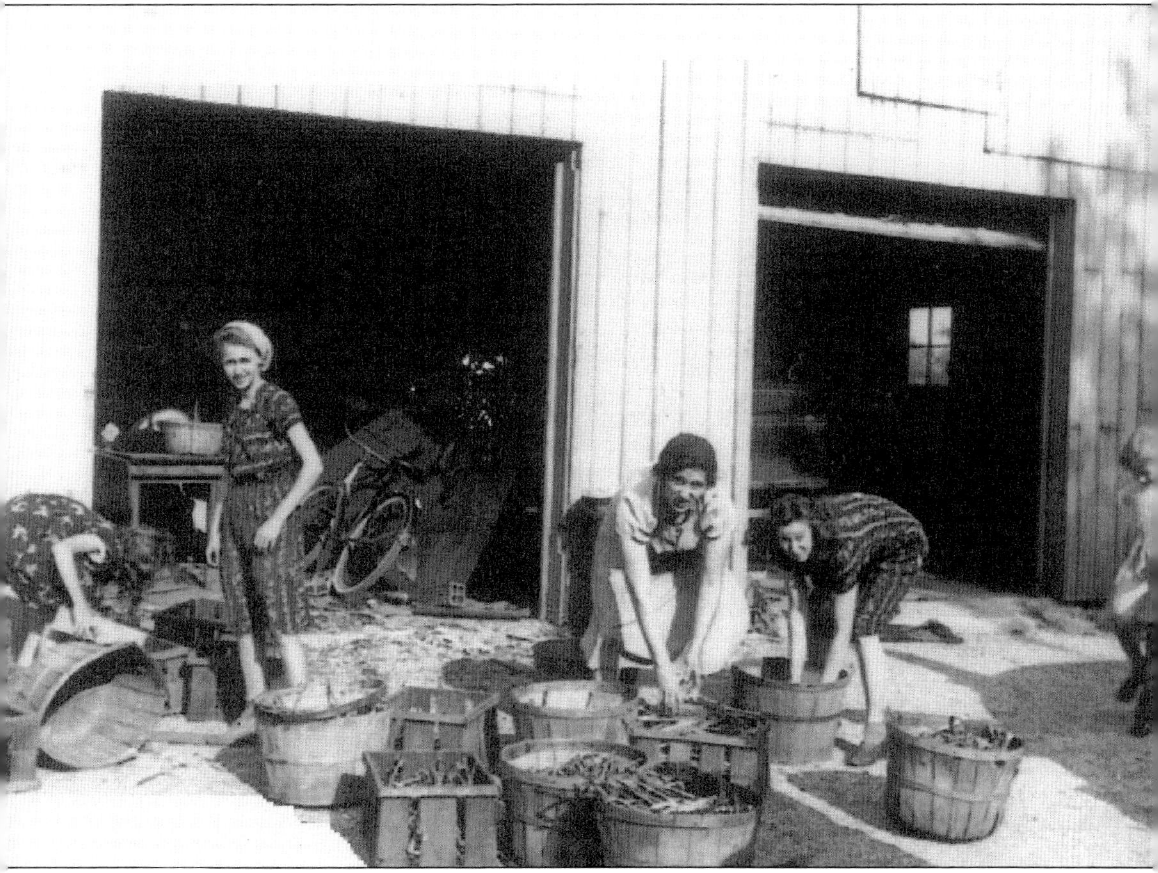

The women in the Van Baren family usually pitched in with farming duties, especially during World War II. Pictured here are Joan Van Baren Vroom (deceased), Agnes Van Baren Kuiper, Anna Holleman Van Baren, Willametta Van Baren Vroegh, and Sylvia Van Baren Hugen. This photo was taken in the early 1940s. (Photo courtesy of Joan Van Baren.)

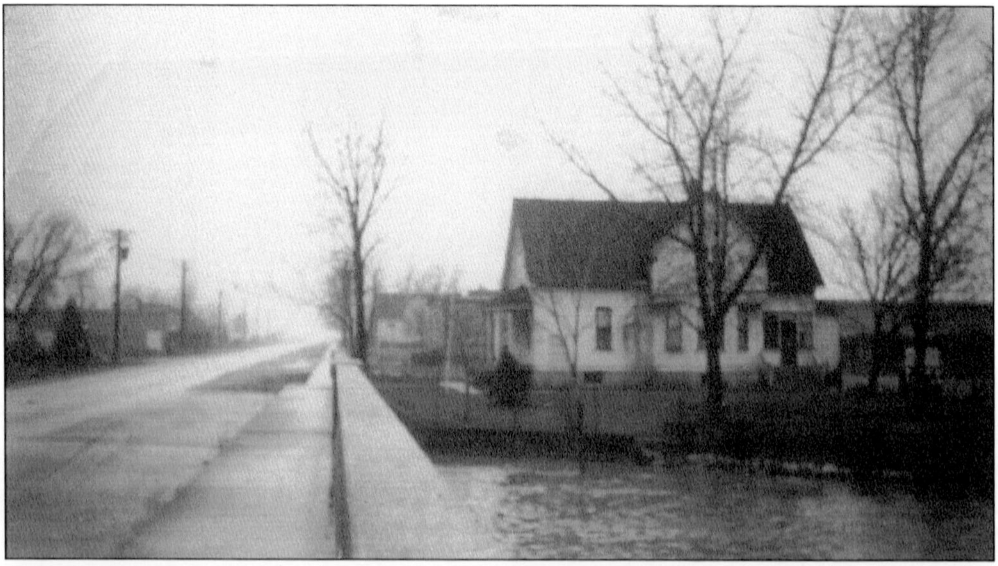

Around 1900, Gise and Alice Van Baren built a home on State Street, which still stands today. As their children got older and married, the family members built additional homes along State Street, where the family farmed. Pictured is the home in 1944. (Photo courtesy of Joan Van Baren.)

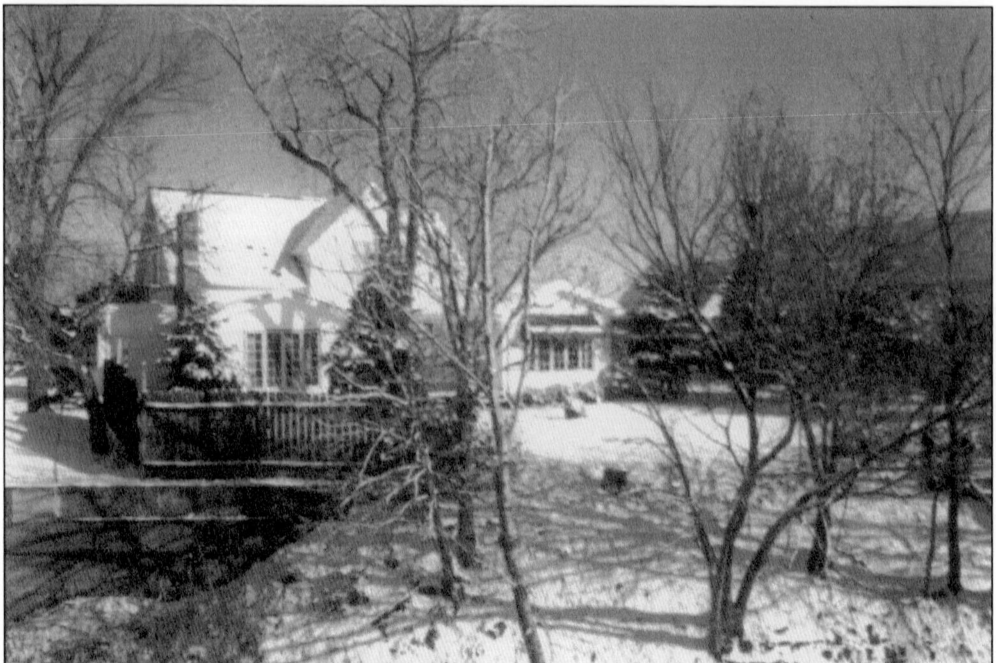

This is the Van Baren home as it looks today. Gilbert Van Baren, the grandson of Gise and Alice Van Baren, resides in the home with his wife, Joan. The family now operates a landscaping business from the property. (Photo courtesy of Joan Van Baren.)

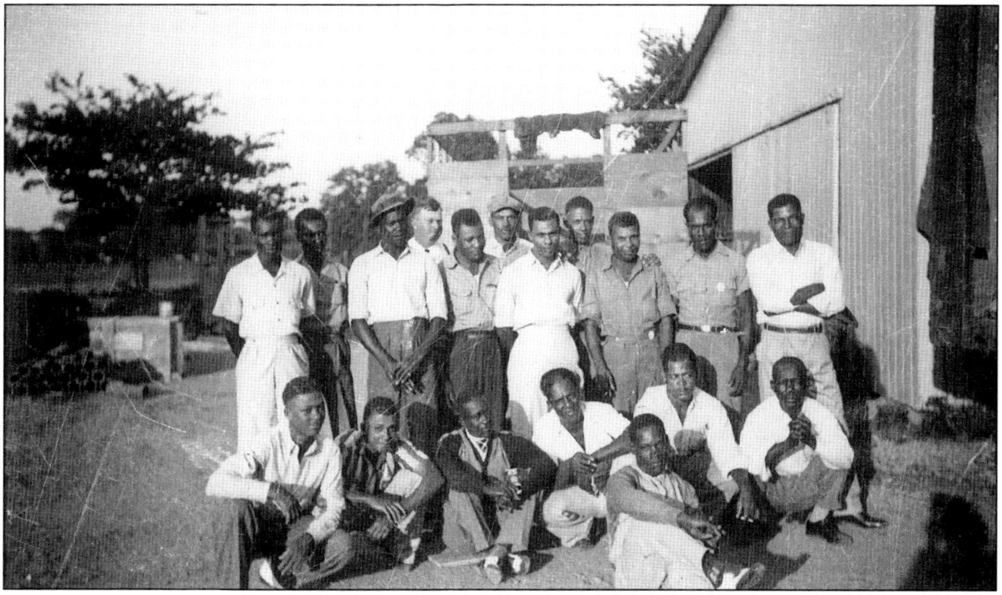

During World War II, when there was a shortage of local men to work on farms, the Van Baren family brought in workers from Jamaica. The group of nearly 20 men lived in a house that was located behind the Van Baren home. One of the men served as the cook and the others tended to farm duties. The workers remained until the late 1940s, when they returned to Jamaica. According to Gilbert Van Baren, many of the men continued to contact the family by mail for years afterwards, looking for work and an opportunity to return to the area. (Photo courtesy of Joan Van Baren.)

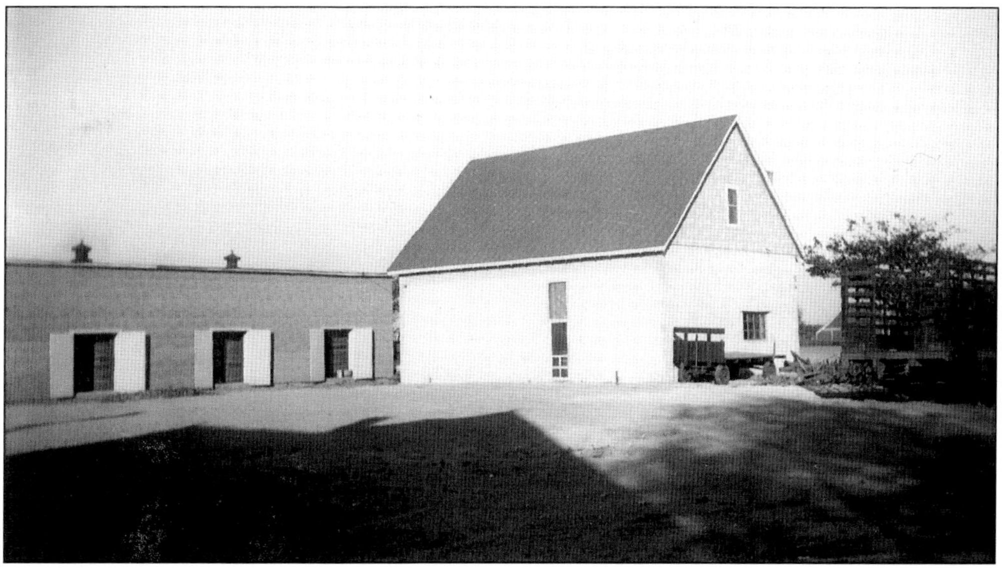

The white building, which was erected in 1944, served as living quarters for the Jamaican workers. The building is still standing and is now used as a garage. (Photo courtesy of Joan Van Baren.)

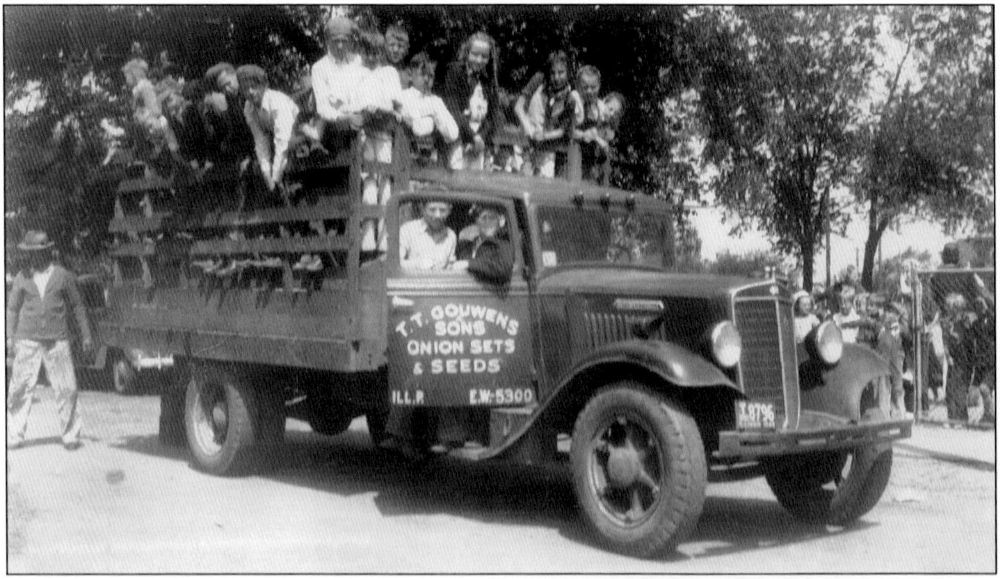

Onions were the major crop in South Holland, which earned the village the title of "Onion Capital of the World." Pictured is one of the trucks of T.T. Gouwens Sons in 1940. (Photo courtesy of Georgian Van Drunen.)

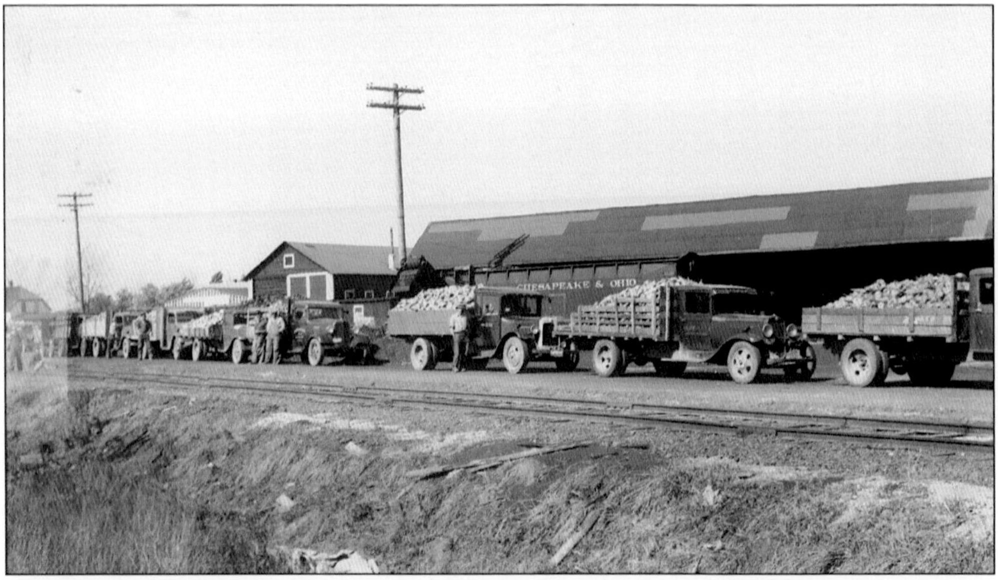

Trucks filled with sugar beets line up near the railroad, waiting to be loaded. According to a marking on the back of the photo, it was taken in October of 1938. (Photo courtesy of Georgian Van Drunen.)

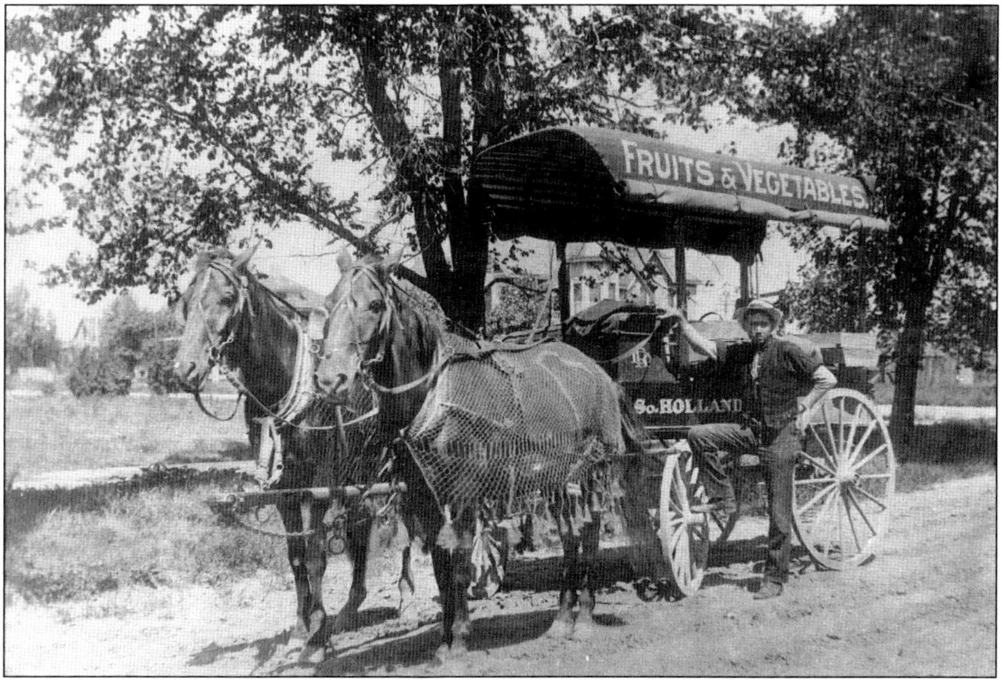

Dave Rinkema stands beside his fruit and vegetable wagon. (Photo courtesy of South Holland Historical Society from the collection of Dr. Carl Walvoord.)

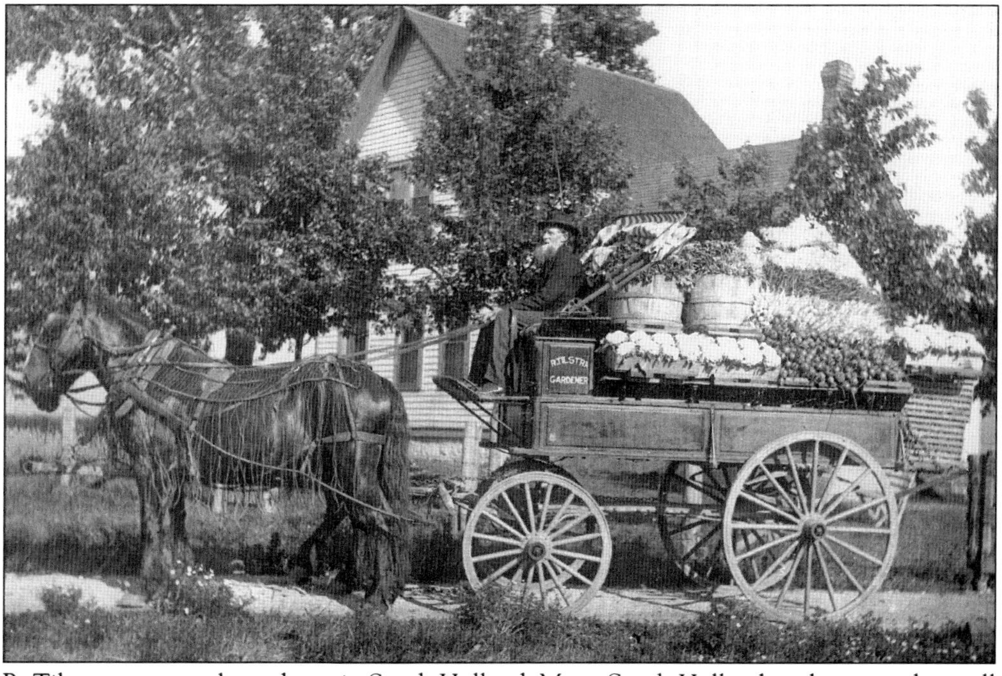

R. Tilstra was an early gardener in South Holland. Many South Holland gardeners made an all day trip to the South Water Street market to sell their crops. Here Mr. Tilstra's wagon is neatly loaded for a trip. (Photo courtesy of South Holland Historical Society from the collection of Dr. Carl Walvoord.)

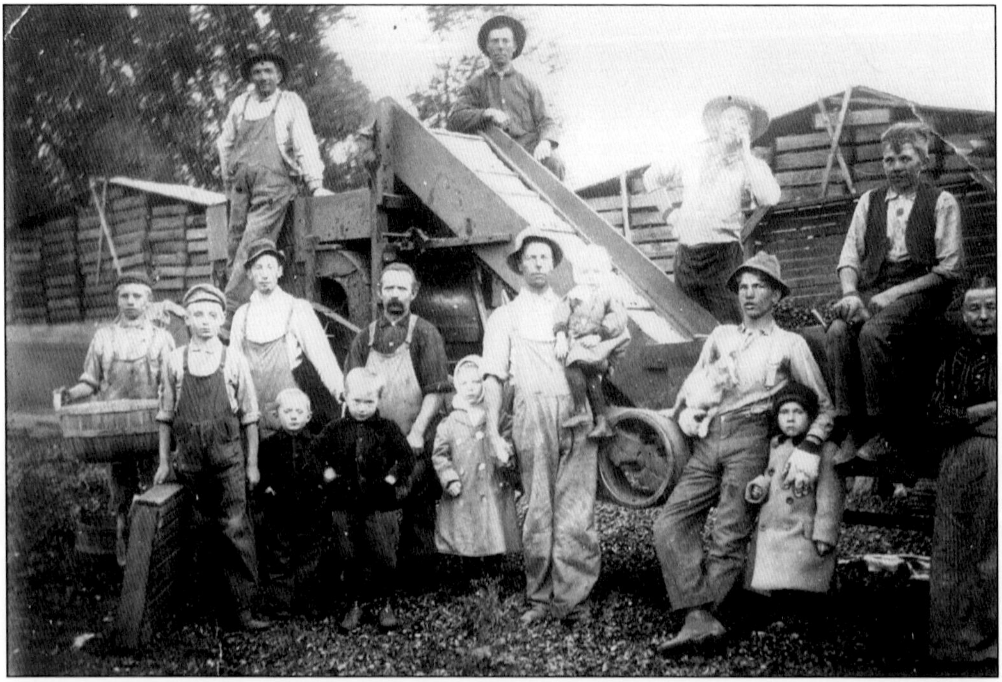

This is an early portable onion mill. Most milling was done in the warehouse, but this mill was also used outside. This picture was taken on the farm of Henry Meyer, who is in the middle holding his son, Gerrit. John Van Der Woude is on the left with his children Clarence and Frank. Mrs. Meyer, Sr. is on the far right. Some of the other individuals in the picture are Nick Ridder, R. Meyer, Herman Van Der Woude, Henry Ridder, Herb Meyer, Minnie Meyer, Ben Voss, and Roy Van Der Woude. (Photo courtesy of South Holland Historical Society from the collection of Dr. Carl Walvoord.)

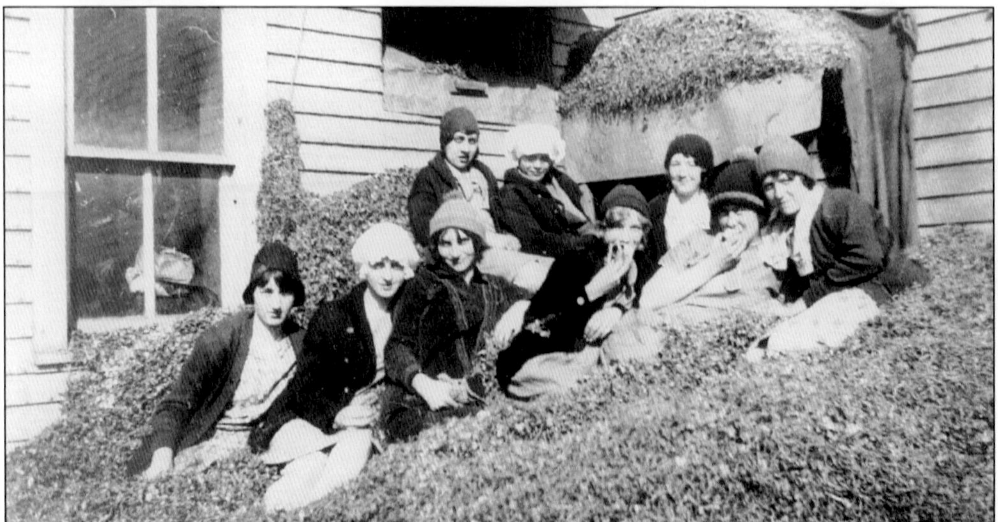

These girls are sitting on the pile of chaff that the onion mill blows out while milling onions. The girls picked out lumps of mud and sprouts while the onions passed by on a belt. (Photo courtesy of South Holland Historical Society from the collection of Dr. Carl Walvoord.)

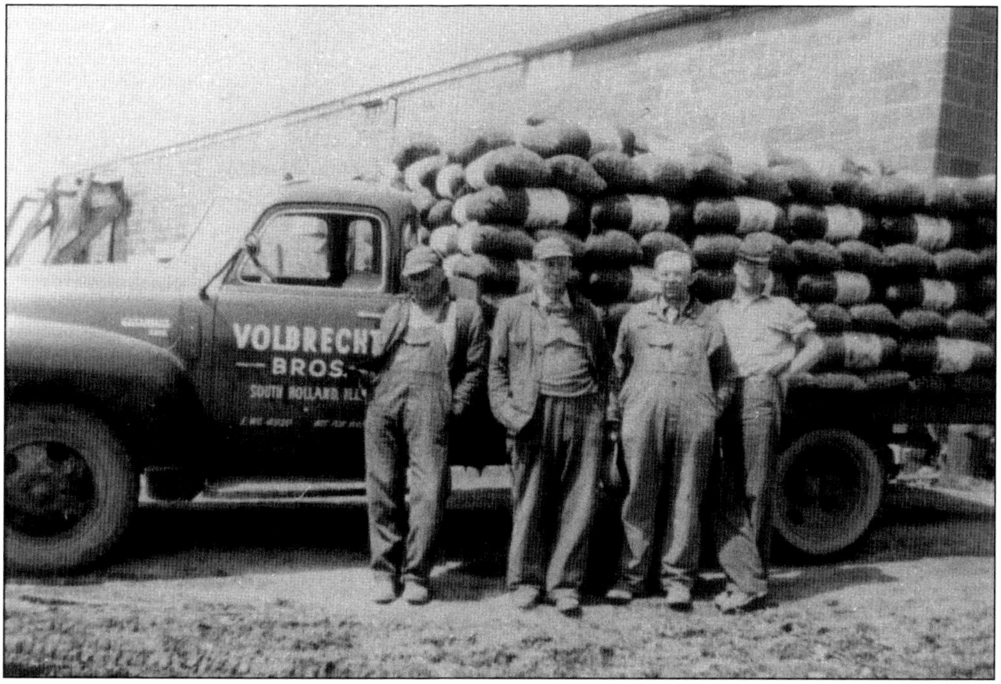

A truck from the Volbrecht farm is ready for delivery. (Photo courtesy of South Holland Historical Society from the collection of Dr. Carl Walvoord.)

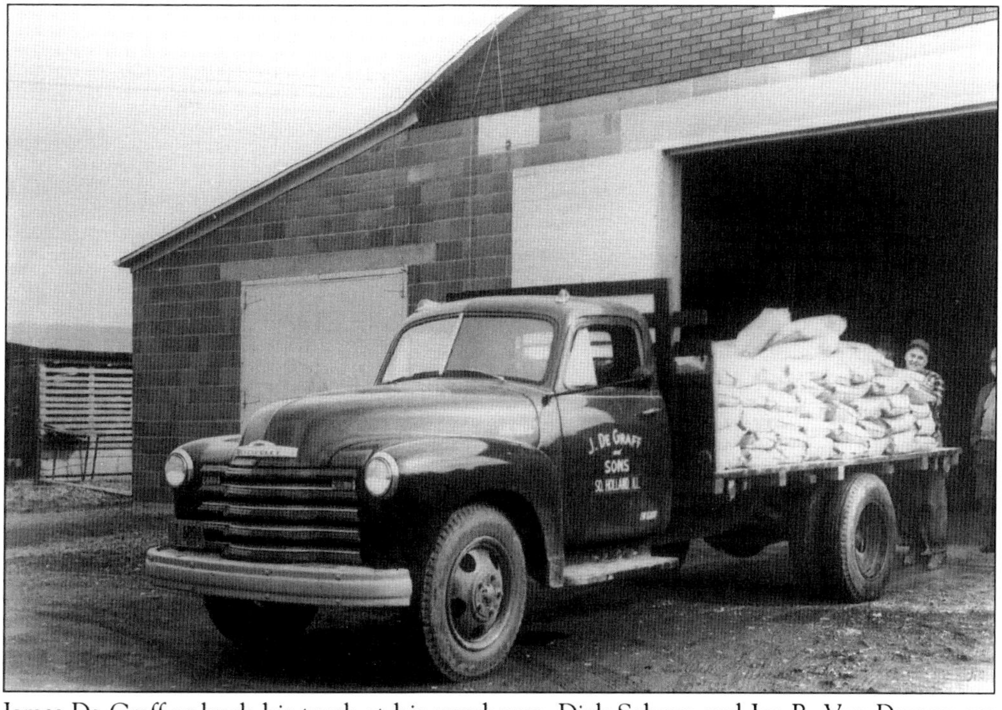

James De Graff unloads his truck at his warehouse. Dick Schaap and Joe R. Van Drunen are standing beside him. (Photo courtesy of South Holland Historical Society from the collection of Dr. Carl Walvoord.)

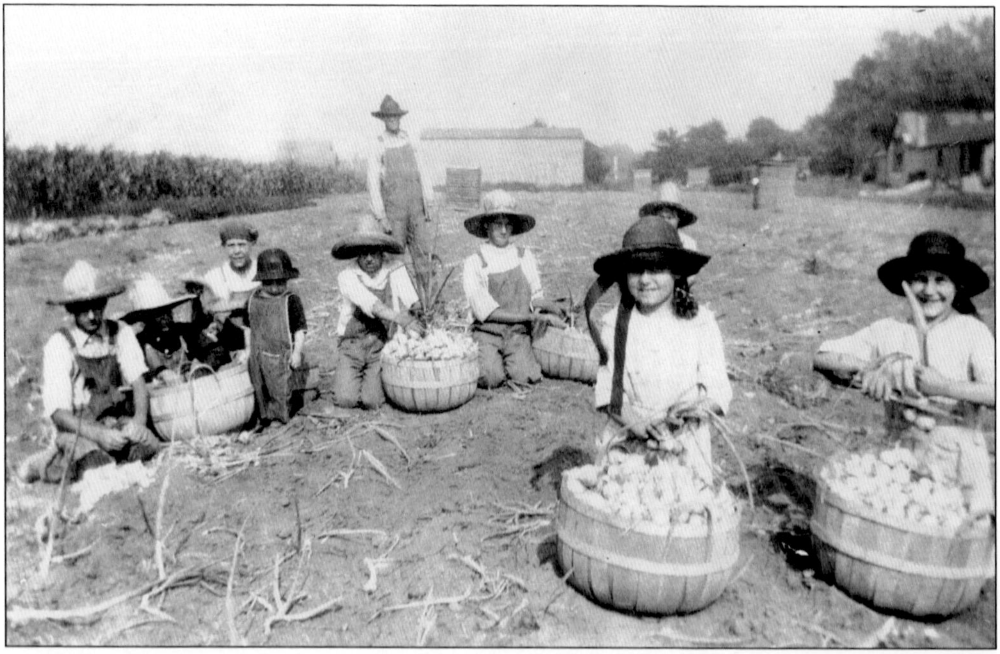

Children work harvesting onion, clipping them by hand with shears. Jacob De Young is the adult standing in the back. The little two year old boy is Gilbert De Young. The photo was taken around 1924. (Photo courtesy of South Holland Historical Society from the collection of Dr. Carl Walvoord.)

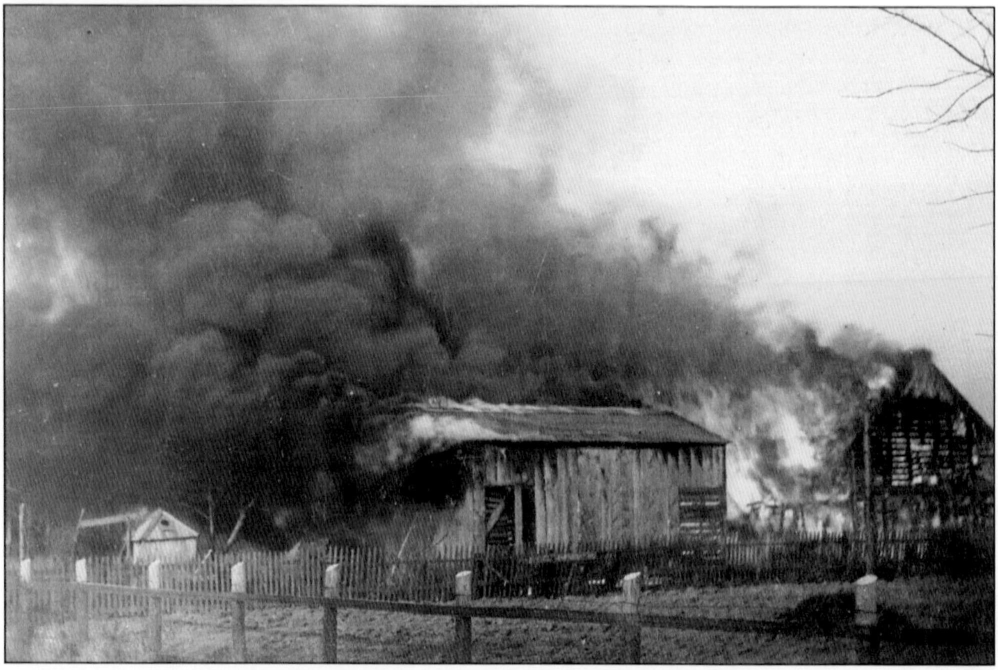

A fire in the barn of Tom De Graff, which was located on the Southeast corner of 159th and Chicago Road (now South Park Avenue). (Photo courtesy of South Holland Historical Society from the collection of Dr. Carl Walvoord.)

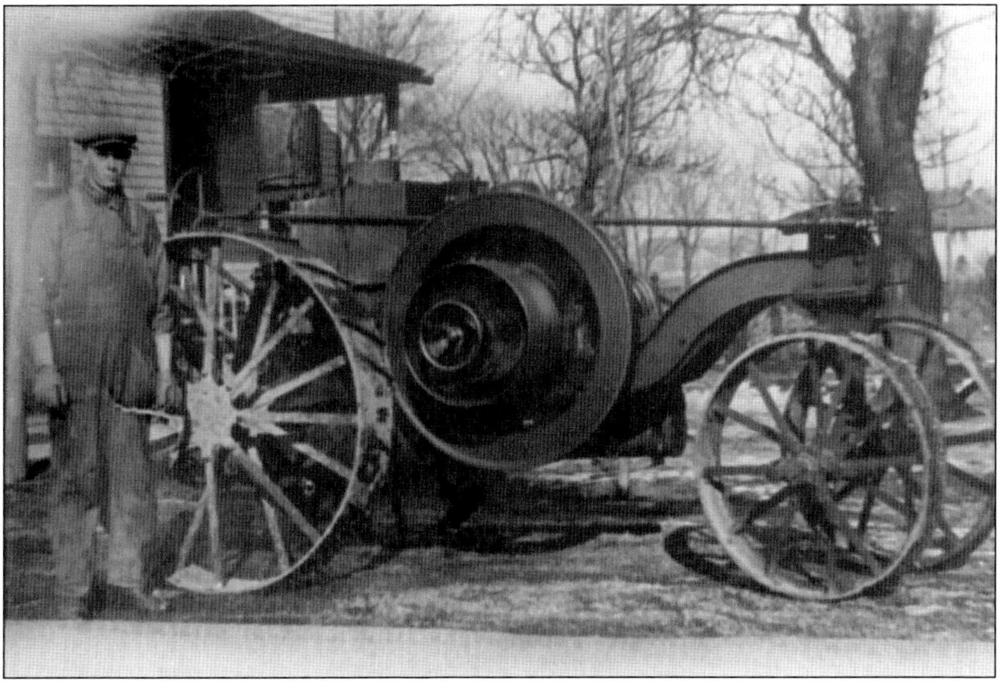

This is the first tractor to be used on the farm of J.H. Veld. It was an International Harvester that was used from about 1915 until 1940. (Photo courtesy of South Holland Historical Society from the collection of Dr. Carl Walvoord.)

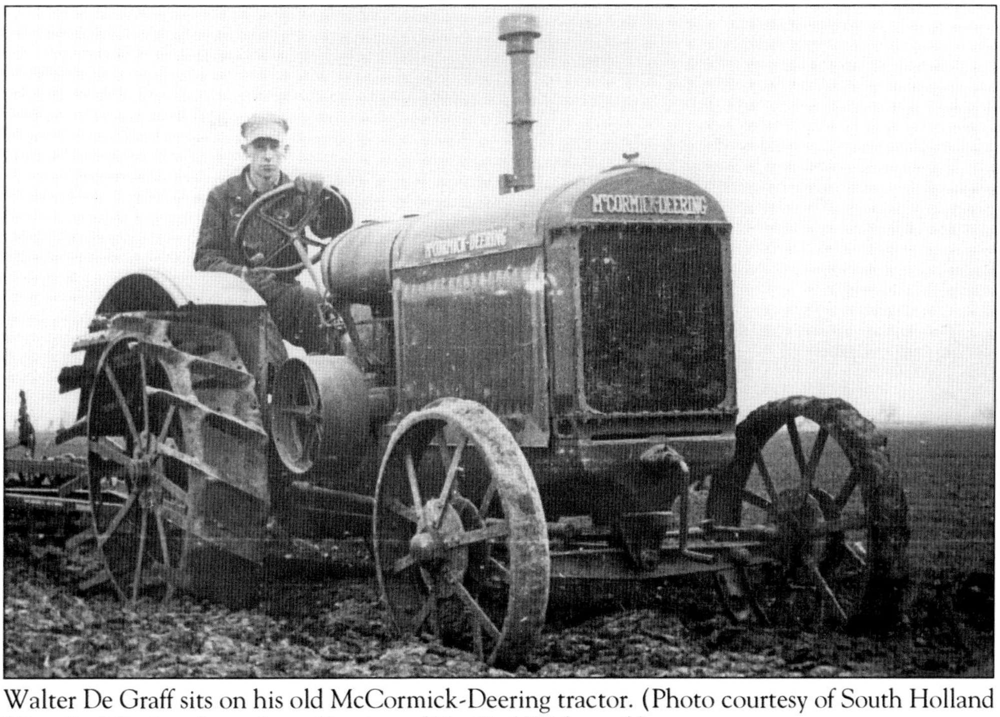

Walter De Graff sits on his old McCormick-Deering tractor. (Photo courtesy of South Holland Historical Society from the collection of Dr. Carl Walvoord.)

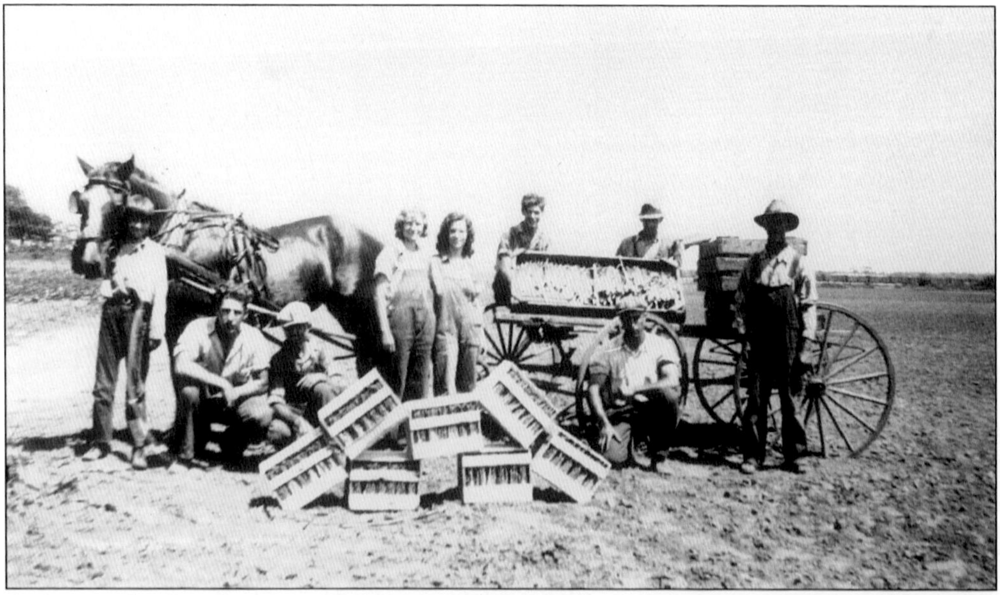

Asparagus developed into an important garden product—it was cut, tumbled and boxed on the farm, usually going to the South Water Street Market. In the third growing season it could be cut until the fourth of July. (Photo courtesy of South Holland Historical Society from the collection of Dr. Carl Walvoord.)

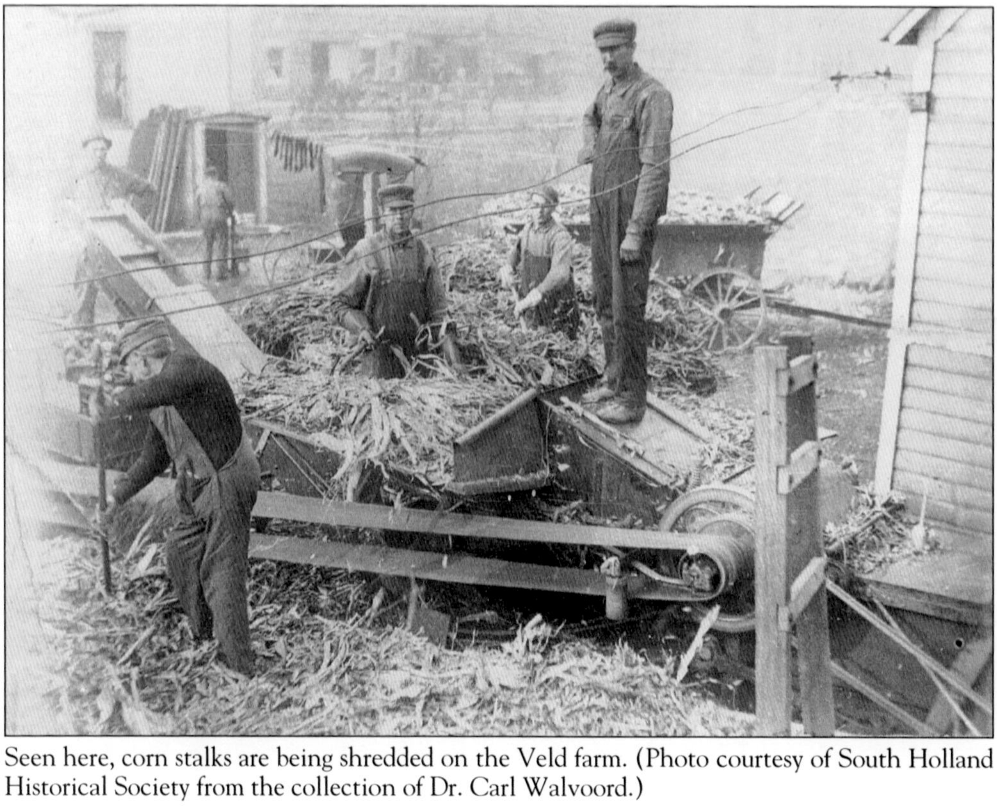

Seen here, corn stalks are being shredded on the Veld farm. (Photo courtesy of South Holland Historical Society from the collection of Dr. Carl Walvoord.)

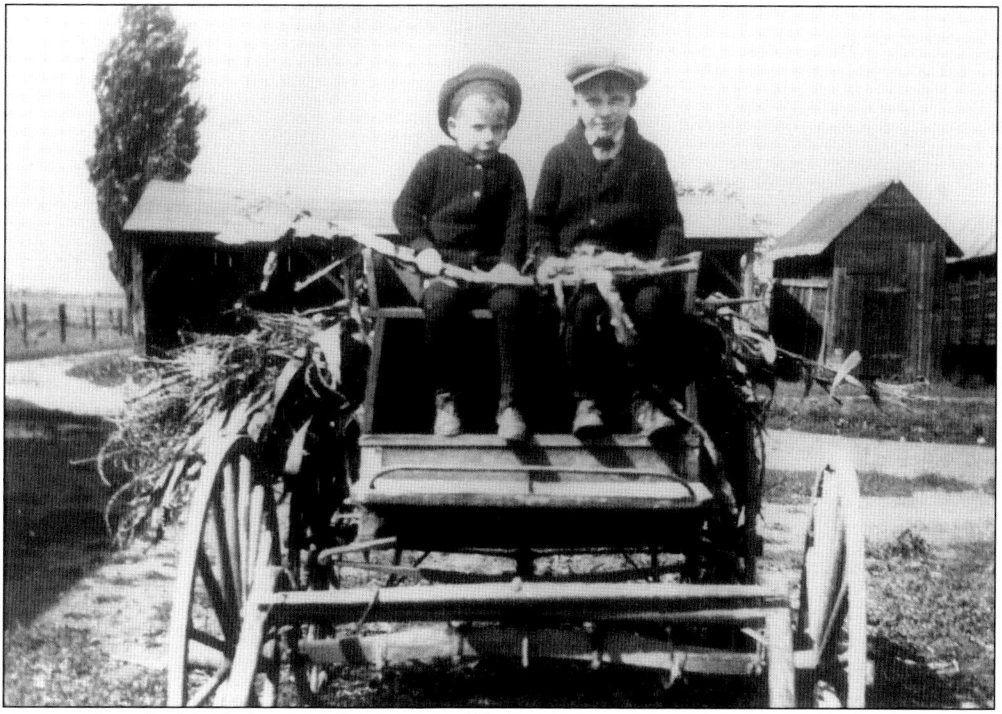

Two unidentified little boys sit on a wagon filled with cornstalks at the farm of Nick Gouwens. (Photo courtesy of South Holland Historical Society from the collection of Dr. Carl Walvoord.)

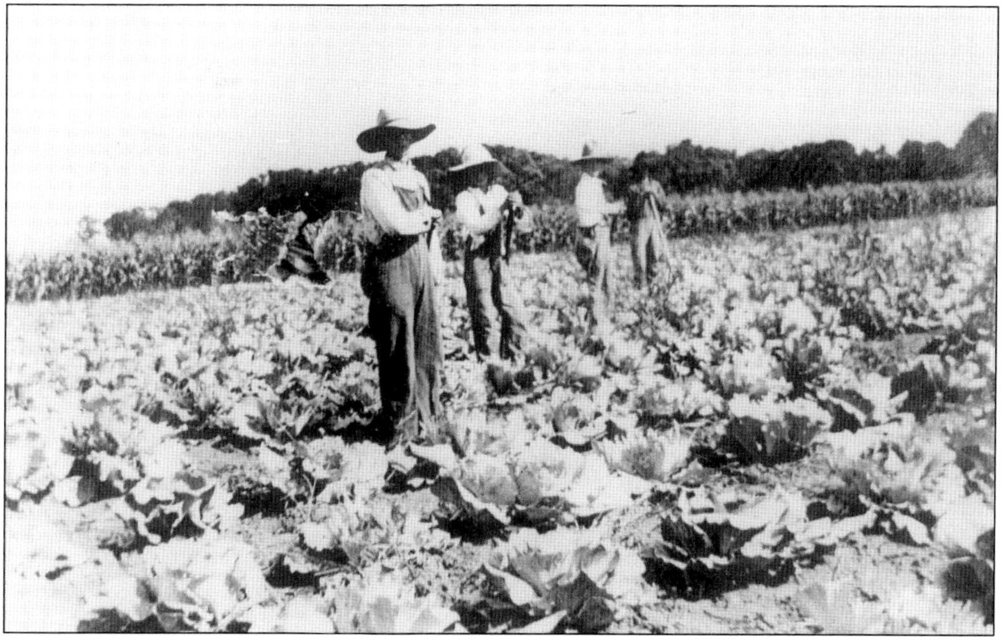

"Cabbages is beautiful?" chuckled farmer Klass Pool, as Selina Peake admired the colors of the vegetables growing in the fields as she arrived in High Prairie in the novel *So Big*, by Edna Ferber. In this photo, workers are hoeing cabbage in a field on the Volbrecht farm. (Photo courtesy of South Holland Historical Society from the collection of Dr. Carl Walvoord.)

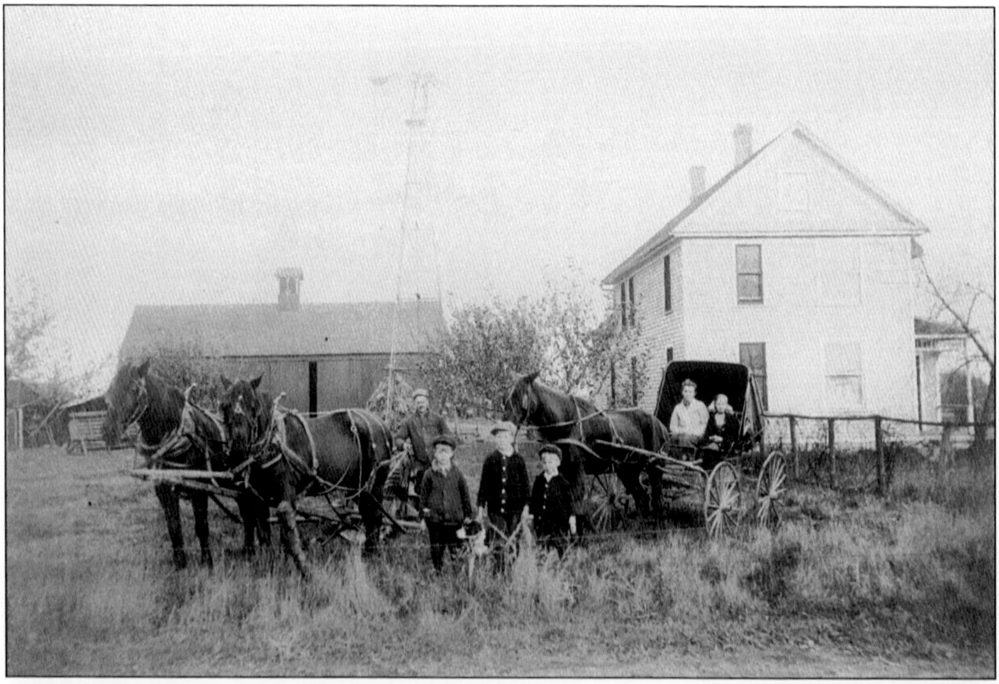

William Paarlberg is standing behind the horses in the farm yard of William Paarlberg. His children Casey, James, and Phillip are standing in front, and his daughter Ruth is seated in the buggy with her mother. (Photo courtesy of South Holland Historical Society from the collection of Dr. Carl Walvoord.)

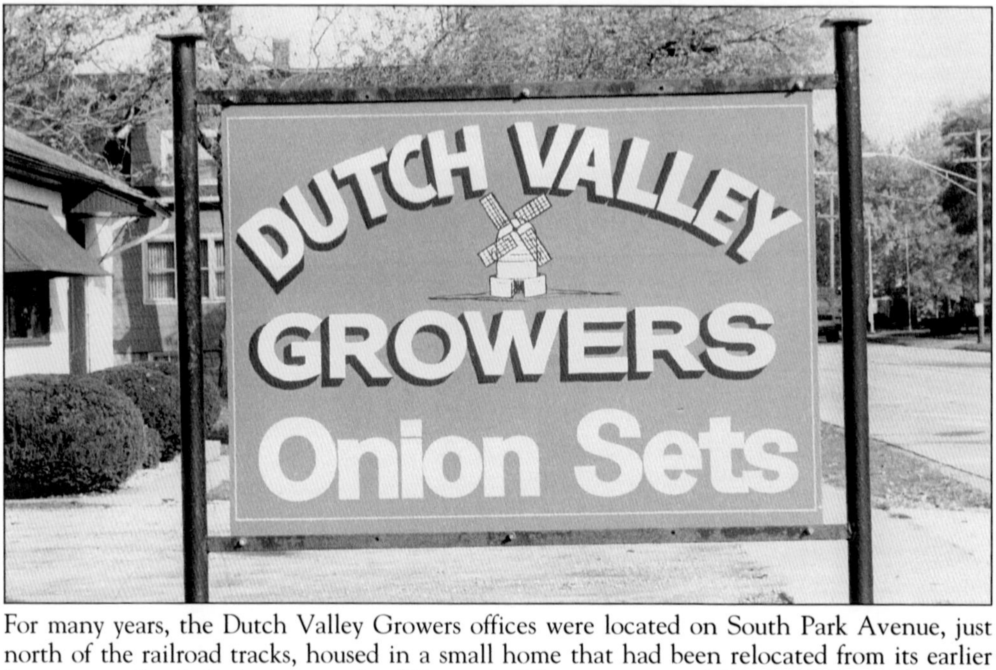

For many years, the Dutch Valley Growers offices were located on South Park Avenue, just north of the railroad tracks, housed in a small home that had been relocated from its earlier location on South Park, just north of Route 6. (Photo courtesy of South Holland Historical Society from the collection of Dr. Carl Walvoord.)

Two

FAMILIES

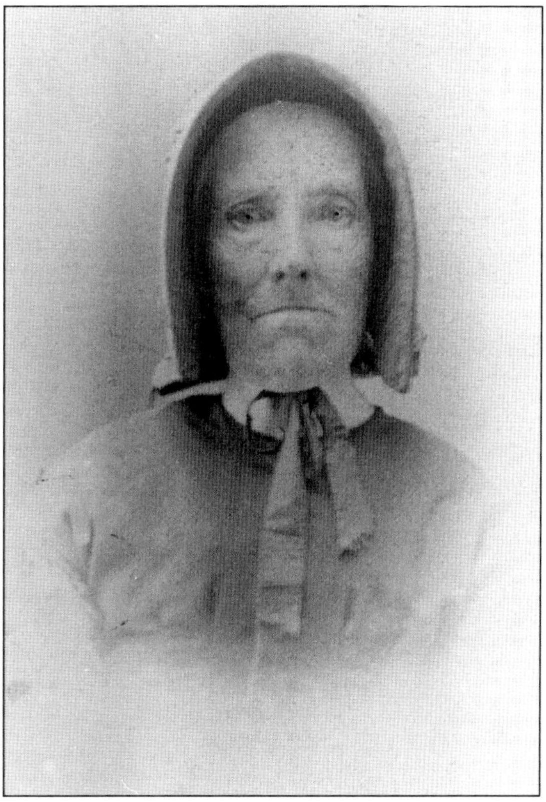

Pictured here is the Paarlberg widow. On her journey to the United States from the Netherlands, she lost her husband three days into the trip. Her three-month-old son then died not long after her arrival in the United States. She arrived in South Holland with several children that she raised alone as she farmed. The main character in the novel *So Big* was based partly on the Paarlberg widow. (Photo courtesy of South Holland Historical Society from the collection of Dr. Carl Walvoord.)

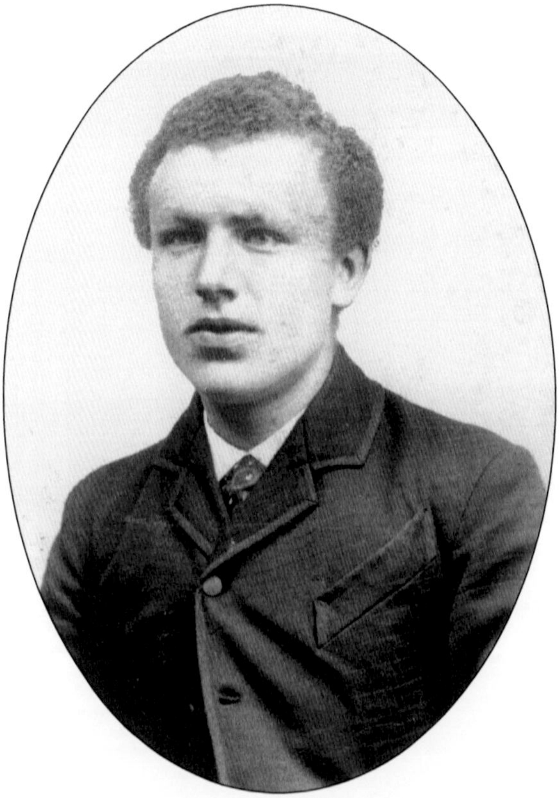

Bert and Johanna Beuzekom, pictured here, had a daughter, who married Gerrit Pals. The couple farmed and had several children. Many of their descendents still reside in South Holland. (Photo courtesy of Harry and Alice Pals.)

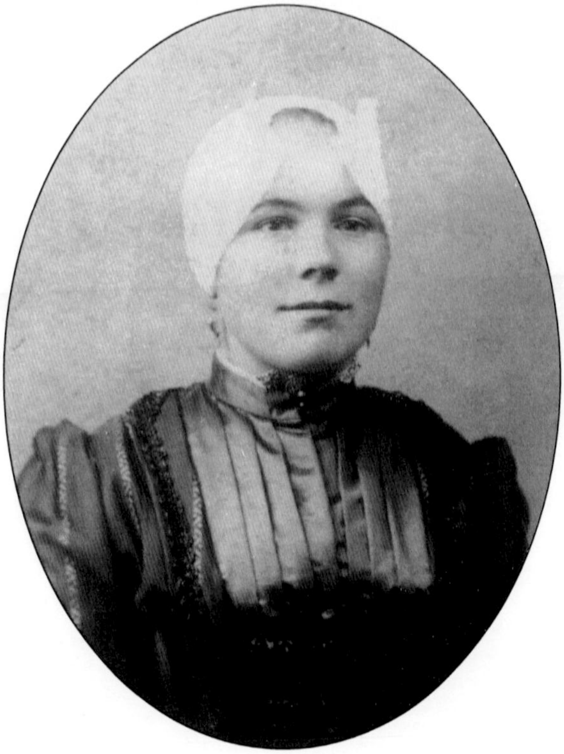

Young brothers Clarence and Tunis De Young, sons of Rich and Kate De Young, dress their best for a professional photograph taken in Chicago. Clarence De Young later taught science courses for many years at Illiana Christian High School in nearby Lansing. (Photo courtesy of Harry and Alice Pals.)

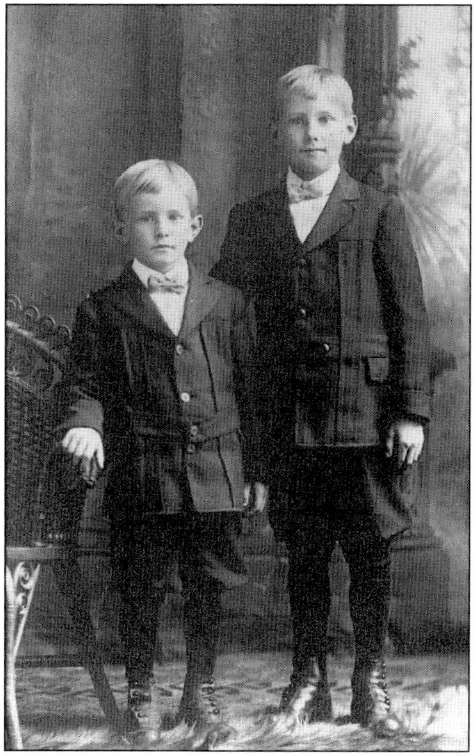

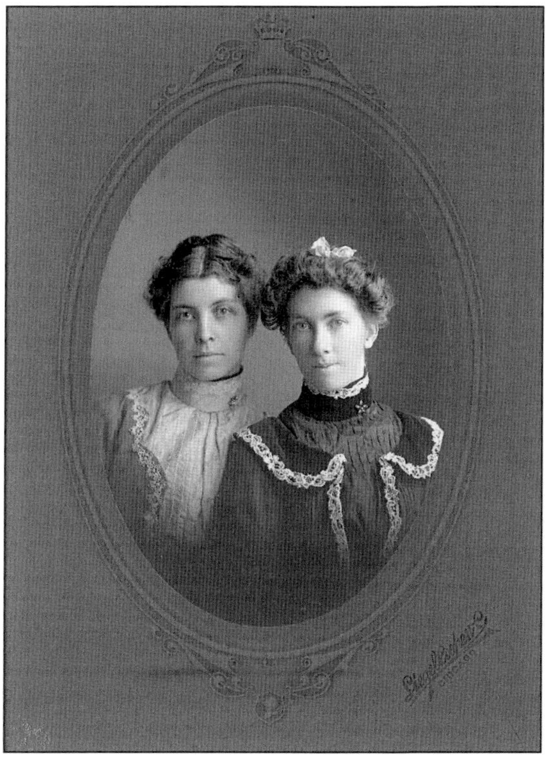

Sisters Annie and Gert De Young are photographed before each of them was married. The sisters were two of a family of ten, which included six boys and four girls. The De Young family attended the True Dutch Church, which still stands on Route 6. Male members of the family conducted readings and played the organ. (Photo courtesy of Harry and Alice Pals.)

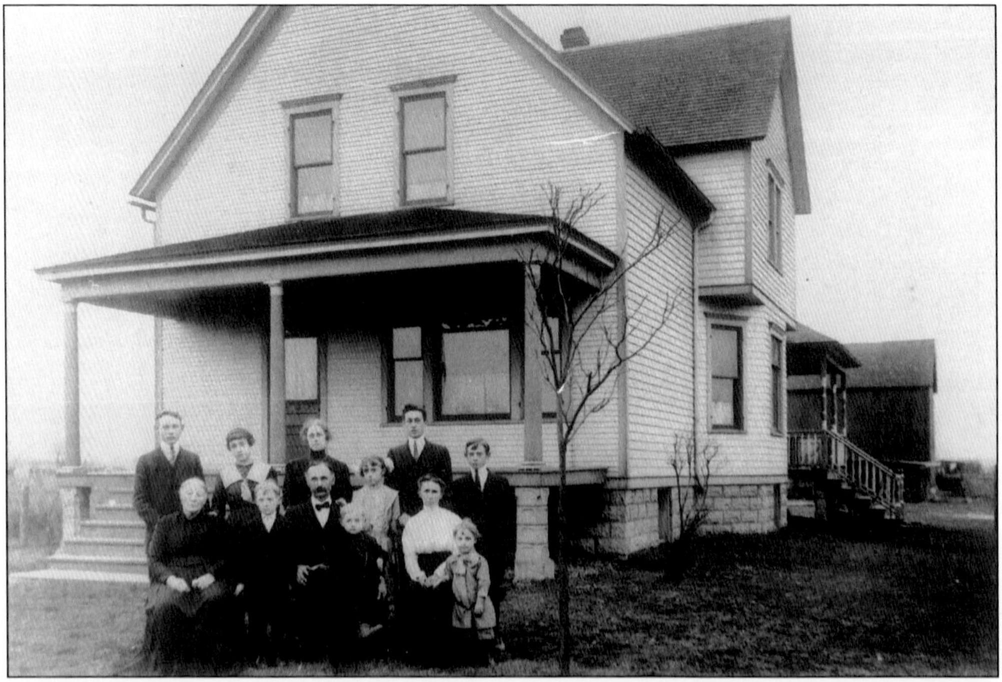

The family of J.J. Gouwens, Sr. is photographed in front of their home on Route 6 in 1914 or 1915. From left to right are: (front row) Grandma Gouwens, Andrew, Mr. J.J. Gouwens, Henry, Jean, Mrs. Gouwens, and William; (back row) Seymour, Elizabeth, Hattie, Jay, and James. (Photo courtesy of South Holland Historical Society from the collection of Dr. Carl Walvoord.)

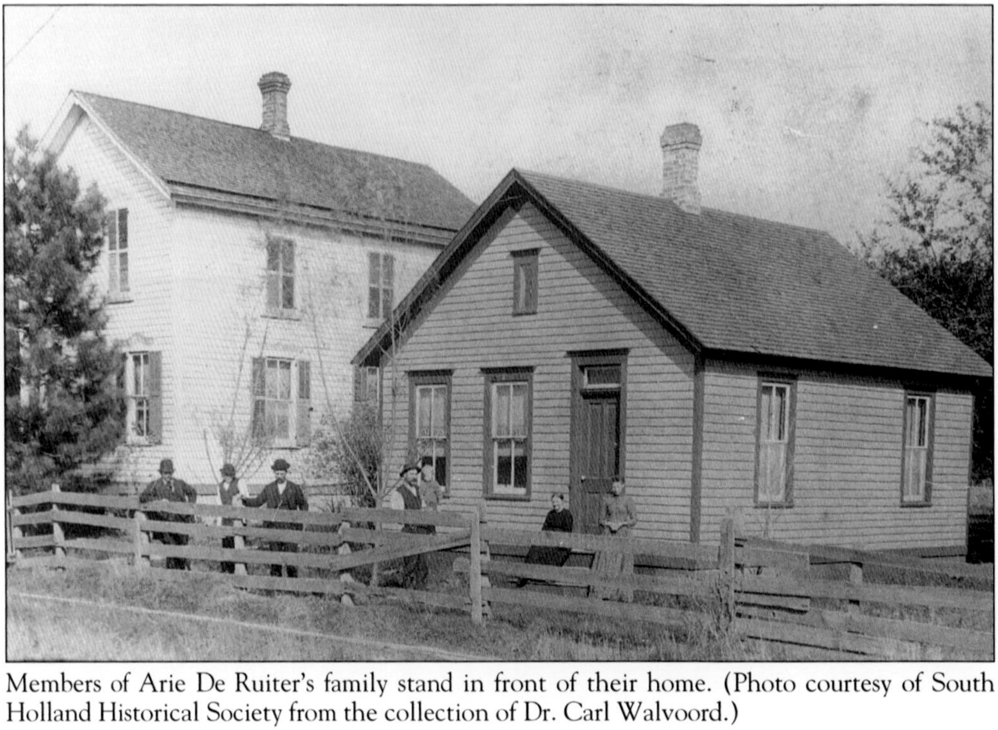

Members of Arie De Ruiter's family stand in front of their home. (Photo courtesy of South Holland Historical Society from the collection of Dr. Carl Walvoord.)

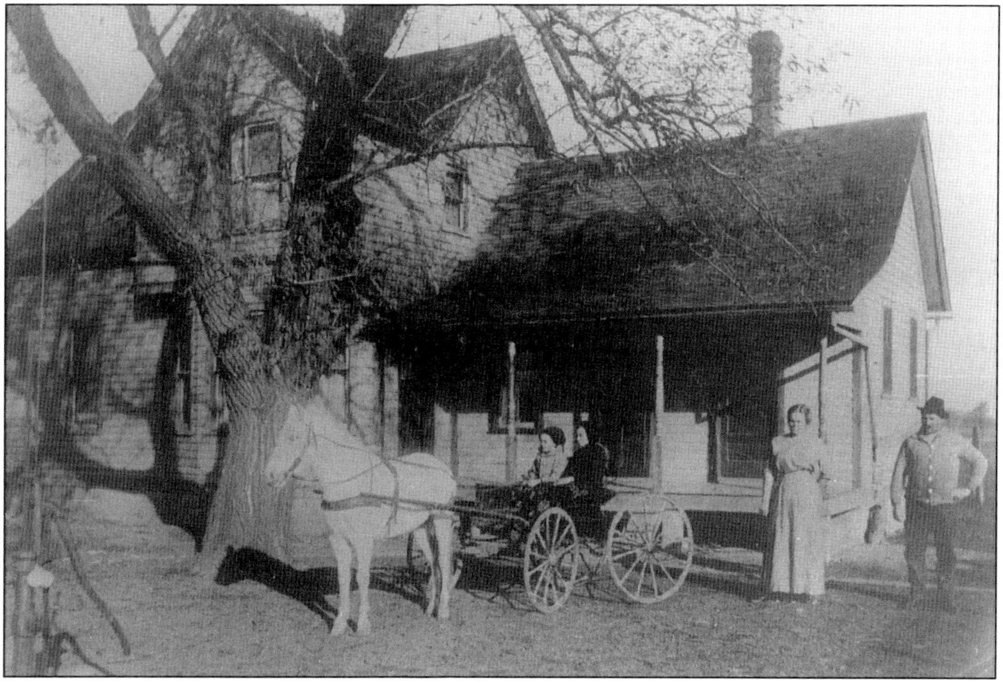

Mr. and Mrs. Issac Shilling stand beside a horse cart with children Hans and Minnie inside. (Photo courtesy of South Holland Historical Society from the collection of Dr. Carl Walvoord.)

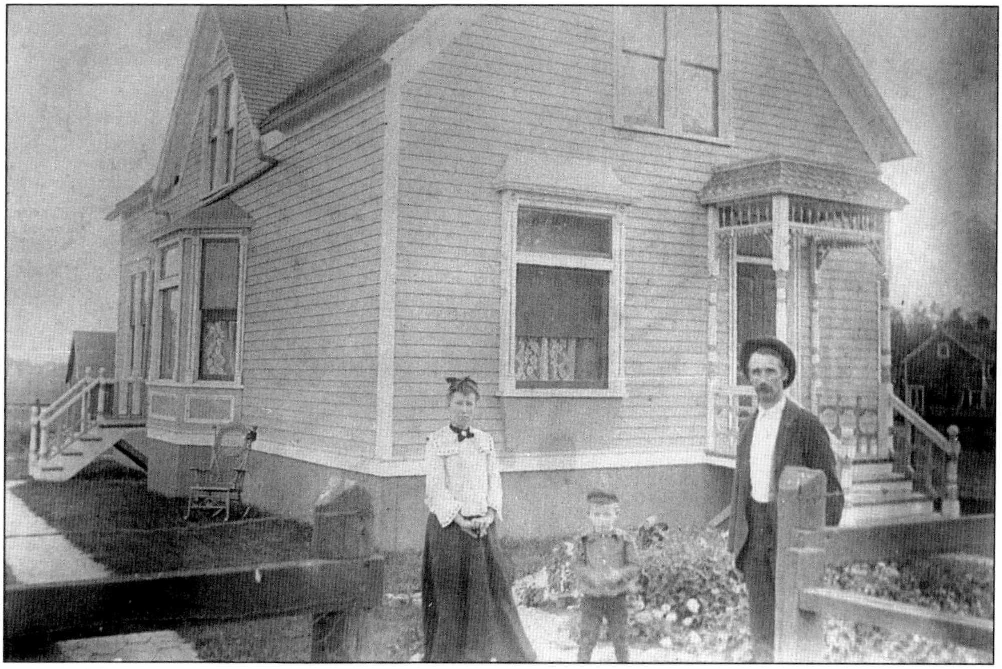

Pictured here are Mr. and Mrs. Peter Jacobs and their son, Hiram, outside their home. It is indicated on the back of the photo that the home was located in the Phoenix subdivision and was built by John Van Drunen in 1899 at a cost of $600. (Photo courtesy of South Holland Historical Society from the collection of Dr. Carl Walvoord.)

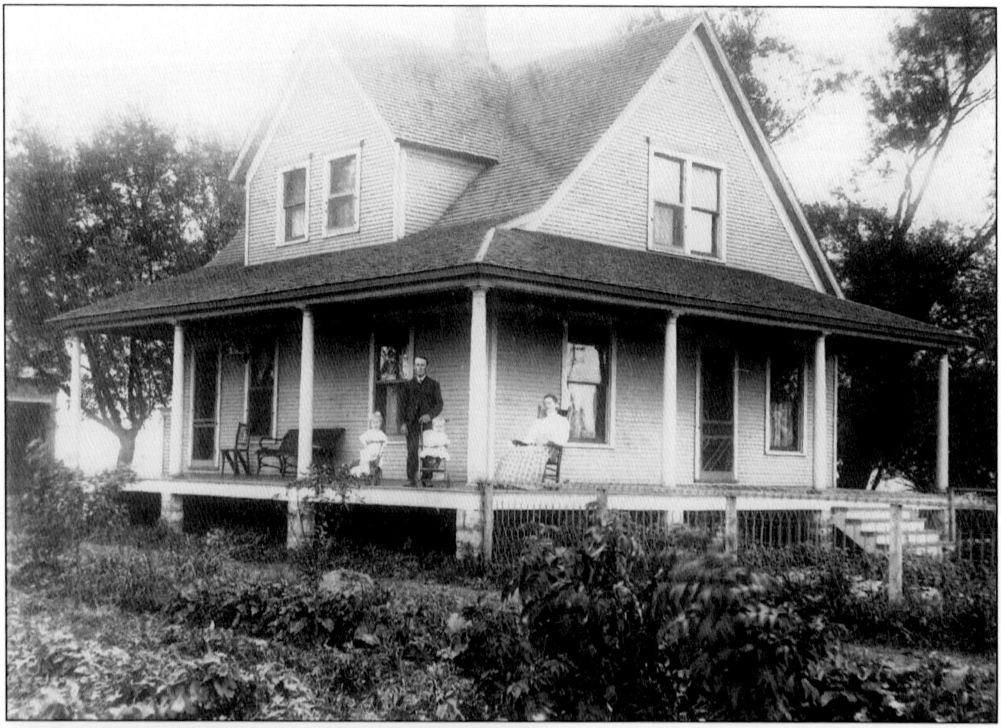

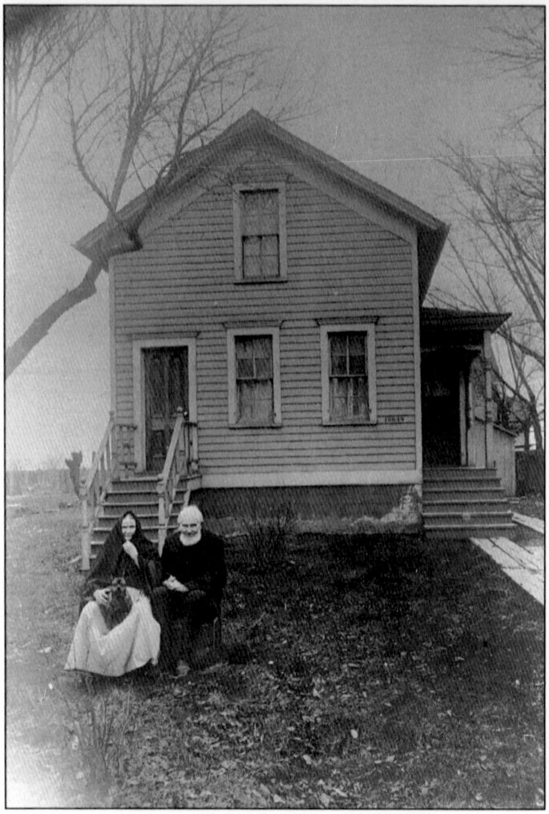

Standing on the porch of their home are J.C. Ravesloot, his wife, Cora, and their children Bertha and Orville. (Photo courtesy of South Holland Historical Society from the collection of Dr. Carl Walvoord.)

Mr. and Mrs. Cornelious Tanis are seated in front of their home at the corner of 160th Place and South Park Avenue. (Photo courtesy of South Holland Historical Society from the collection of Dr. Carl Walvoord.)

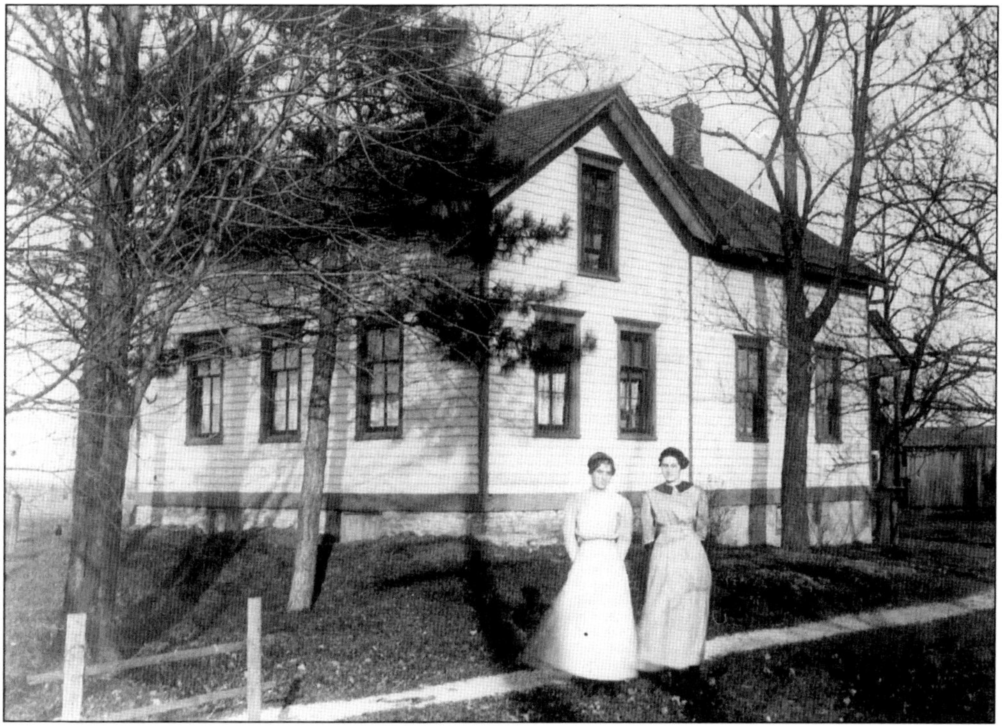

Margaret and Nellie Blink stand in front of their home at 170th Street and South Park Avenue. (Photo courtesy of South Holland Historical Society from the collection of Dr. Carl Walvoord.)

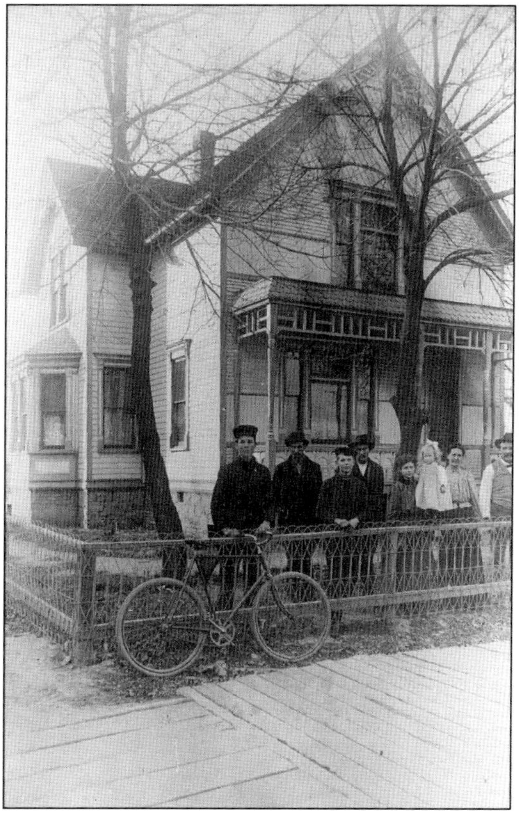

This is the home of Mr. and Mrs. Henry P. De Young in the early 1900s. It was located on South Park Avenue about a block south of Route 6 on the west side of the street. Pictured are Peter De Young, unidentified, Dick De Young, unidentified, Alice De Young, Anna Eenigenberg, Mrs. Henry P. De Young, and Mr. Henry P. De Young. (Photo courtesy of South Holland Historical Society from the collection of Dr. Carl Walvoord.)

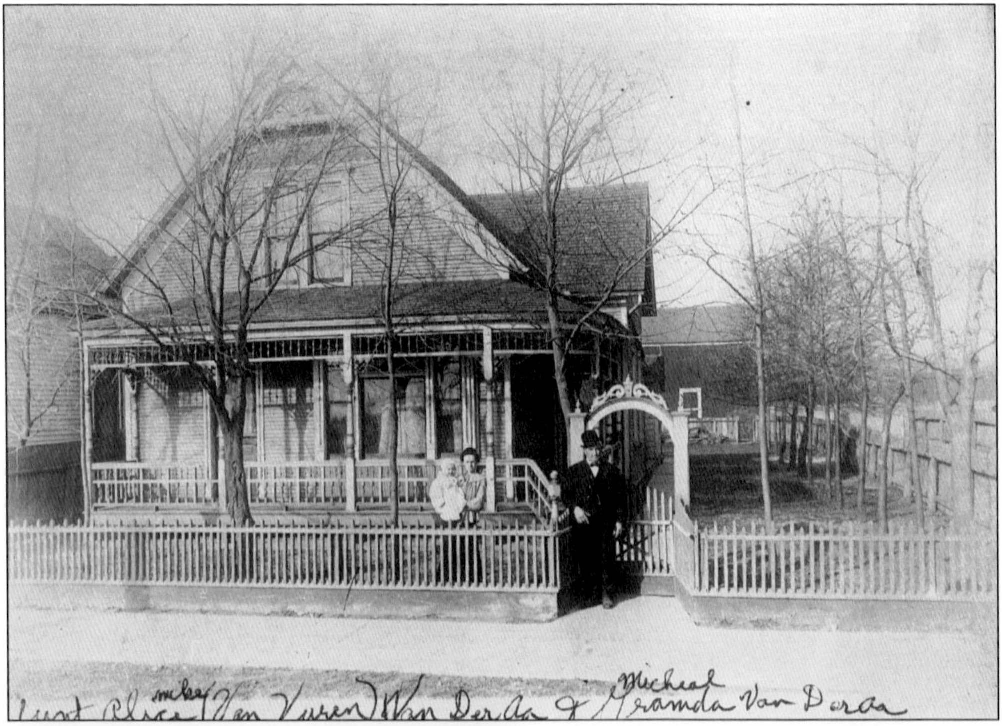

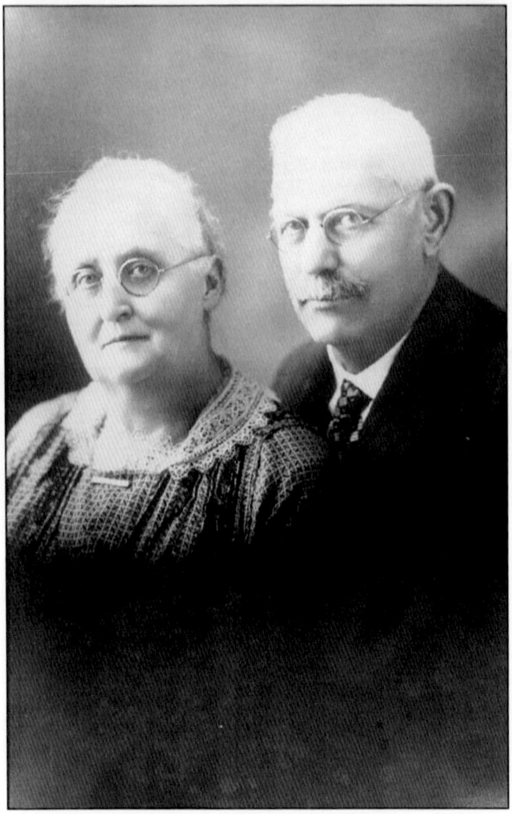

Pictured in this photo are Michael Van Der Aa and his wife, Alice Van Der Aa, holding their son, Teddy. Teddy Van Der Aa had an ice cream parlor that was located at 158th and South Park Avenue. Mike Van Der Aa served as the South Holland fire chief for many years. (Photo courtesy of South Holland Historical Society from the collection of Dr. Carl Walvoord.)

Pictured here are Mr. and Mrs. John Vinke. Mr. Vinke was the owner of Wausau Lumber and Coal Co. (Photo courtesy of South Holland Historical Society from the collection of Dr. Carl Walvoord.)

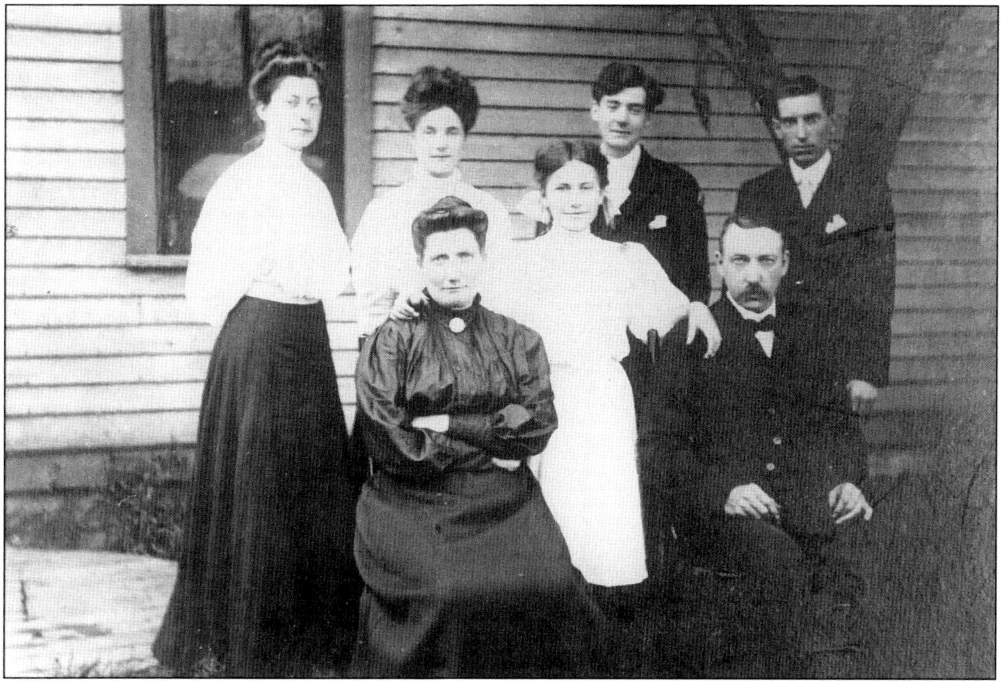

This photograph is of the Vorst family. Mr. Vorst worked as a butcher for John Schilling at his meat market. (Photo courtesy of South Holland Historical Society from the collection of Dr. Carl Walvoord.)

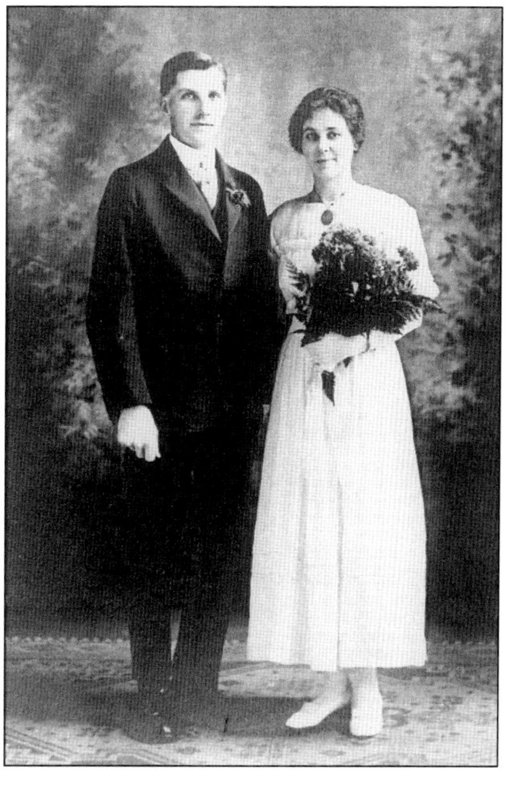

Taken around 1918, this is the wedding photo of John K. De Young and Helen Van Der Giessen. (Photo courtesy of South Holland Historical Society from the collection of Dr. Carl Walvoord.)

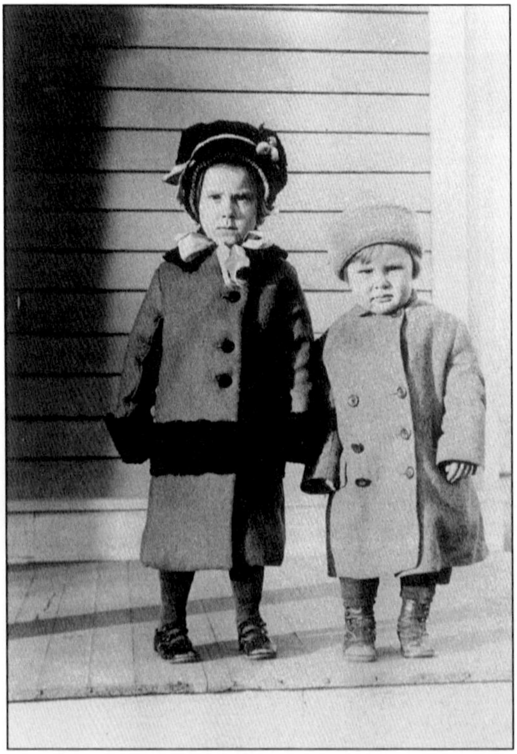

Elizabeth and William Jacobs. (Photo courtesy of South Holland Historical Society from the collection of Dr. Carl Walvoord.)

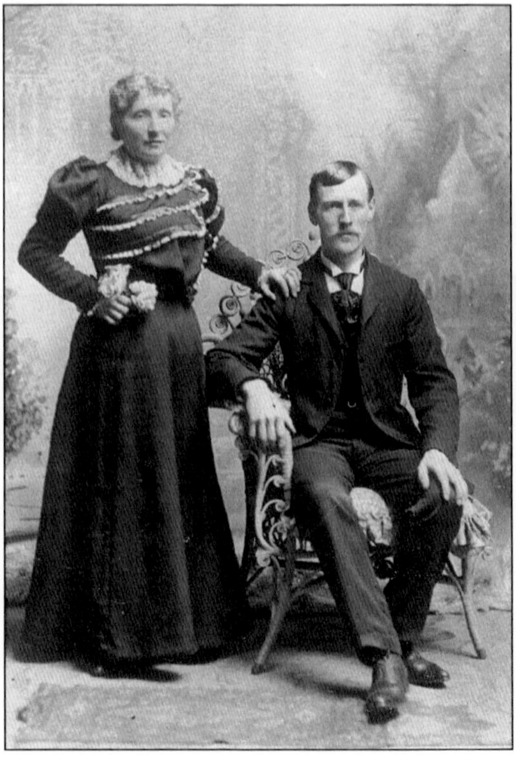

Mr. and Mrs. Peter Smit—Mr. Smit and his brother Albert were painters in South Holland. Peter's sons Richard and Henry were also painters and for many years ran a paint store on South Park Avenue. The building later changed hands a couple times before it was demolished in 1981 to make space for parking for the South Holland Trust and Savings. (Photo courtesy of South Holland Historical Society from the collection of Dr. Carl Walvoord.)

A photo from the wedding of Gerrit Richveld and Hattie Anker. (Photo courtesy of South Holland Historical Society from the collection of Dr. Carl Walvoord.)

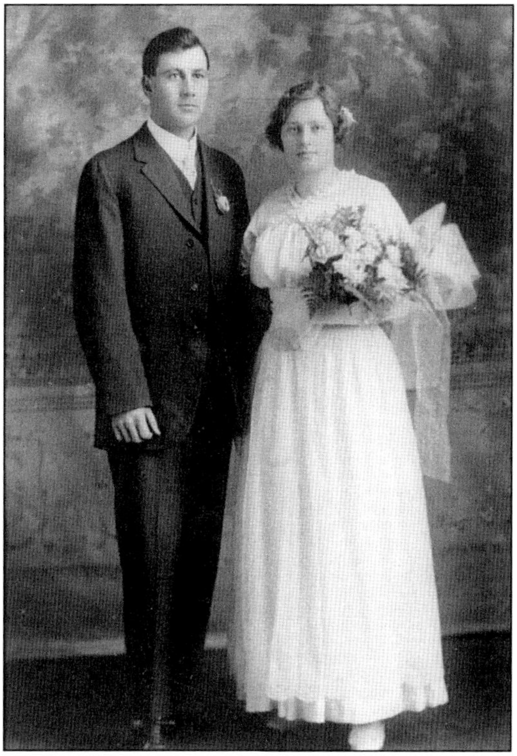

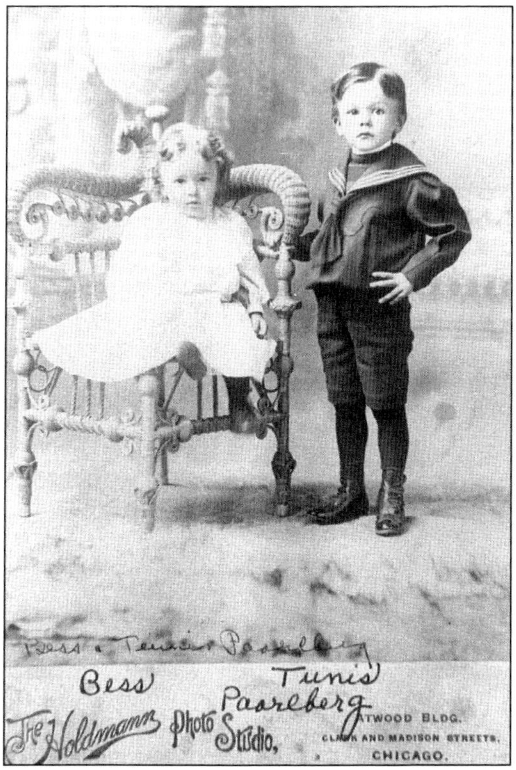

Bess and Tunis Paarlberg, children of Nick Paarlberg, are professionally photographed in Chicago. (Photo courtesy of South Holland Historical Society from the collection of Dr. Carl Walvoord.)

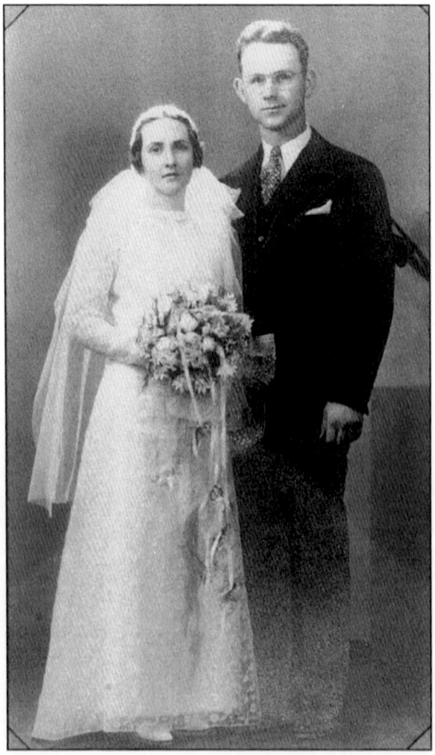

A 1935 wedding photo of Henry Gouwens and Cornelia De Young. (Photo courtesy of South Holland Historical Society from the collection of Dr. Carl Walvoord.)

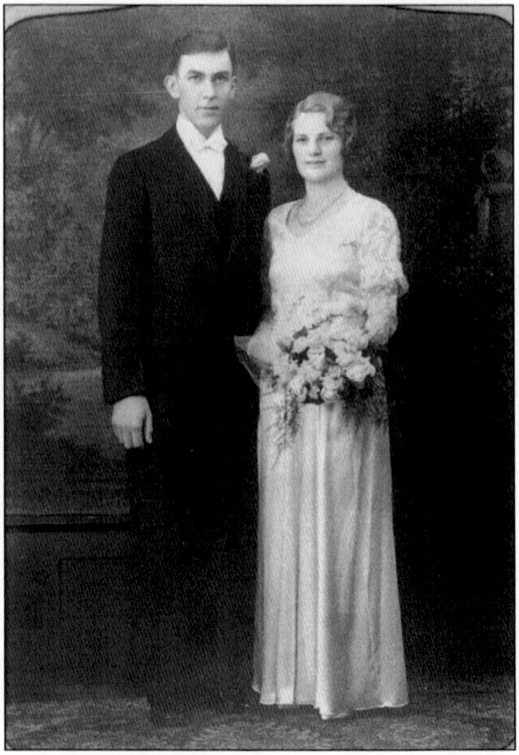

A 1933 wedding photo of Clarence De Young and Jeanette Van Oosten. (Photo courtesy of South Holland Historical Society from the collection of Dr. Carl Walvoord.)

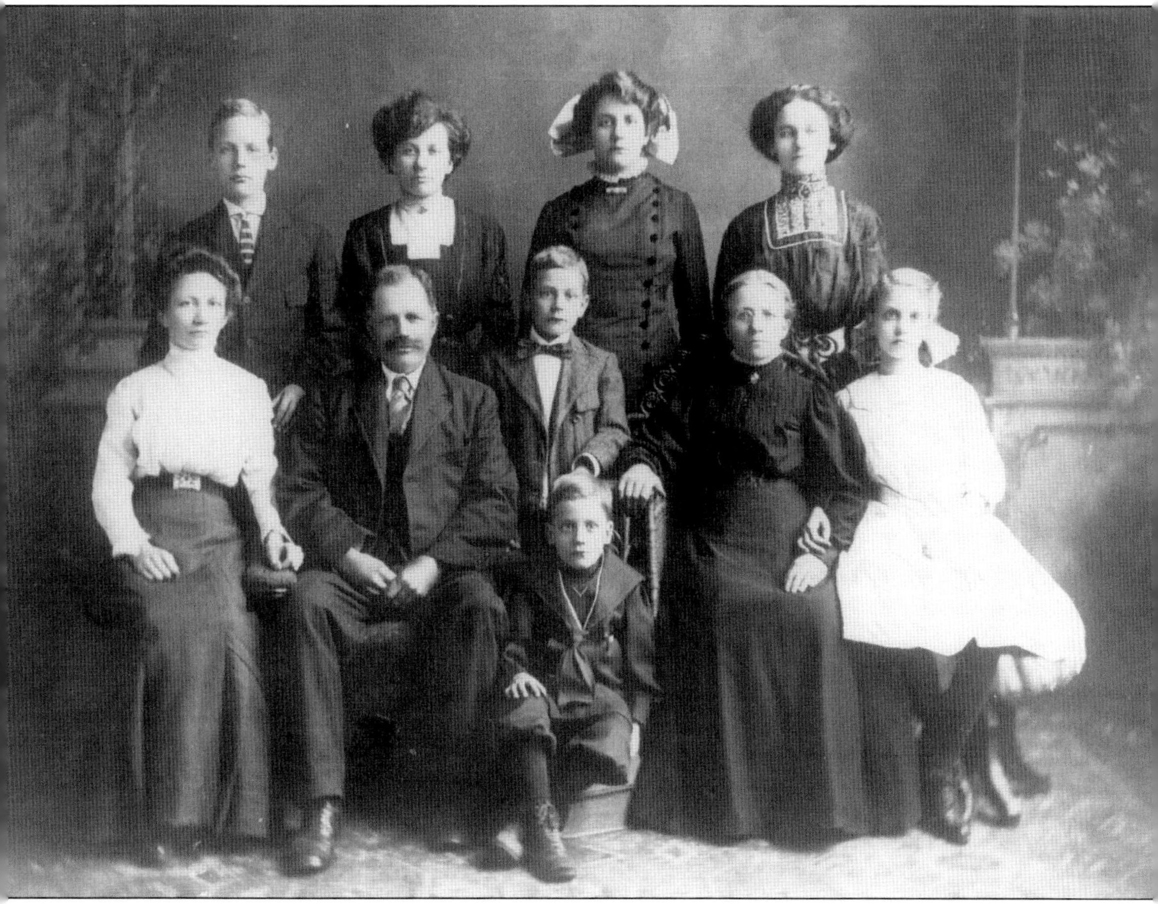

The Cornelius Van Etten family. Pictured, from left to right, are: (front row) Gertrude Van Etten Mall Smith (daughter), Cornelius Van Etten (father), Cornelius Mall (grandson, standing), Clarence Mall (grandson, seated), Anna Van Etten (mother), and Pearl Mall (granddaughter); (back row) Fred Mall (grandson), Clara Van Etten (daughter), Jamie Van Etten (daughter—married Bert Bruggeman), and Anna Mall (granddaughter). (Photo courtesy of South Holland Historical Society from the collection of Dr. Carl Walvoord.)

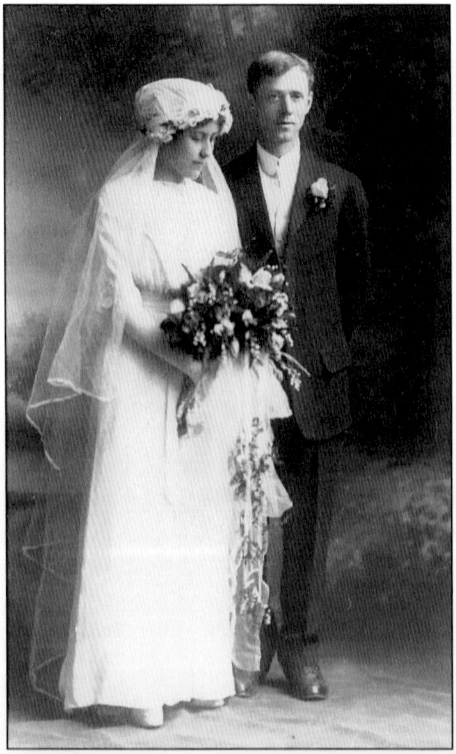

The wedding photo of Nelson and Elizabeth Dalenberg, from 1913. The couple had four children—Marie, born in 1914, Ruth Ann, Paul Nelson, born in 1921, and Lois Ruth, born in 1930. (Photo courtesy of South Holland Historical Society from the collection of Dr. Carl Walvoord.)

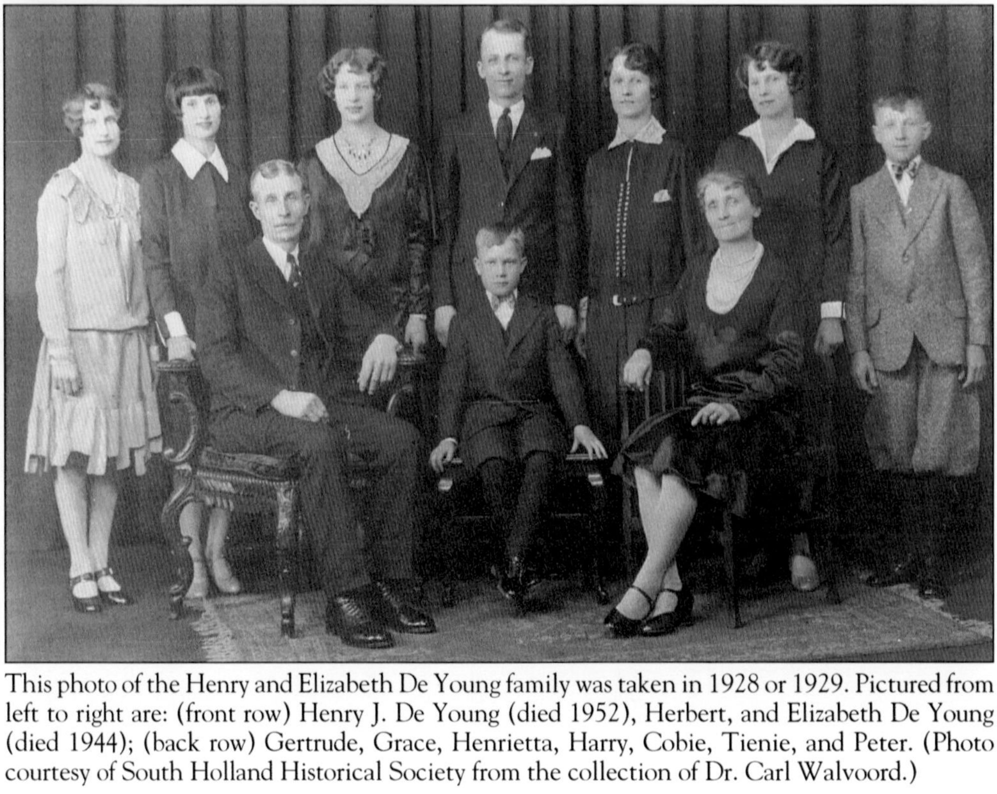

This photo of the Henry and Elizabeth De Young family was taken in 1928 or 1929. Pictured from left to right are: (front row) Henry J. De Young (died 1952), Herbert, and Elizabeth De Young (died 1944); (back row) Gertrude, Grace, Henrietta, Harry, Cobie, Tienie, and Peter. (Photo courtesy of South Holland Historical Society from the collection of Dr. Carl Walvoord.)

A 1914 wedding photo of Tunis Paarlberg and Bessie Gouwens. After the death of Bessie Paarlberg, Tunis married Grace Schaffers. (Photo courtesy of South Holland Historical Society from the collection of Dr. Carl Walvoord.)

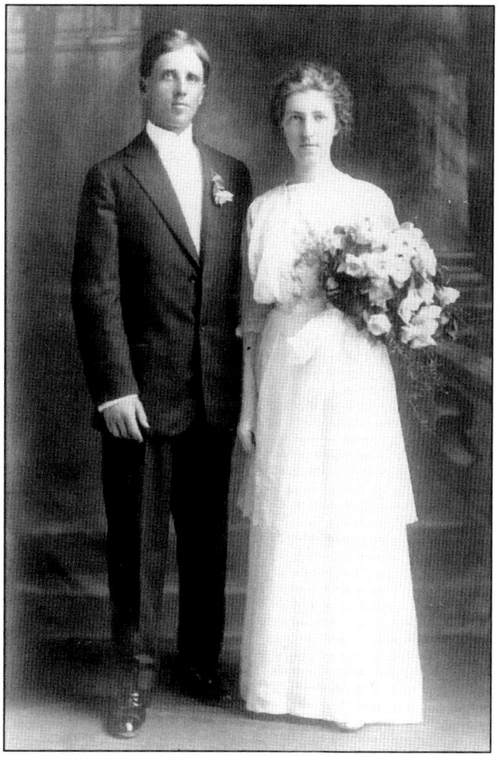

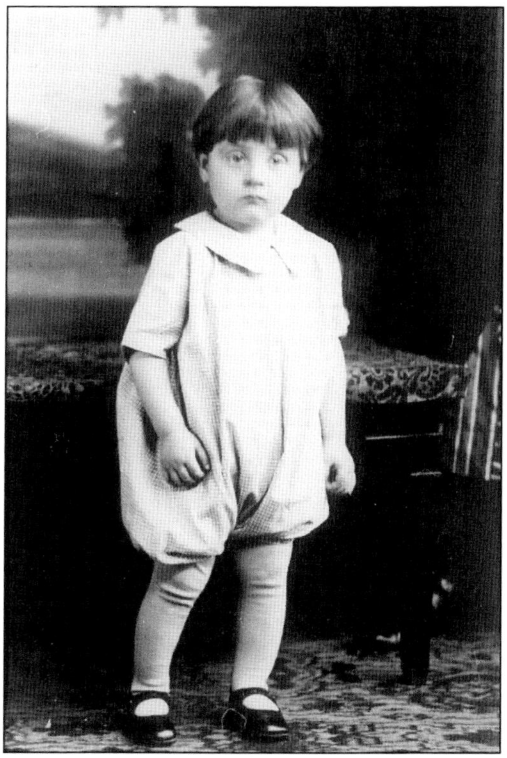

Clifford Gerrit Blink at age two. (Photo courtesy of South Holland Historical Society from the collection of Dr. Carl Walvoord.)

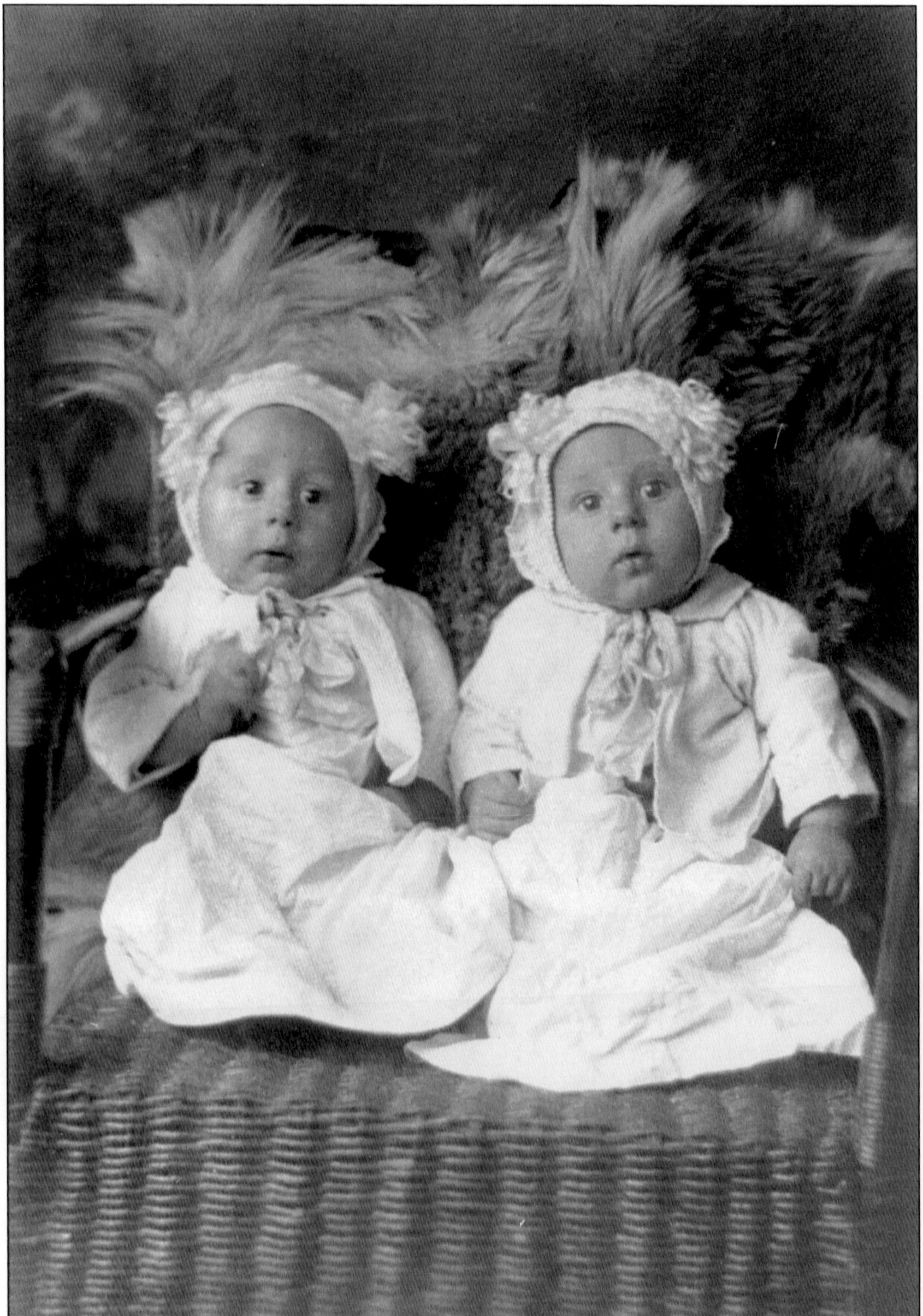

Despite the gowns and frilly bonnets, these two babies are brothers—twins Luke and John Jacobs. They were brothers of Hiram Jacobs. (Photo courtesy of South Holland Historical Society from the collection of Dr. Carl Walvoord.)

Mr. Nick De Young and his wife. Mr. De Young bought the old Schilling residence on South Park Avenue and converted it to the village's first funeral home. After some additions to the building a line of furniture was added to the business. Eventually, he left the funeral home business and the business remains as a furniture store today. The business still operates at the same location. (Photo courtesy of South Holland Historical Society from the collection of Dr. Carl Walvoord.)

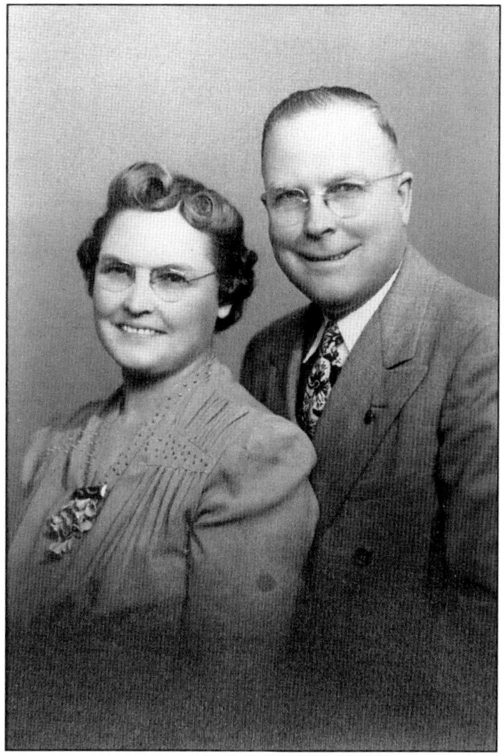

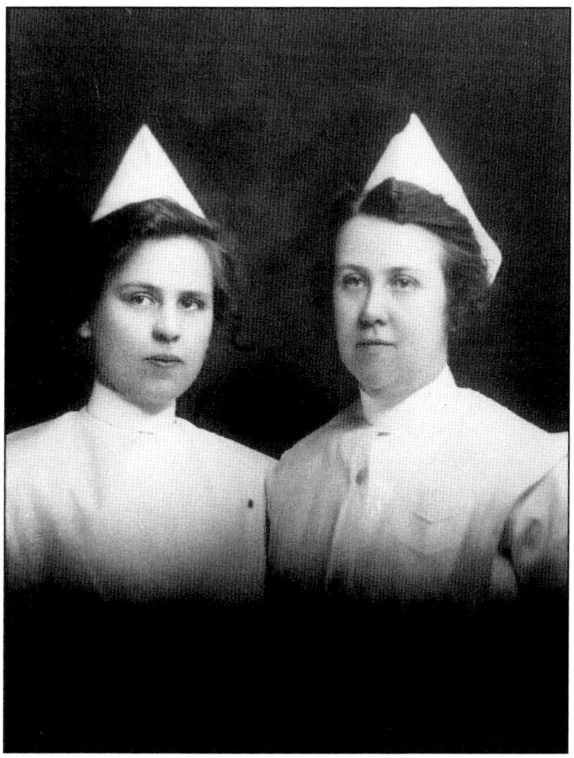

Mary and Ann Paarlberg both served as U.S. Army nurses during World War I. They are nieces of the widow Paarlberg. (Photo courtesy of South Holland Historical Society from the collection of Dr. Carl Walvoord.)

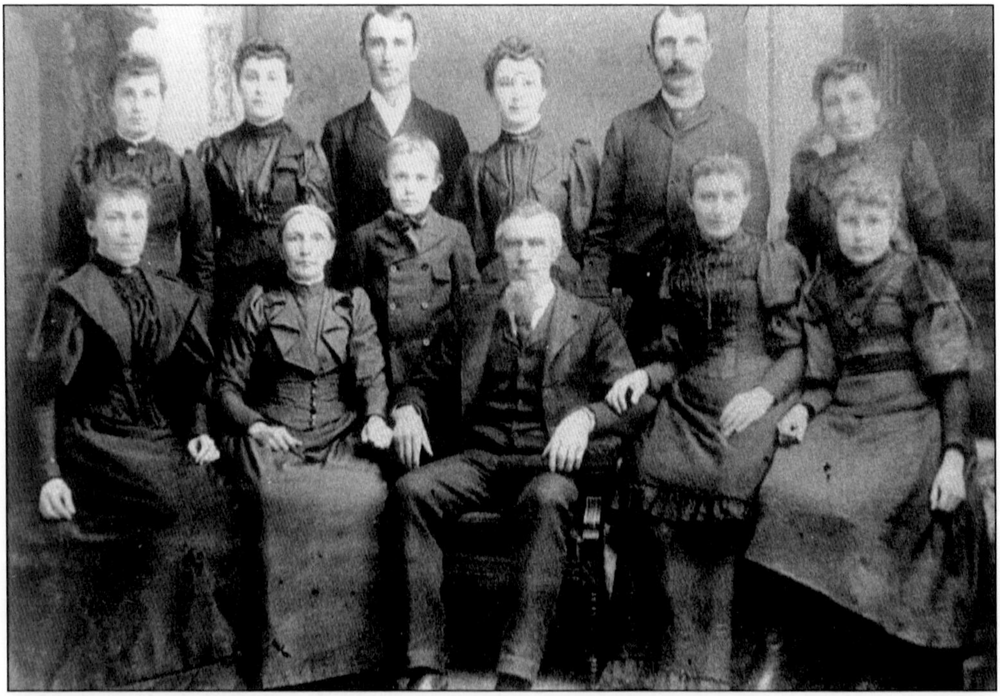

Hiram Jacobs and his wife Elizabeth (De Young) Jacobs are pictured with their children, Margaret, Minnie, Peter, Kate, Henry, Gertie, Anna, Anthony, Susan, and Corena. (Photo courtesy of South Holland Historical Society from the collection of Dr. Carl Walvoord.)

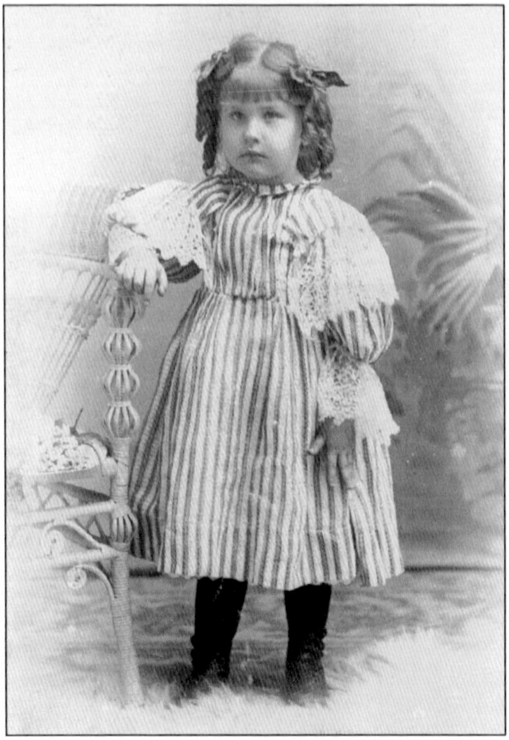

A young Maude De Young is pictured in this professional photograph. (Photo courtesy of South Holland Historical Society from the collection of Dr. Carl Walvoord.)

This photo was taken around 1906 of Mrs. Jennie Hillegonds, who was the mother of Mrs. William Paarlberg. She is pictured with her grandchildren Casey and Ruth Paarlberg. (Photo courtesy of South Holland Historical Society from the collection of Dr. Carl Walvoord.)

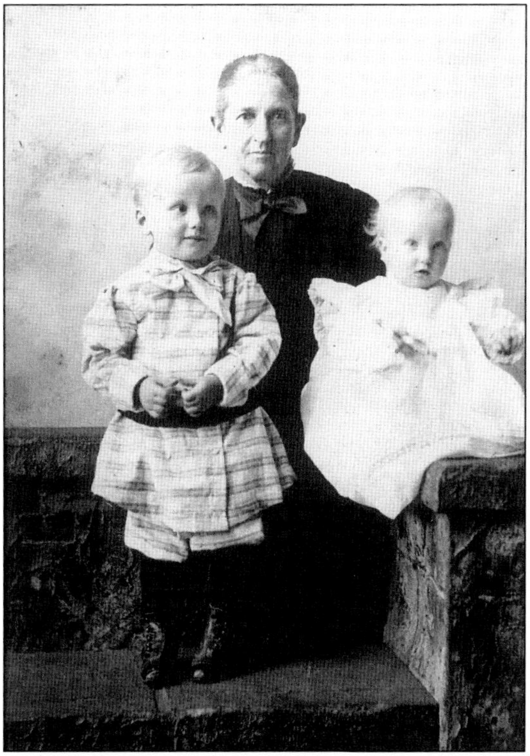

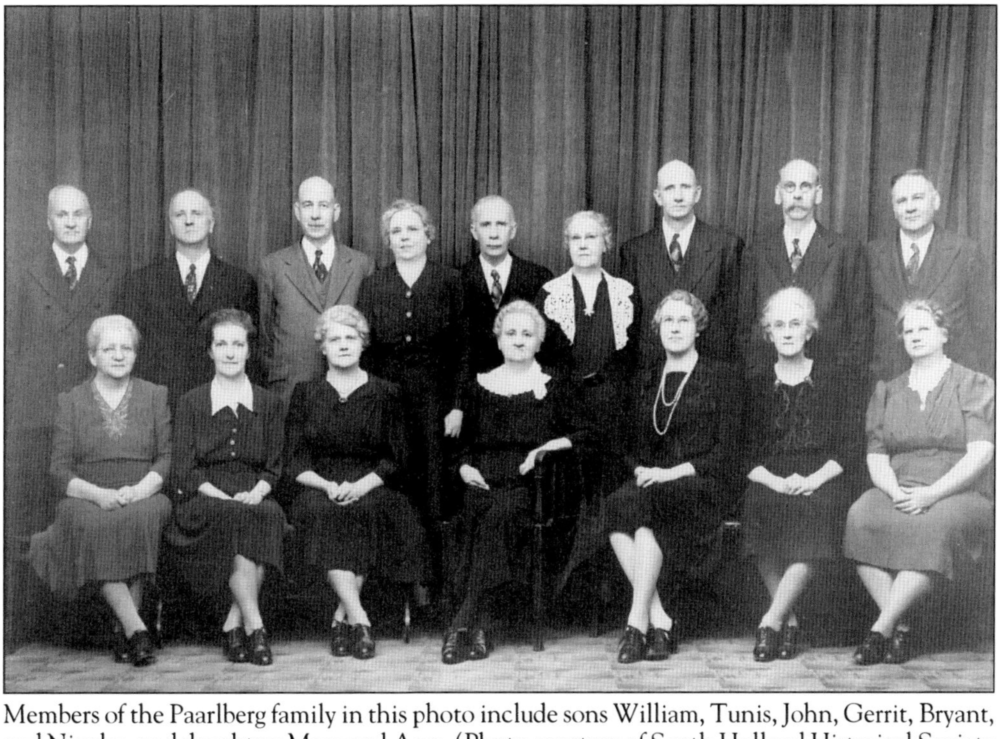

Members of the Paarlberg family in this photo include sons William, Tunis, John, Gerrit, Bryant, and Nicolas, and daughters Mary and Ann. (Photo courtesy of South Holland Historical Society from the collection of Dr. Carl Walvoord.)

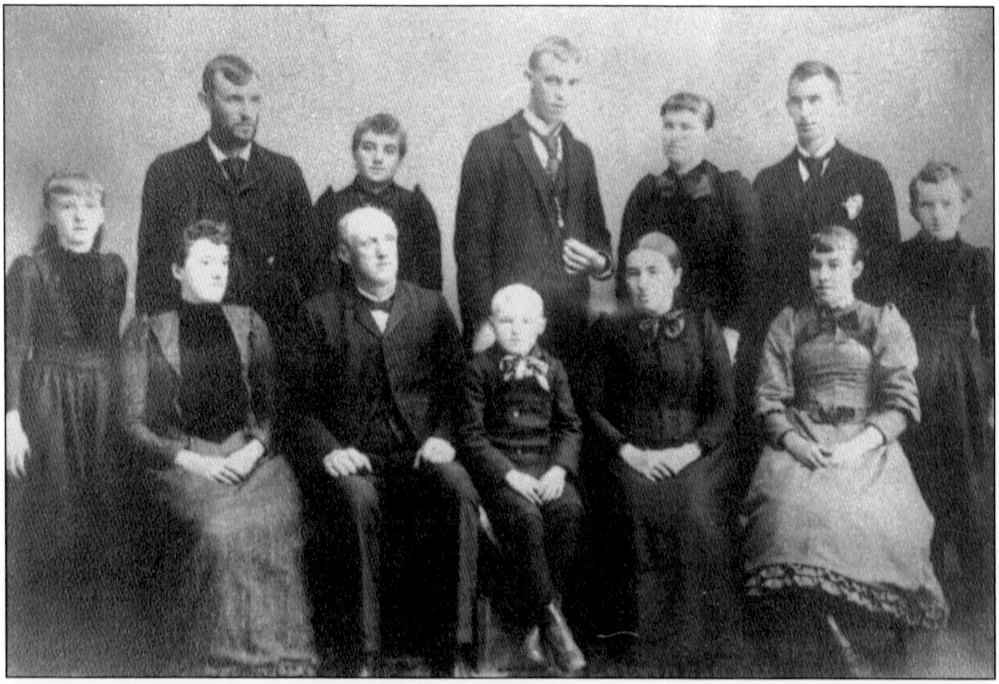

The Family of Arie Bardwick, from left to right: (front row) Cora, Mr. and Mrs. Bardwick, Nicolas, Yarrmitje, Nellie, and Caroline; (back row) John, Tellie, Harry, Alice, Garrit, and Carrie. The Bardwicks ran a store on South Park Avenue for years, ran by Mr. Bardwick and later managed by Carrie and Nellie. (Photo courtesy of South Holland Historical Society from the collection of Dr. Carl Walvoord.)

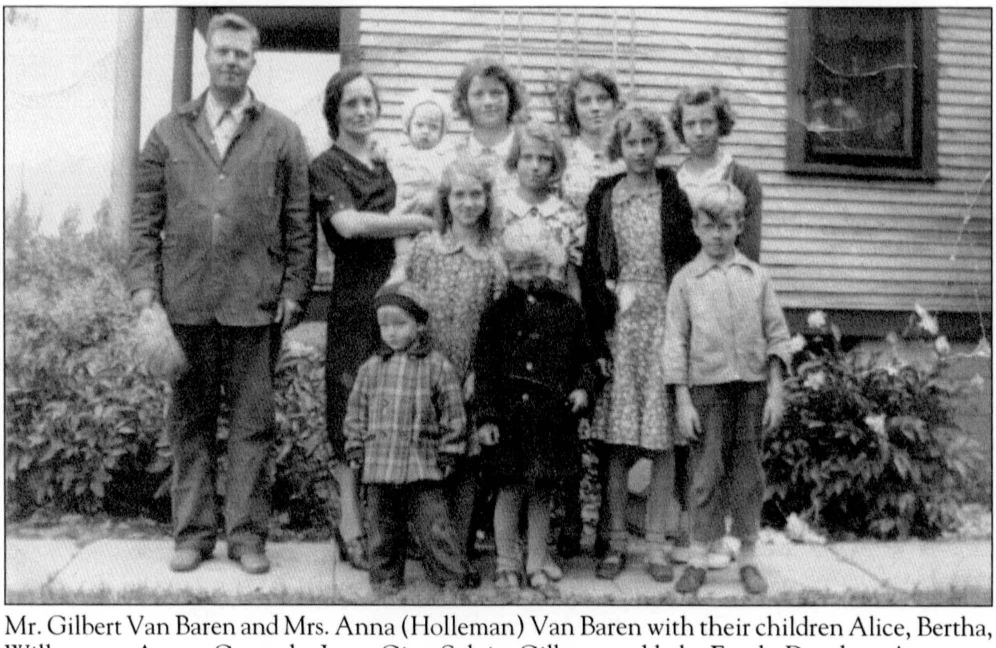

Mr. Gilbert Van Baren and Mrs. Anna (Holleman) Van Baren with their children Alice, Bertha, Willametta, Agnes, Gertrude, Joan, Gise, Sylvia, Gilbert, and baby Frank. Daughter Anna was not yet born. (Photo courtesy of Joan Van Baren.)

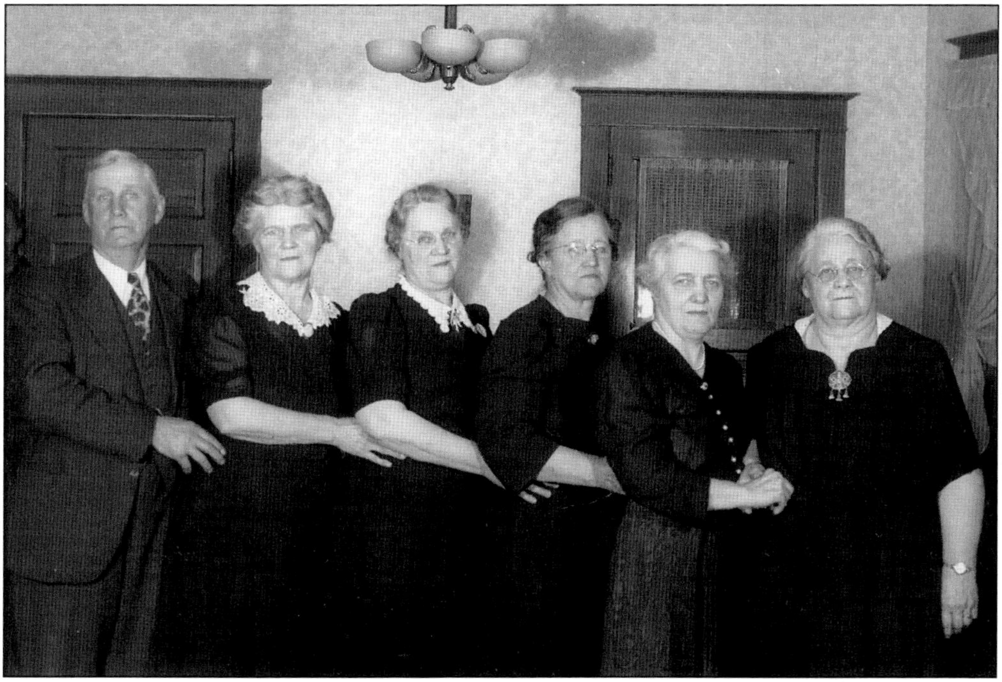

The Anker siblings, children of Peter W. Anker and Hermina (Rietveld) Anker, from left to right, are William P. Anker (youngest), Mrs. John Paarlberg, Mrs. Nick De Boer, Mrs. Isaac Shilling, Mrs. Albert Gouwens, and Mrs. R. J. Van Drunen. Mrs. Nick De Boer and Mrs. Albert Gouwens were twins. (Photo courtesy of Georgian Van Drunen.)

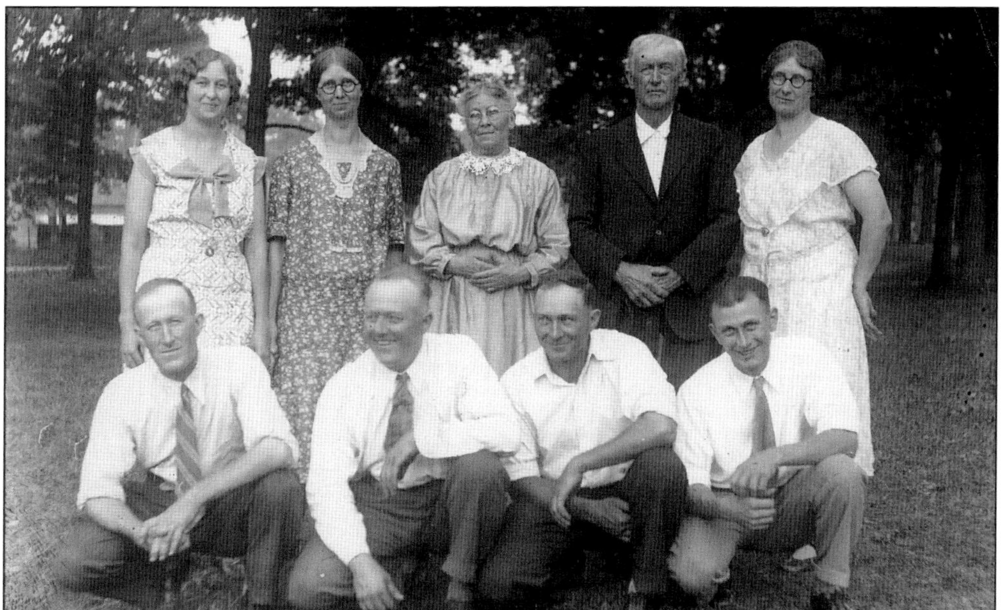

Pictured are Anna Van Drunen Vanderbilt (back row, middle) and Reinder Vanderbilt (back row, to right of Anna). The couple had an orchard in the area of Route 6 and Cottage Grove, where the Jewel store stands today. (Photo courtesy of Georgian Van Drunen.)

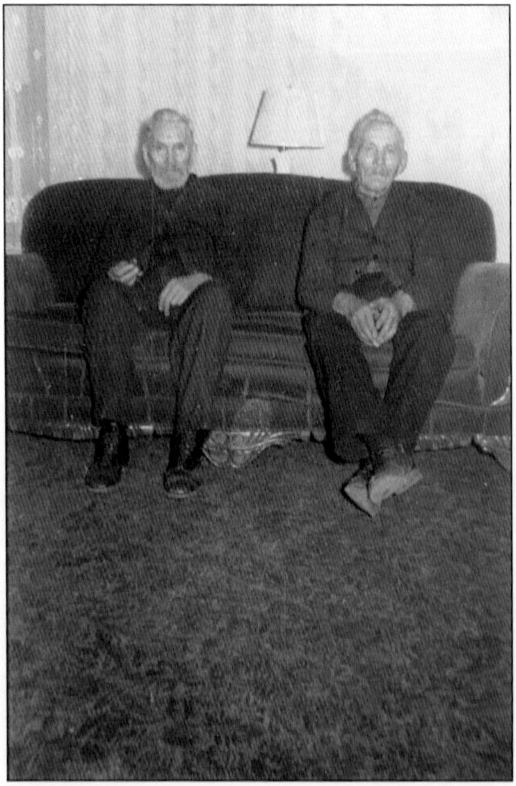

Brothers Peter and Simon Van Duersen came to the United States from Holland in 1893 and settled in South Holland. Peter and his wife, Johanna, had eight children—three girls and five boys. Only two of the boys lived to adulthood. (Photo courtesy of Georgian Van Drunen.)

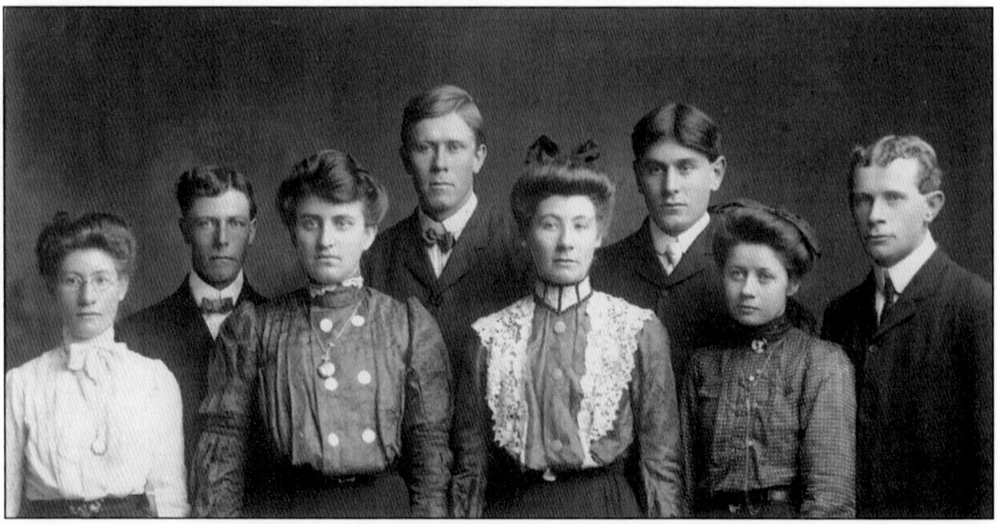

Siblings of the Voss family. The first three females are Voss sisters, with their husbands standing behind them. The fourth male is Henry Voss, with wife Henrietta Gouwens Voss standing in front of him. (Photo courtesy of Georgian Van Drunen.)

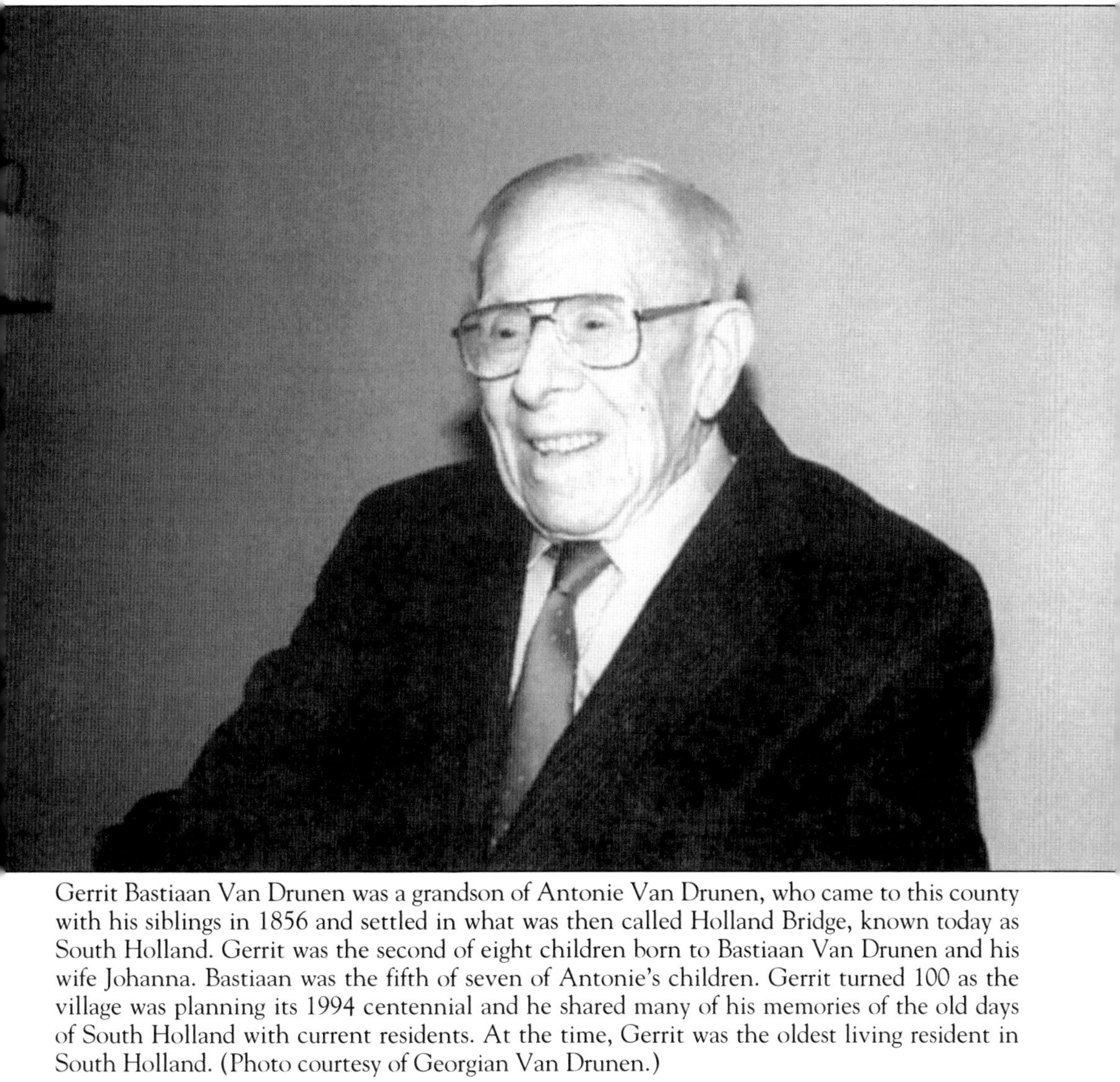

Gerrit Bastiaan Van Drunen was a grandson of Antonie Van Drunen, who came to this county with his siblings in 1856 and settled in what was then called Holland Bridge, known today as South Holland. Gerrit was the second of eight children born to Bastiaan Van Drunen and his wife Johanna. Bastiaan was the fifth of seven of Antonie's children. Gerrit turned 100 as the village was planning its 1994 centennial and he shared many of his memories of the old days of South Holland with current residents. At the time, Gerrit was the oldest living resident in South Holland. (Photo courtesy of Georgian Van Drunen.)

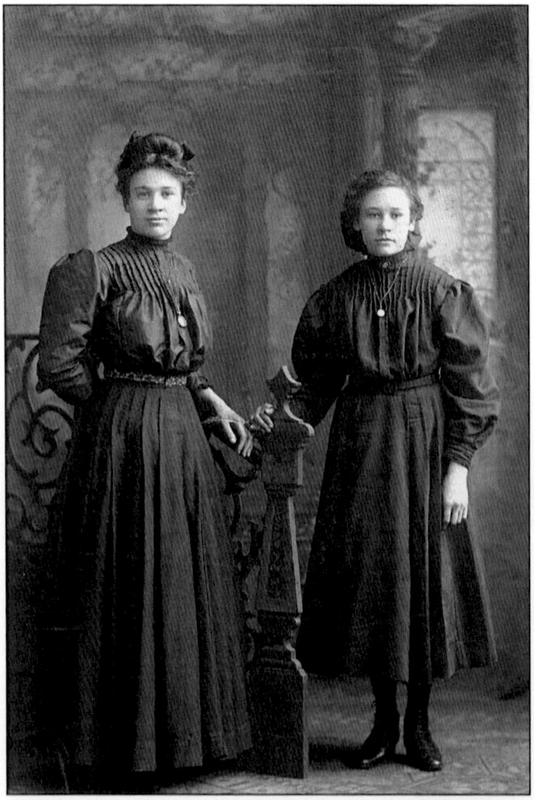

Sisters Nellie Van Deursen Vanderbilt and Cora Van Deursen Van Drunen. (Photo courtesy of Georgian Van Drunen.)

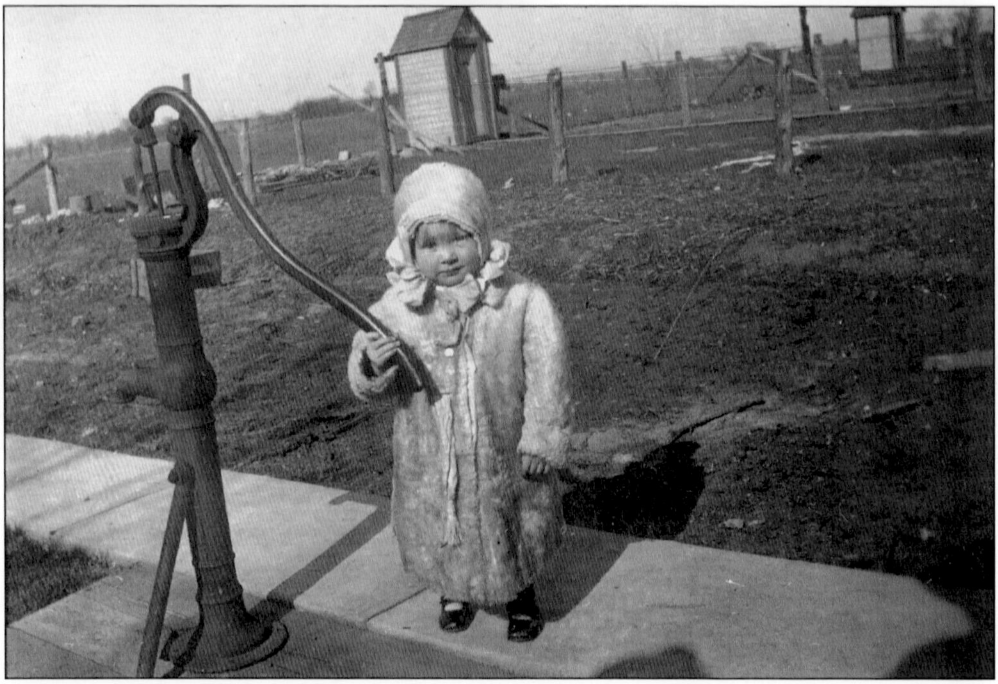

Anna Vanderbilt Voss in about 1913 at around age two. (Photo courtesy of Georgian Van Drunen.)

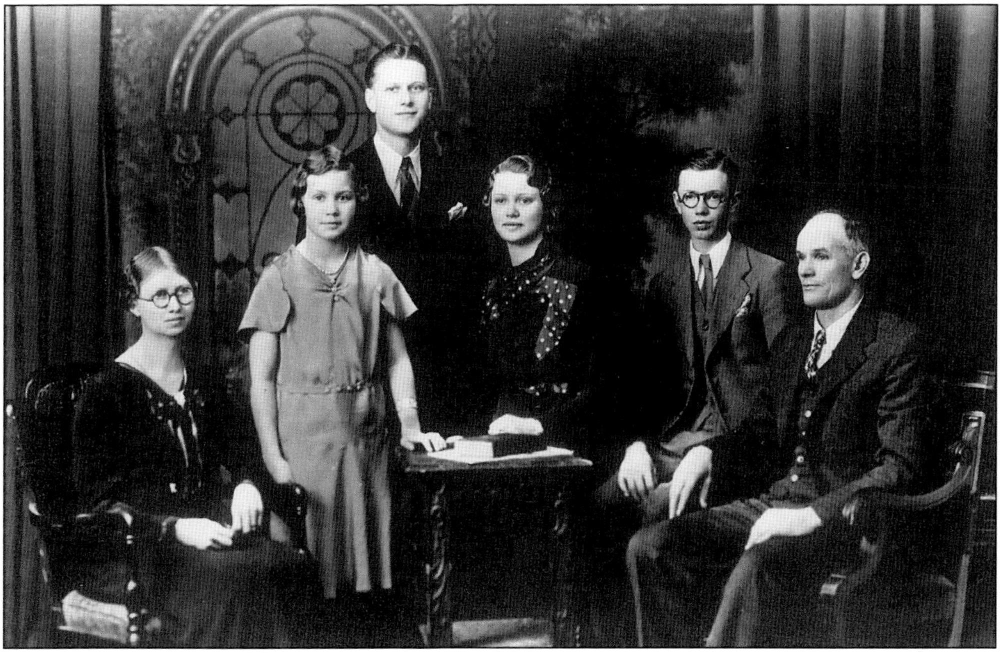

Henry and Hester De Young are pictured with their four children. (Photo courtesy of Georgian Van Drunen.)

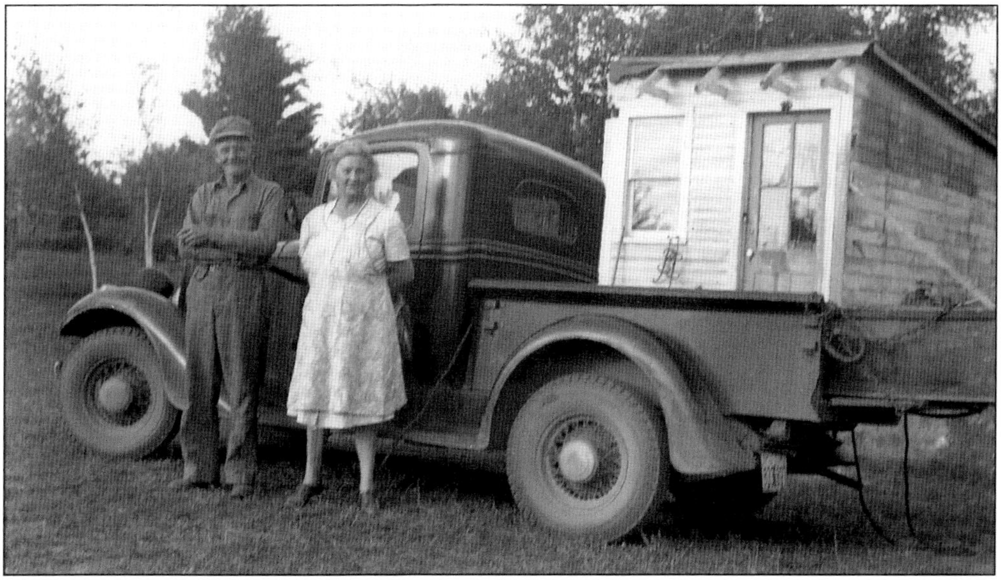

Ben and Nellie De Young had both been previously married and Ben had seven boys and Nellie had three girls and two boys. The couple raised the 12 children together, and did not have any other children. (Photo courtesy of Georgian Van Drunen.)

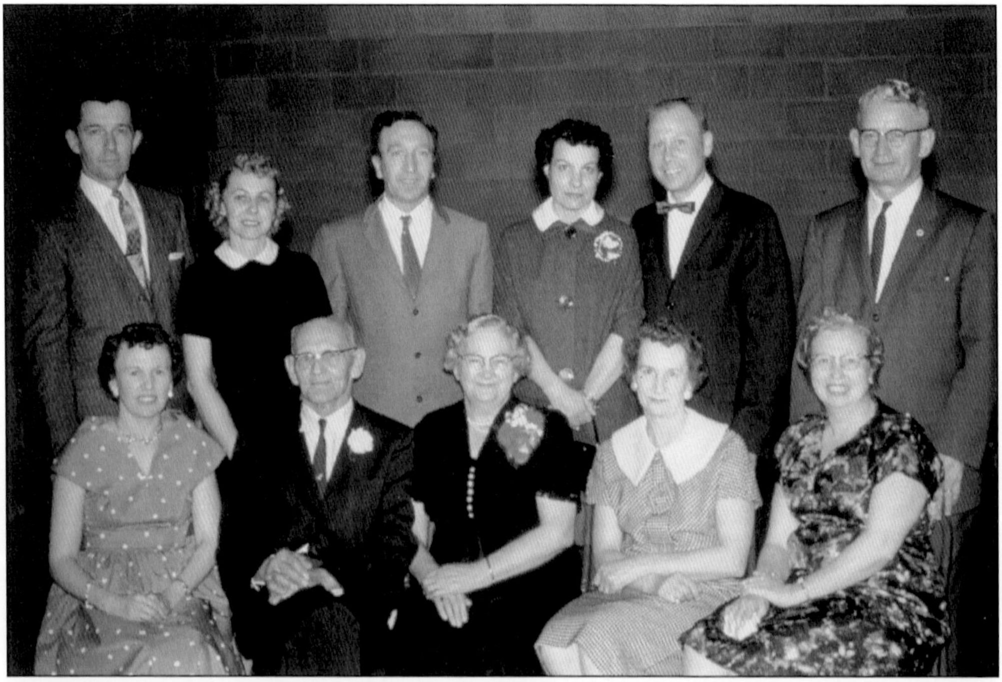

Ben and Nellie De Young (front row, second and third from left) celebrate their 25th anniversary in 1959. (Photo courtesy of Georgian Van Drunen.)

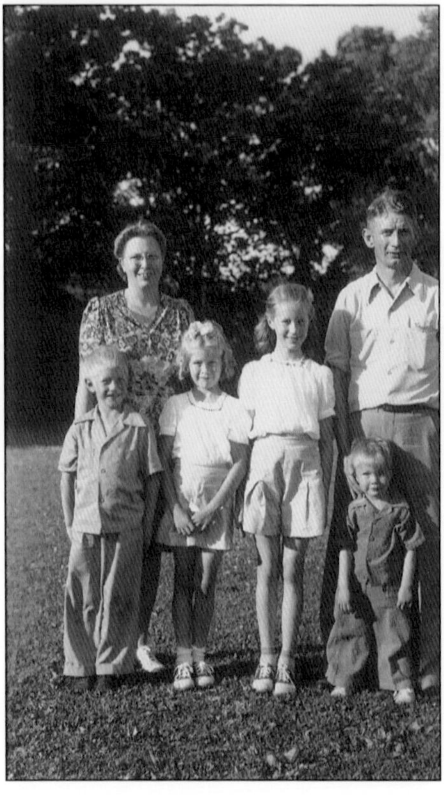

Ann Vanderbilt Voss, George Voss, and their children, from left to right, Paul, Marlene, Georgian, and Eugene. The photo was taken around 1947. (Photo courtesy of Georgian Van Drunen.)

The wedding photo of Ann Vanderbilt Voss and George Voss, married July 12, 1935. (Photo courtesy of Georgian Van Drunen.)

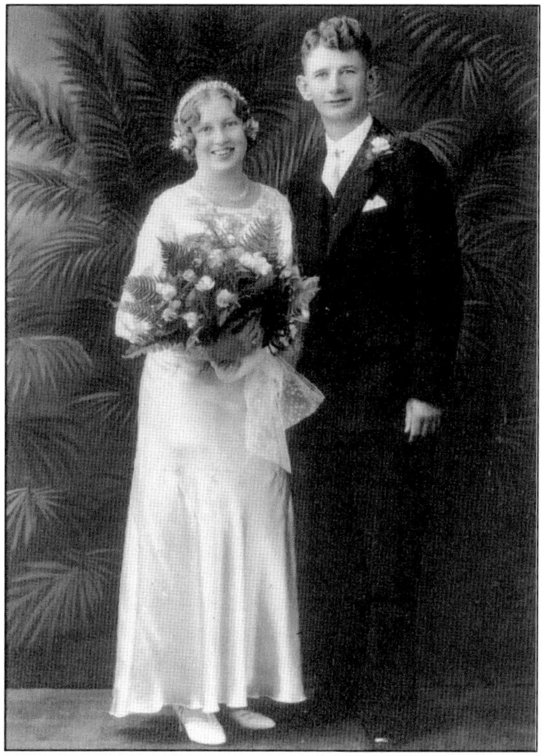

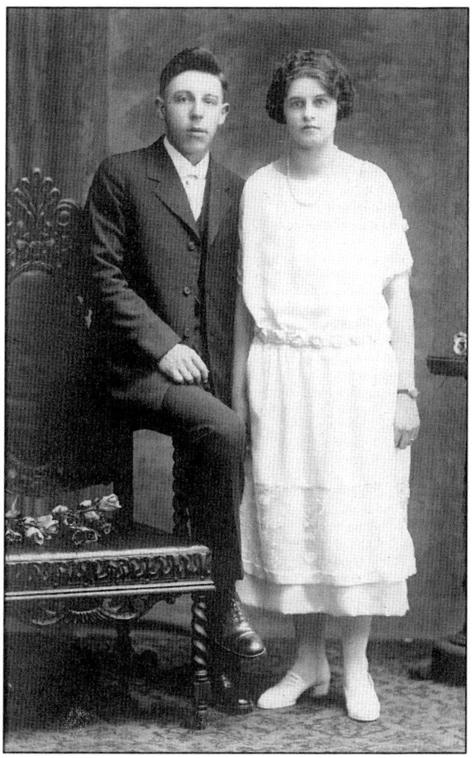

The wedding photo of Anthony Van Drunen and Nellie Van Der Aa in the 1920s. (Photo courtesy of Georgian Van Drunen.)

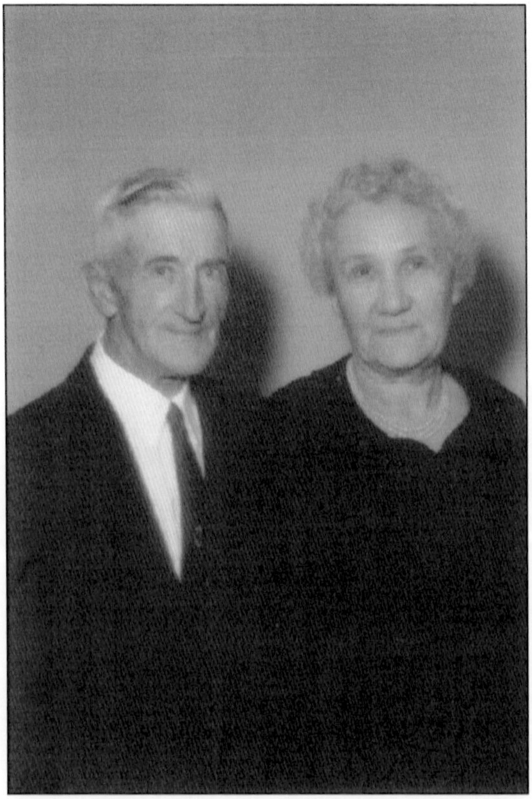

Bill Vroegh and his wife Johanna had one son, Sam, and two daughters, Nellie and Ada. Ada married a member of the Wognum family, which owns and operates Wognum Electric on Van Dam Road. (Photo courtesy of Joan Van Baren.)

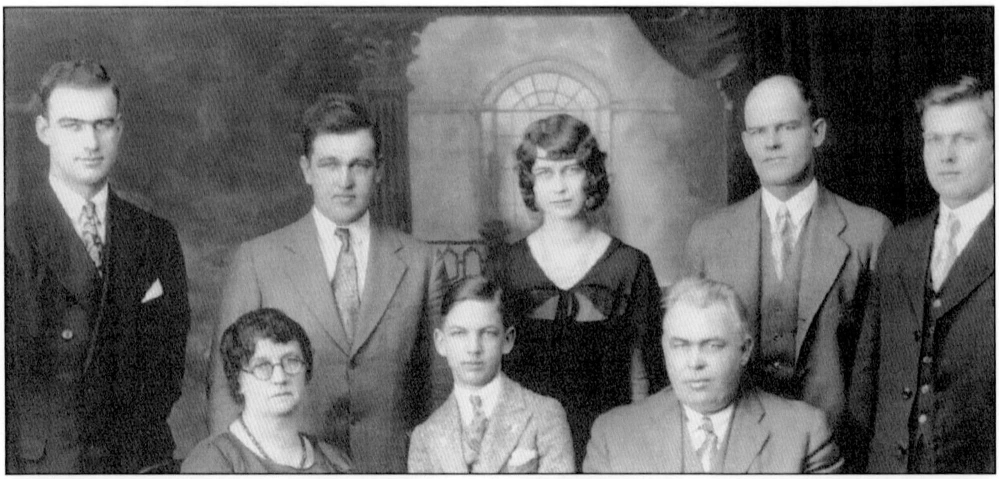

An early 1930s photo of the Gise Van Baren Family. Pictured from left to right are: (front row) Alice (mother), Gerrit (who just passed away in the Spring of 2003), and Gise (father); (back row) John, Art, Agnes Van Drunen, Frank, and Gilbert. (Photo courtesy of Joan Van Baren.)

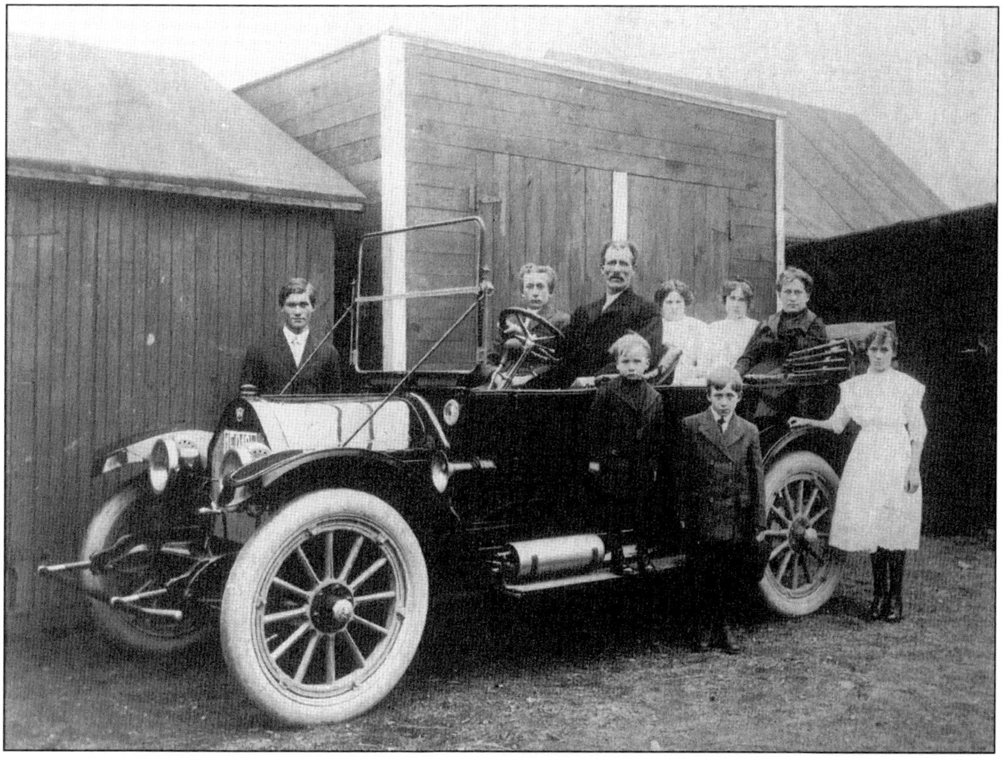

A 1916 photo of the Holleman family shows, from left to right, John, Egbert, William (father, in driver seat), Sophie, Alice, Bertha (mother), and Anna (age 16). The boys in front are Anthony and Herbert. (Photo courtesy of Joan Van Baren.)

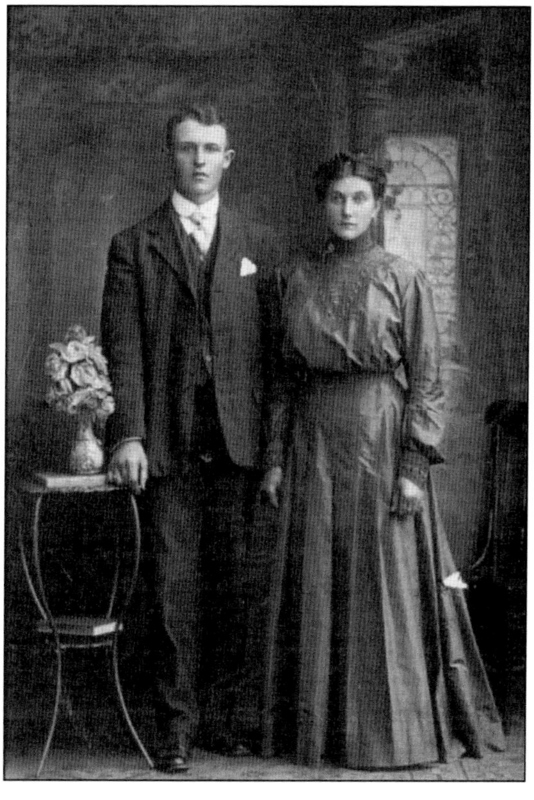

Jerry Lenting, a farmer, is pictured with his wife, Ida. (Photo courtesy of Joan Van Baren.)

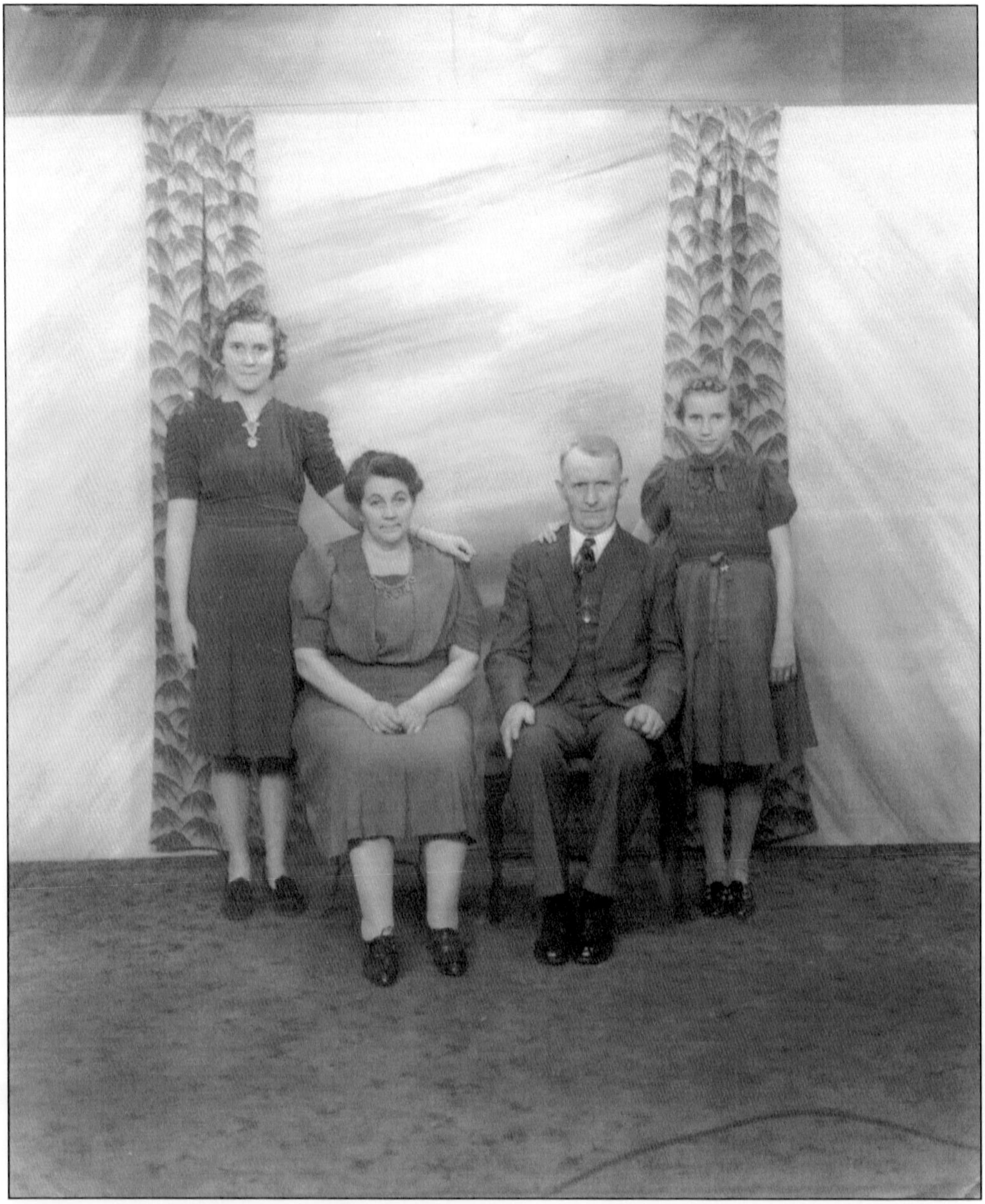

Jerry and Ida Lenting had no children of their own, but took care of two nieces after the death of their parents. The nieces are Tina Bruisma (left) and Clara Couwenhoven (right). (Photo courtesy of Joan Van Baren.)

Three

FAITH

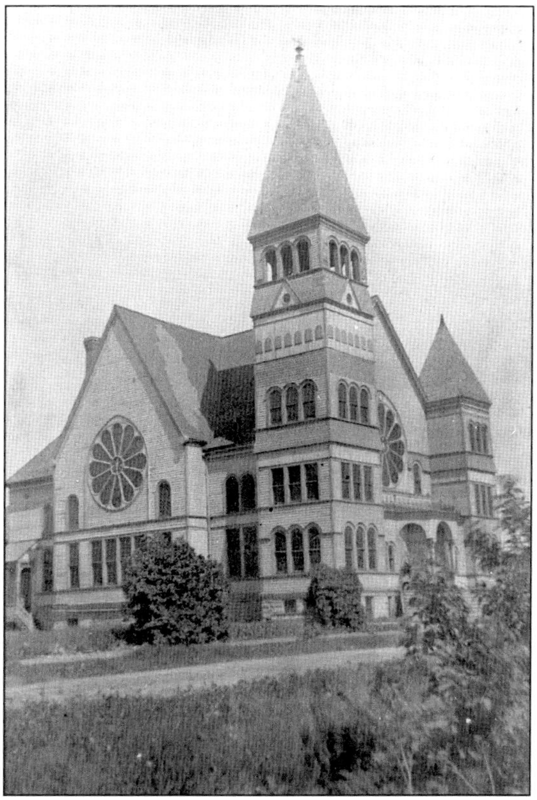

The First Reformed Church of South Holland has seen four buildings occupy its current site. The first church, which was called Low Prairie Church, was formed by fourteen families of Dutch immigrants and the first church was erected in 1848. Another church was rebuilt in 1863 and a third in 1891. In 1899, the name of the church became the First Reformed Church of South Holland. Pictured is the third church building, dedicated on February 29, 1891. The high steeple was later removed. (Photo courtesy of South Holland Historical Society from the collection of Dr. Carl Walvoord.)

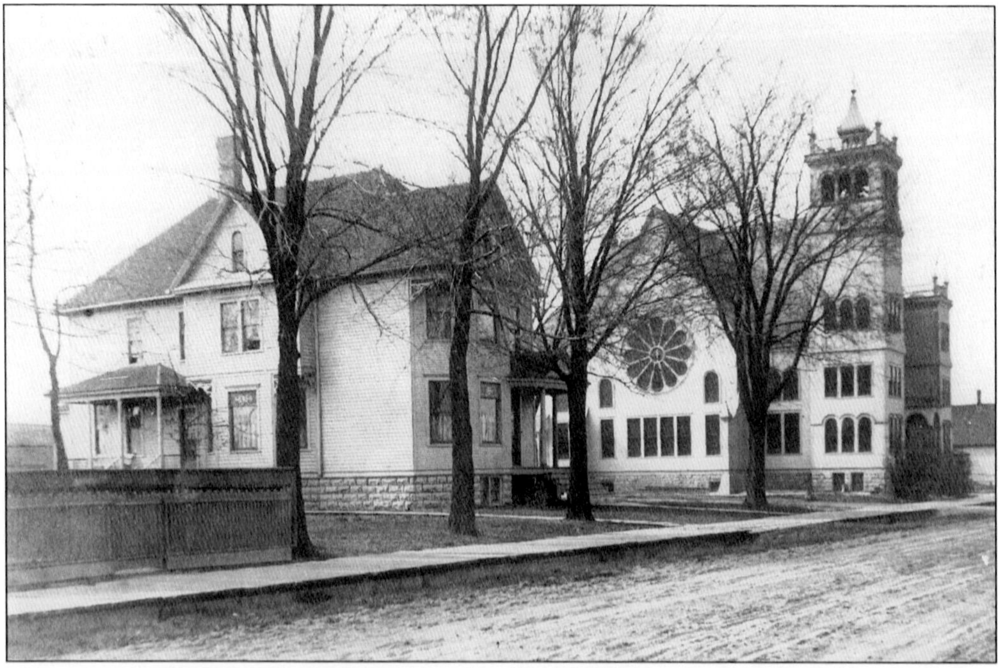

This picture, taken prior to 1920, shows the third building of the First Reformed Church and parsonage. (Photo courtesy of South Holland Historical Society from the collection of Dr. Carl Walvoord.)

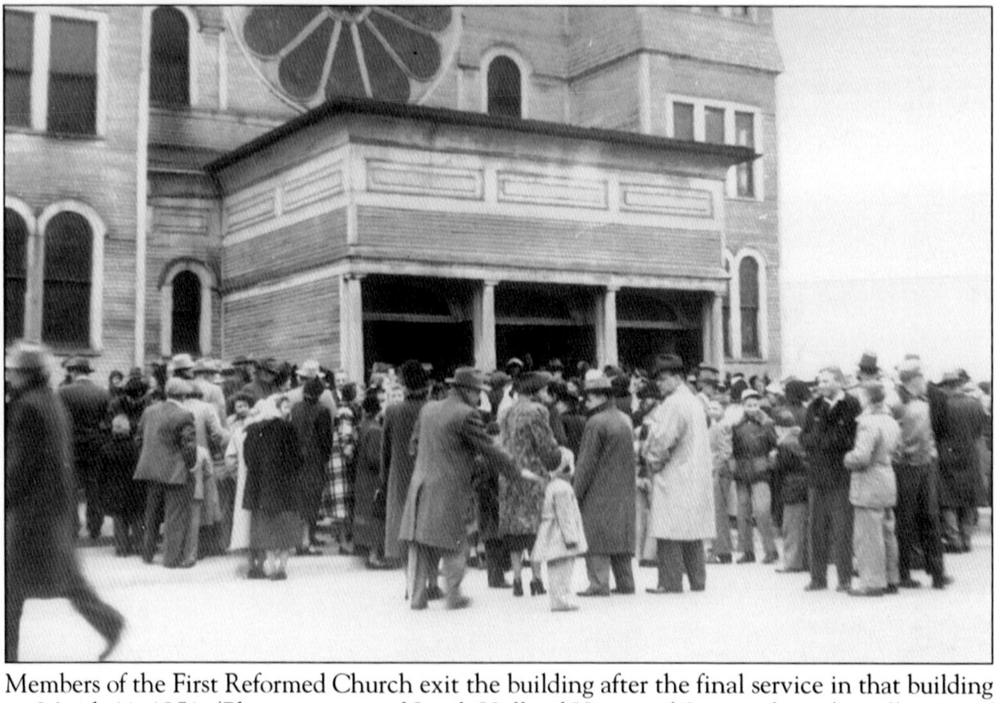

Members of the First Reformed Church exit the building after the final service in that building on March 11, 1951. (Photo courtesy of South Holland Historical Society from the collection of Dr. Carl Walvoord.)

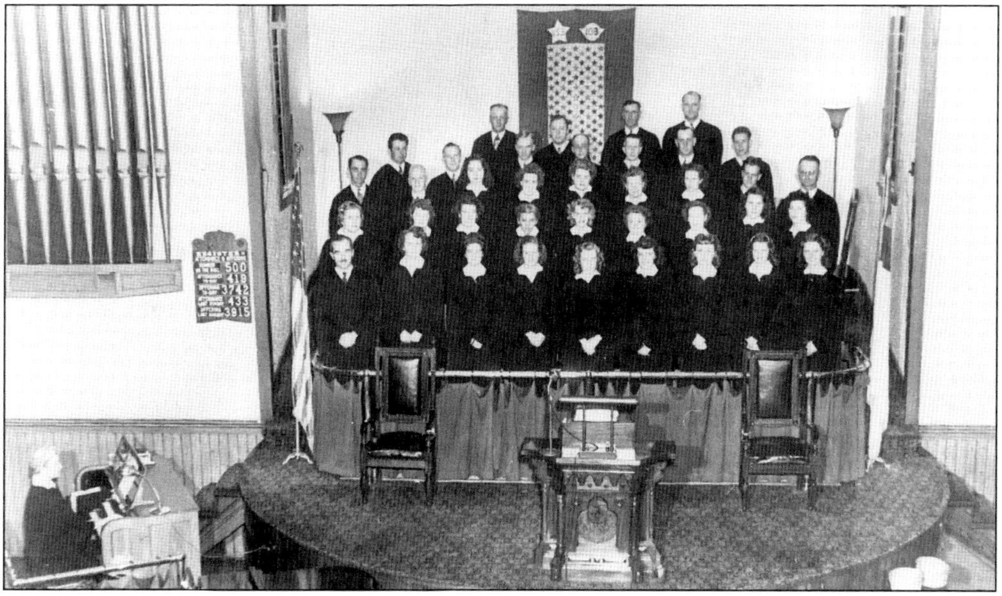

Members of the First Reformed Church Pulpit and Choir are: (front Row) Mr. Lambert, director, G. Bottema, Ethel Reinkma, Julia De Young, Jane Ellen Rietvelt, Joanne Paarlberg, Dorothy Prince, Harriet Santefort, and Carol De Graff; (second row) Florence Gouwens, Queenie Gouwens, Alice Cook, Abbie Anker, Lorraine De Groot, Cora Van Dyke, Margaret Cook, Caryl Paarlberg, and Ruth Jansma; (third row) Cornelius Ven Druin, Richard G. De Young, Susan de Jong, Dorothy Verchught, Viola Veld, Esther Van Milligan, Jeanette Van Kley, David Paarlberg, and Henry Gouwens; (fourth row) Harold Ver Druin, Bert Van Kley, Matt Van Der Wolf, William Rietvelt, Henry Reitvelt, Tel Paarlberg, and Dick Jansma; (back row) Casey Paarlberg, Art Van Kley, John Santefort, and Rob Gouwens. M. Rietvelt is at the organ. Leona Paarlberg is at the piano. (Photo courtesy of South Holland Historical Society from the collection of Dr. Carl Walvoord.)

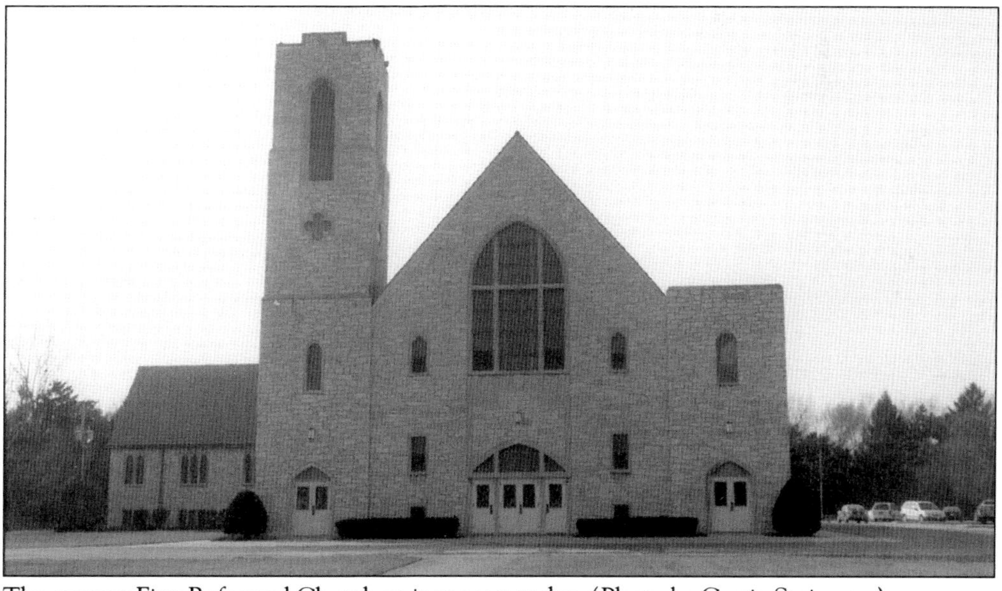

The current First Reformed Church as it appears today. (Photo by Carrie Steinweg.)

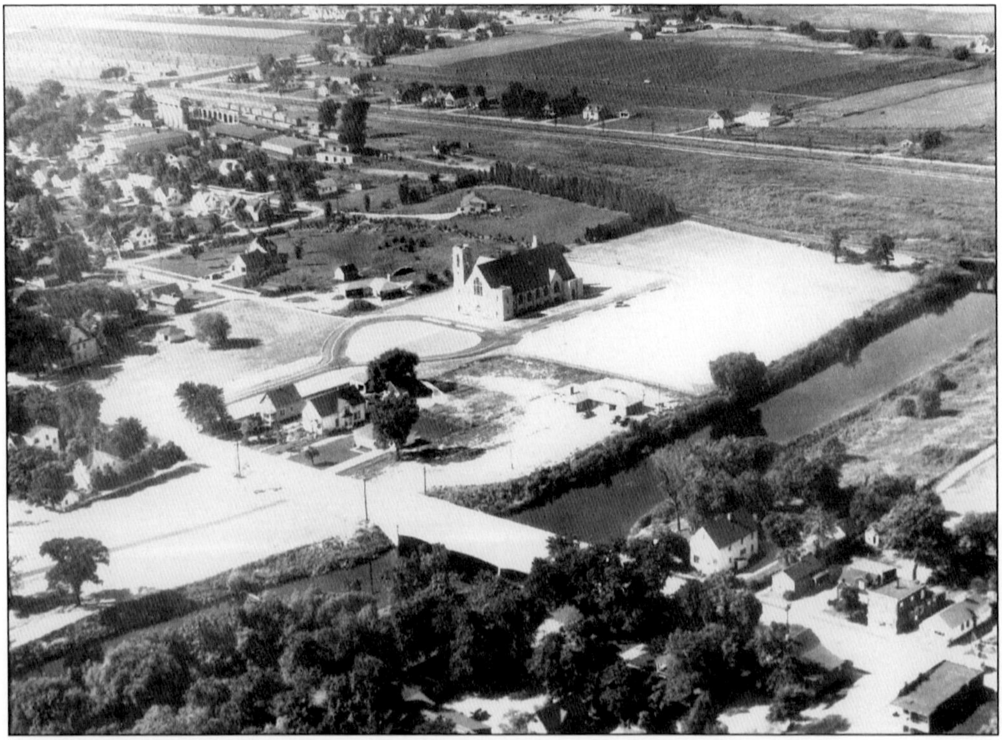

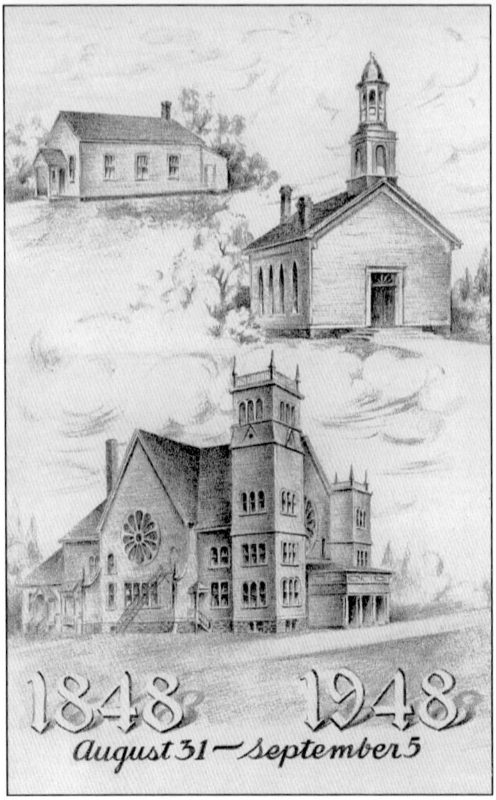

An aerial view of the current First Reformed Church. (Photo courtesy of South Holland Historical Society from the collection of Dr. Carl Walvoord.)

This flyer for the First Reformed Church's centennial service includes sketches of the first three buildings on the cover of the program. (Courtesy of Jim Veld.)

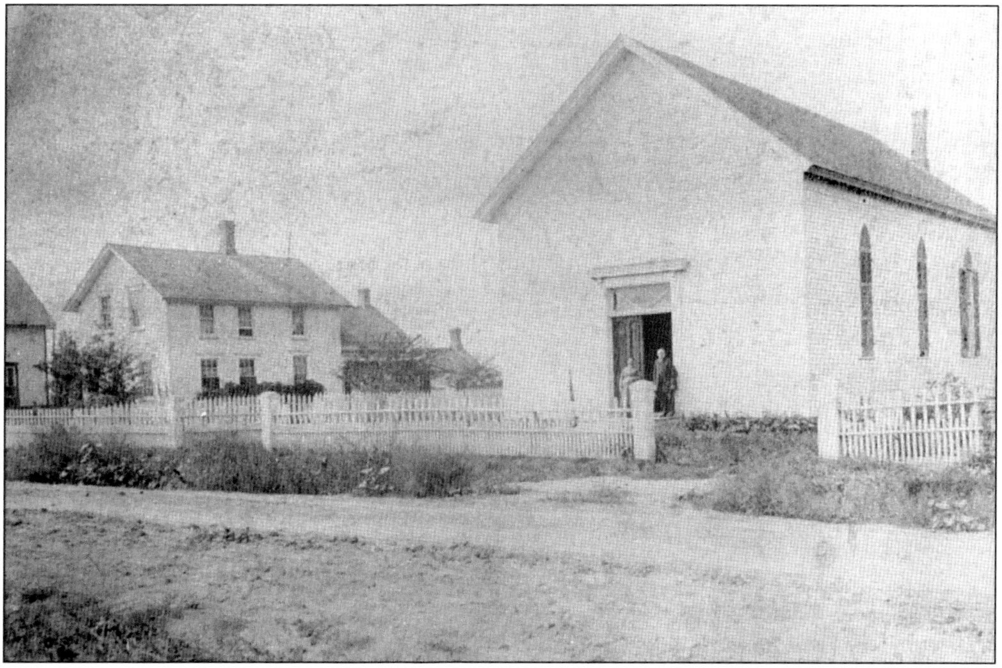

The small True Dutch Reformed Church has been a place of worship for South Hollanders for over 125 years. (Photo courtesy of South Holland Historical Society from the collection of Dr. Carl Walvoord.)

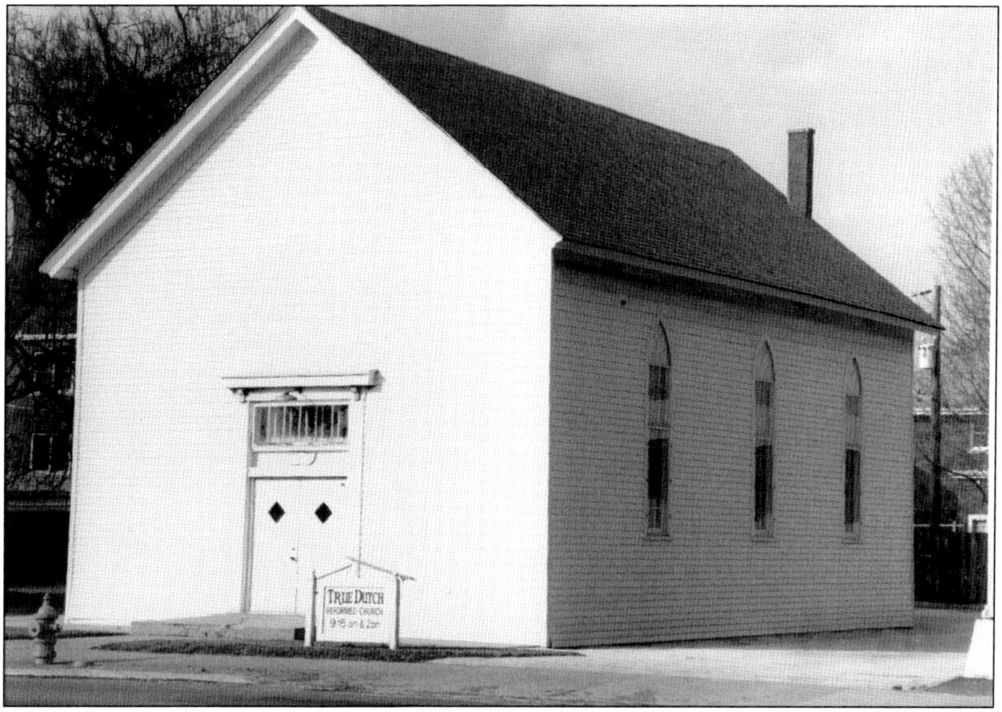

The True Dutch Reformed Church has not changed in appearance, although many of the homes and buildings along Route 6 have seen changes or been demolished. (Photo by Carrie Steinweg.)

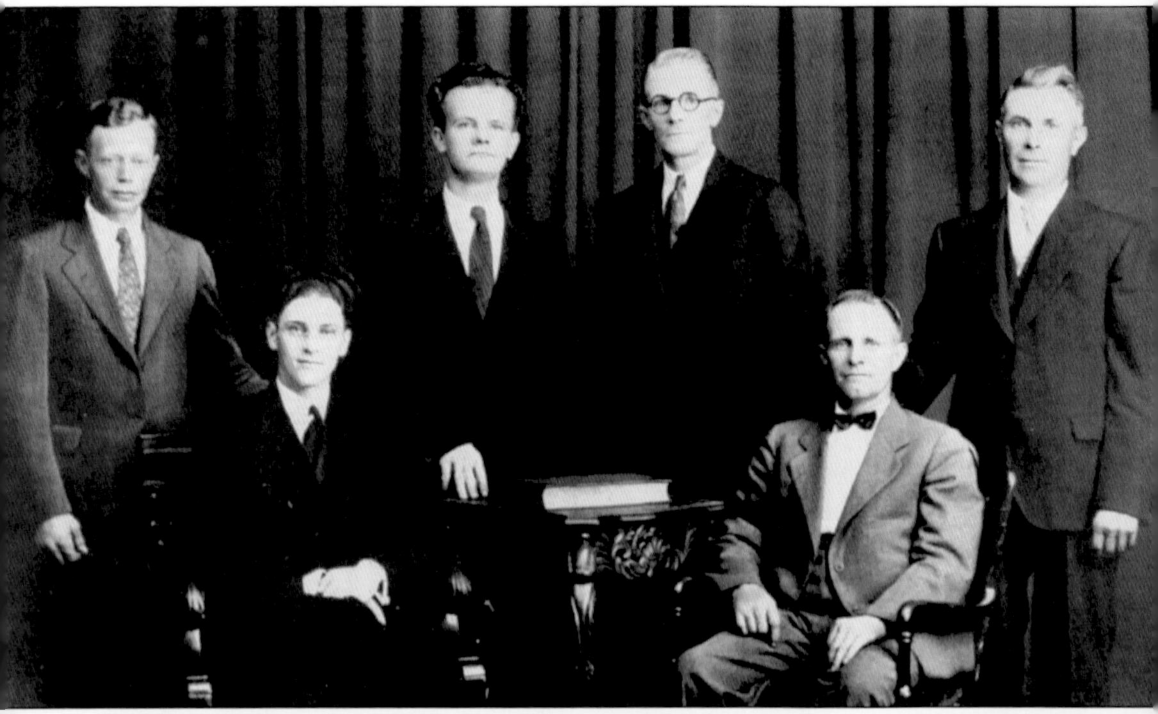

The first pastor and consistory of the Protestant Reformed Church, which was organized in 1926. Pictured from left to right are: (front row) A. Poortenga and Rev. Peter De Boer; (back row) A. Miedema, W. Terpstra, A. Hoeksema, and L. Lanting.

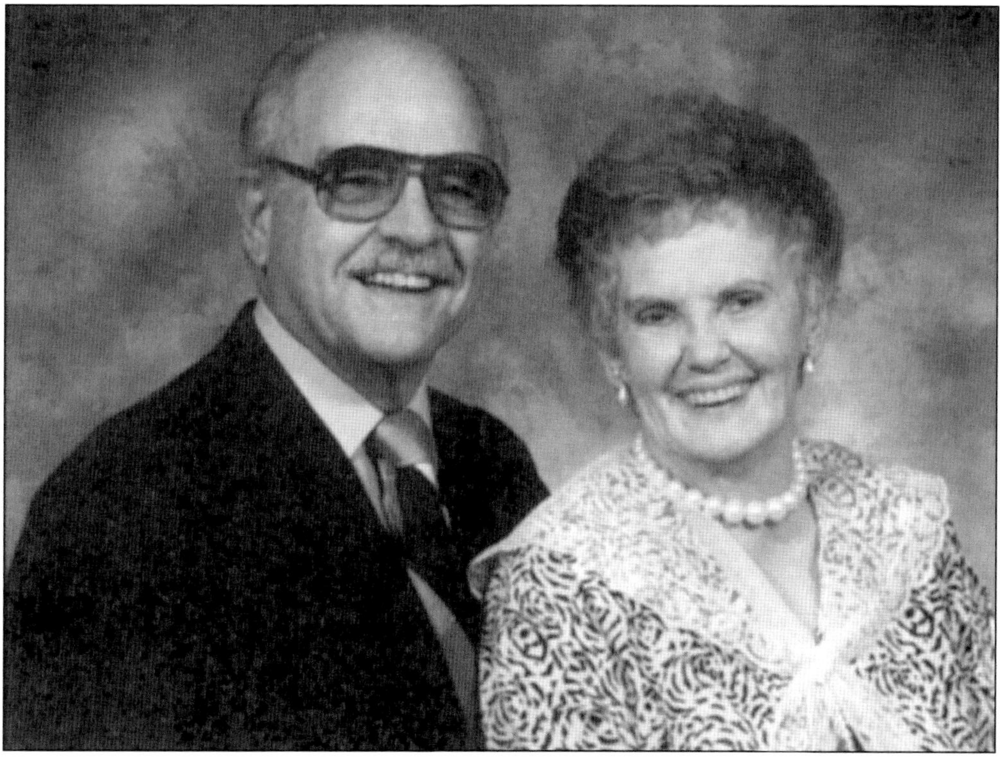

Herman Rosenberg, the first full-time pastor of Faith Reformed Church, is pictured here with his wife, Flora.

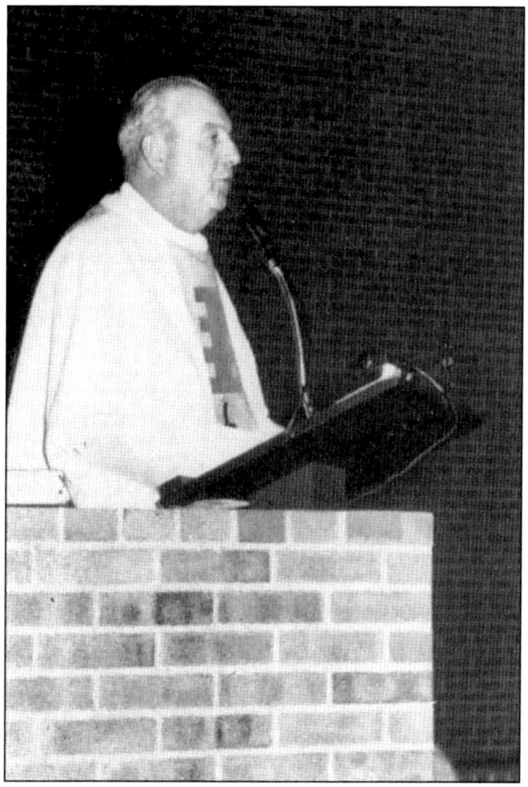

Father Thomas Gorman was the founding pastor of Holy Ghost Parish, pictured here at the dedication ceremonies on May 16, 1971.

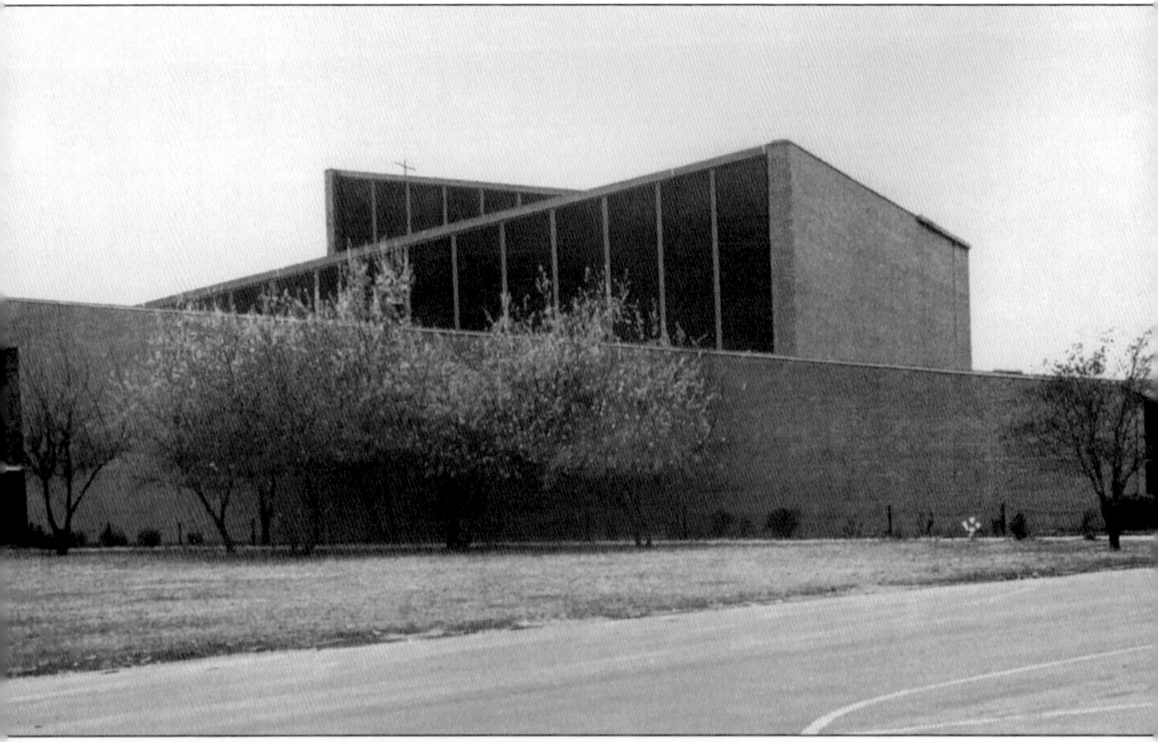

Holy Ghost Parish at the time of its opening.

Four

EDUCATION

As far as education, these words always stuck with me: "Those who teach children, labor in God's workshop."

—Jim Veld, longtime Board member of School District 205

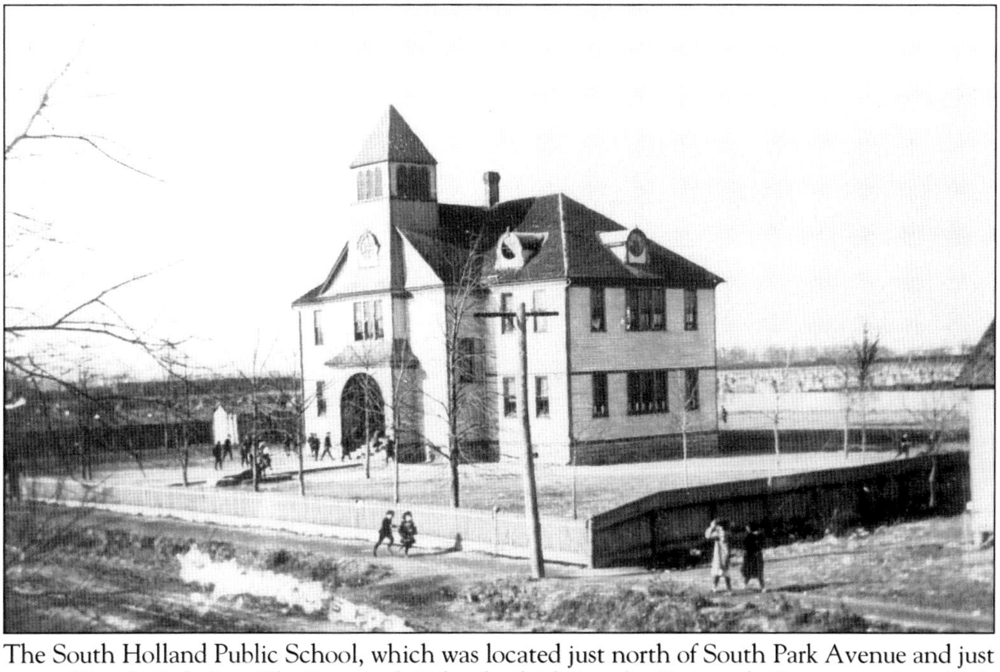

The South Holland Public School, which was located just north of South Park Avenue and just west of South Park Ave. The Roosevelt School, which is today Roosevelt Center, was later built on the grounds. Bessie and Tunis Paarlberg are in front of the school, going home for lunch. (Photo courtesy of South Holland Historical Society from the collection of Dr. Carl Walvoord.)

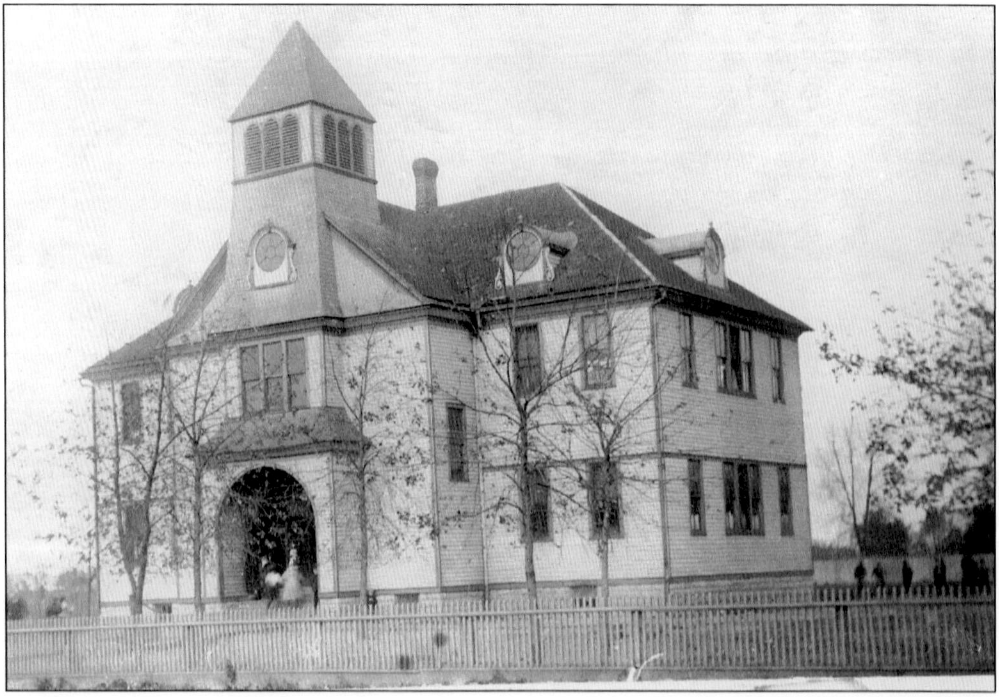

Later photographs of the South Holland Public School are seen here. (Photo courtesy of South Holland Historical Society from the collection of Dr. Carl Walvoord.)

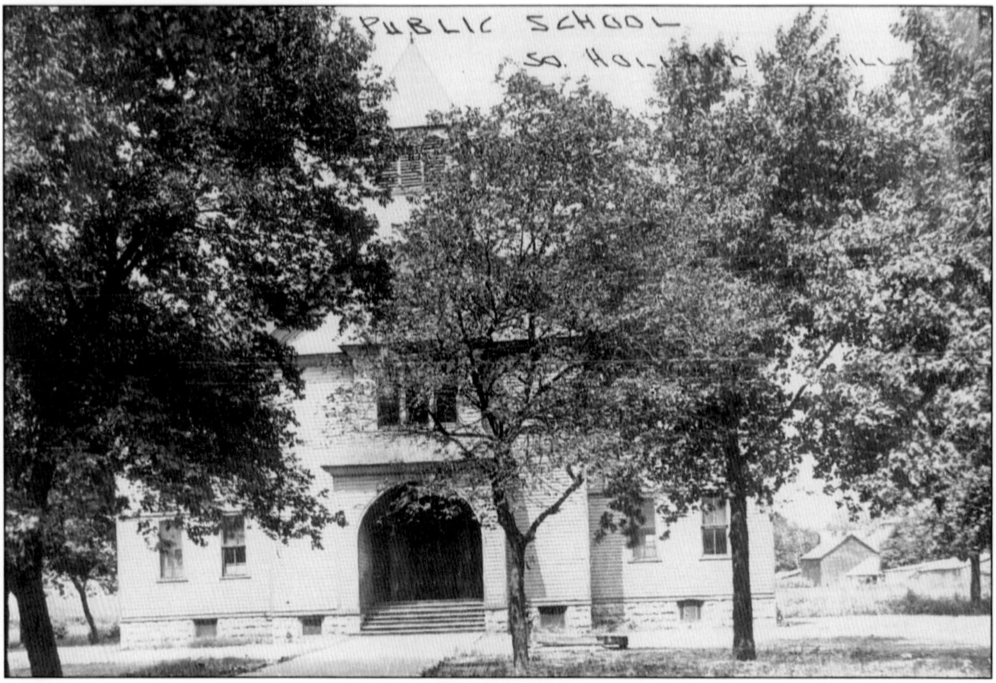

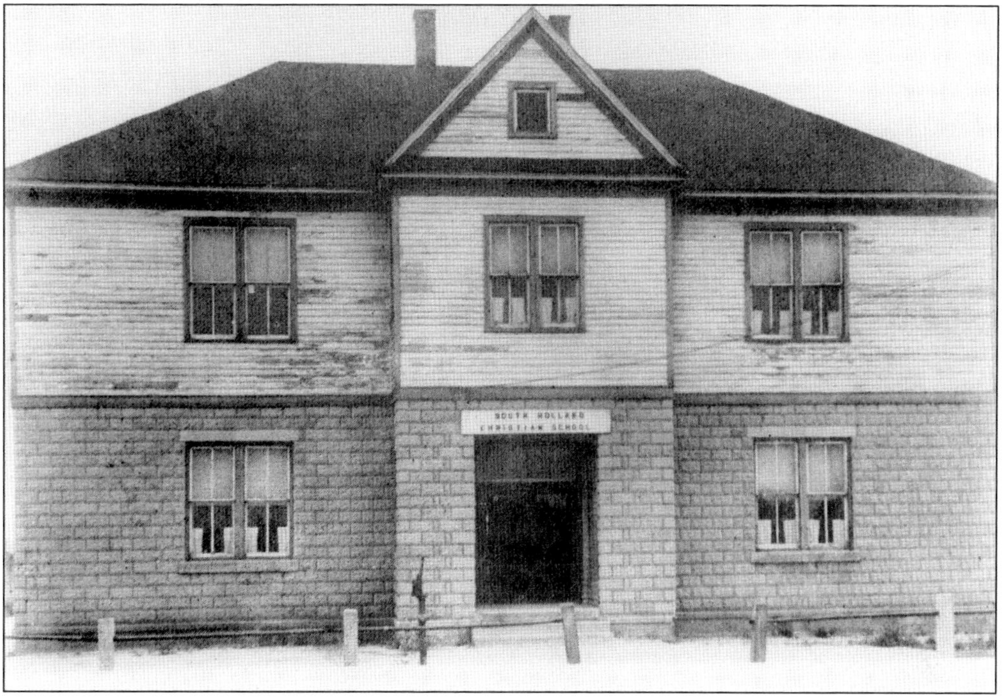

The South Holland Christian School was located on Route 6. (Photo courtesy of South Holland Historical Society from the collection of Dr. Carl Walvoord.)

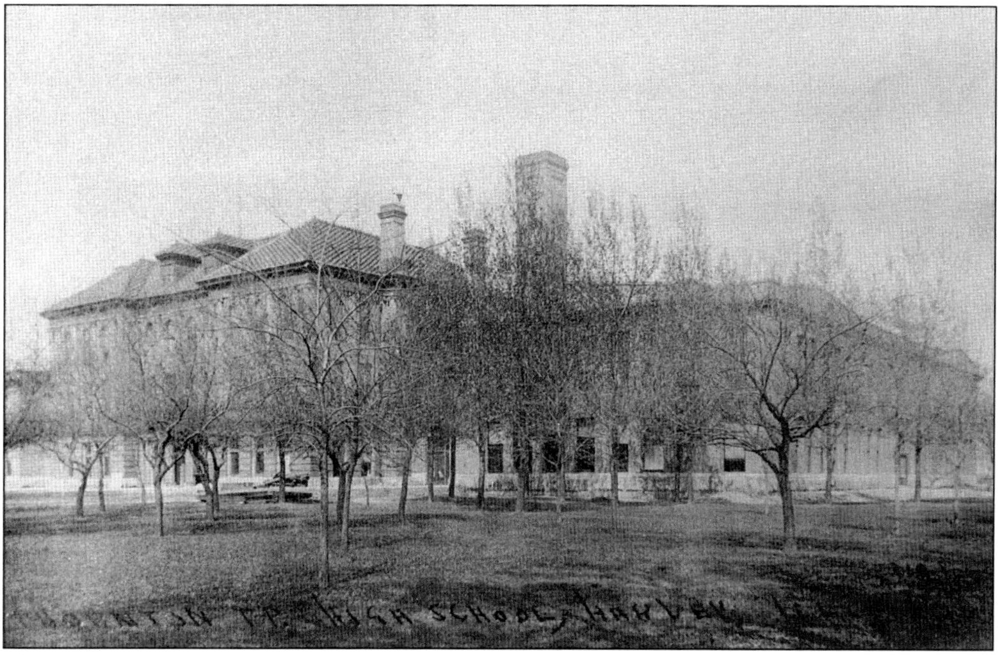

This photo was taken long before Thornridge and Thornwood high schools existed. Prior to 1924, when additions were made to the building, teenagers in South Holland attended Thornton High School in Harvey. (Photo courtesy of South Holland Historical Society from the collection of Dr. Carl Walvoord.)

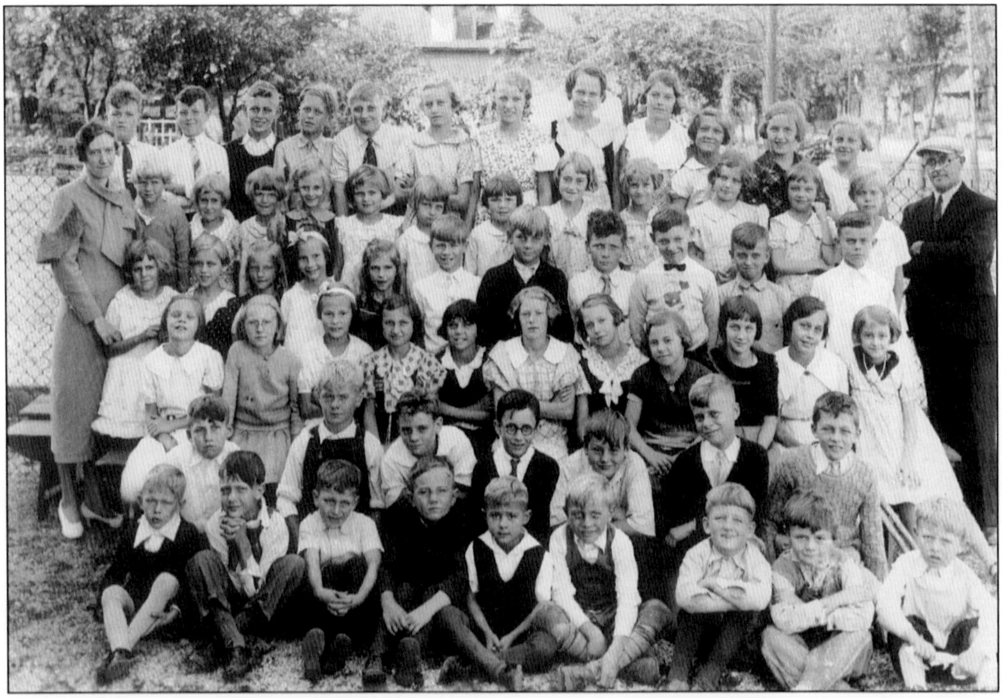

A 1935 photo of students of the South Holland Christian School. (Photo courtesy of South Holland Historical Society from the collection of Dr. Carl Walvoord.)

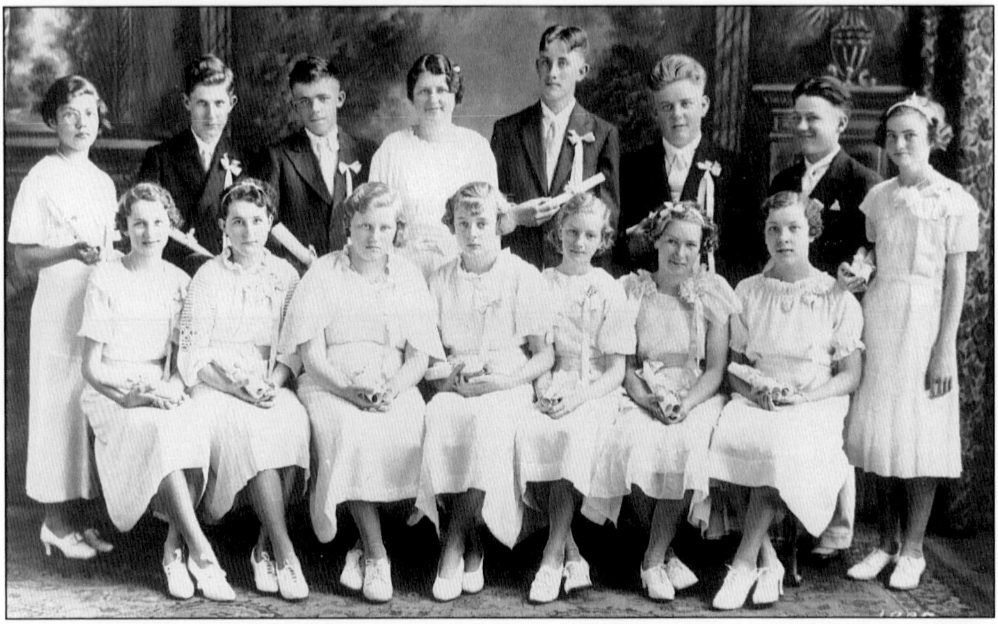

The last graduating class of the Gouwens School in 1935 is, from left to right: (front row) Marie Van Der Giessen, Ann ?, Katherine Hoekstra, Vivian Blink, Irene Bernowski, Cornilia Van Hoort, and Anna Marie Van Milligan; (back row) Maie Owenwald, Gerald Veld, John Kusay, Miss Dorothy Bobhuis, Peter Van Milligan, Clarence Veld, unidentified, and Willabell Robinson. (Photo courtesy of South Holland Historical Society from the collection of Dr. Carl Walvoord.)

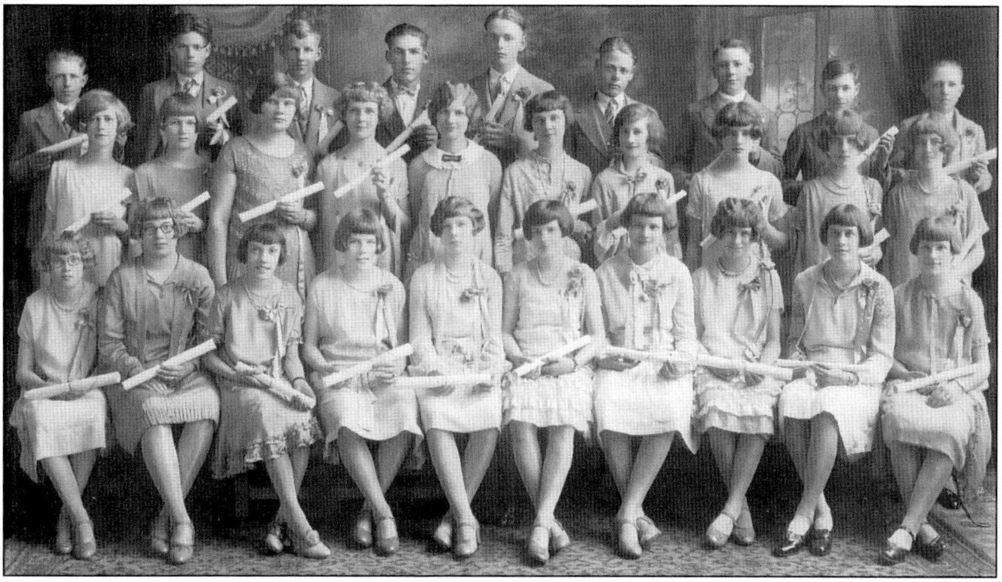

The 1925 graduating class of the Roosevelt School. (Photo courtesy of Georgian Van Drunen.)

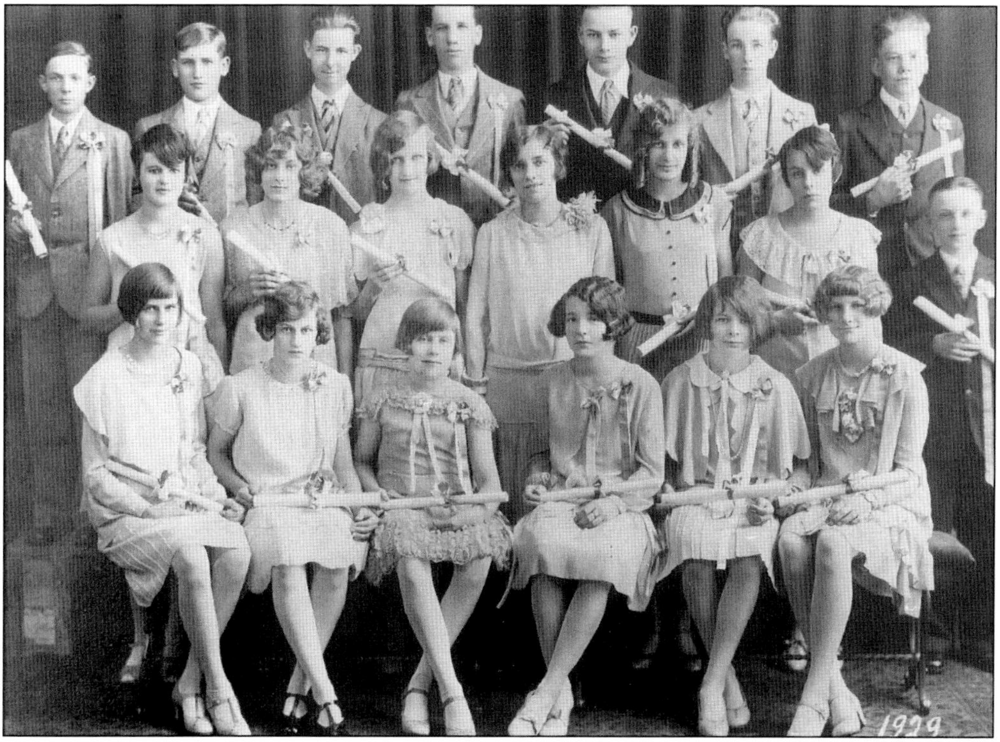

The 1929 Graduating Class of Roosevelt School, is, from left to right: (front row) Marian Newell, Ruth Shilling, Grace Meyer, Alice Gouwens, Ruth Voss, and Carrie Van Der Grind; (second row) Agnes Bottema, Mary Van Der Aa, Marie Triemstra, Miss Peck, Grace Brown, Marian Butler, and Sonny Triemstra; (back row) Bill Santefort, Gerrit Koster, Gerrit Van Kley, Ted Van Der Aa, Nick Topp, and unidentified. (Photo courtesy of South Holland Historical Society from the collection of Dr. Carl Walvoord.)

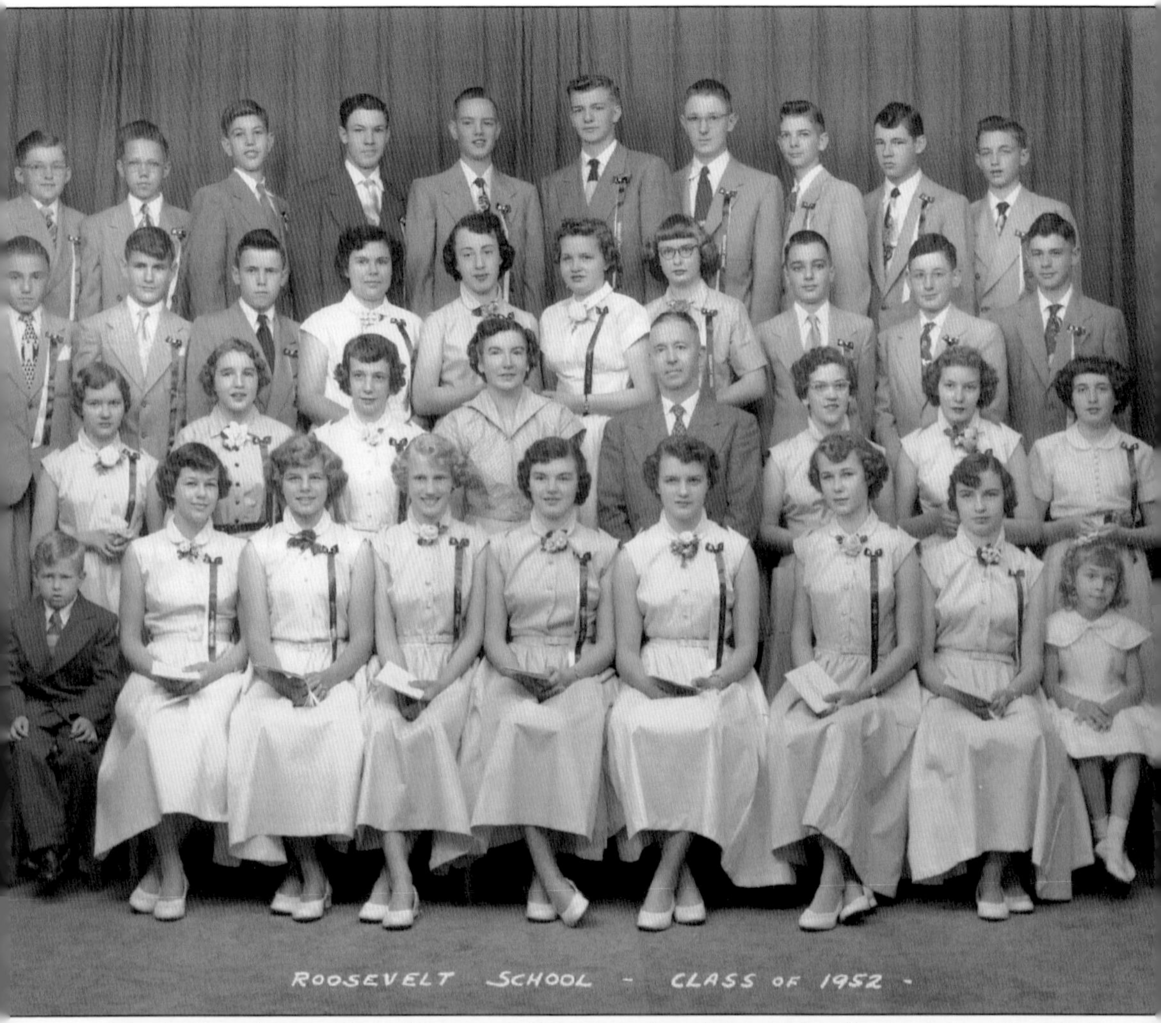

The 1952 graduating class of Roosevelt School, is, from left to right: (front row) unidentified, Cheryl Turgren, Ruth Tysee, Lenora De Ward, Joan Koeksema, Ellen Visser, Audrey Veld, Trucy Voss, and unidentified; (second row) Judy Kazen, Mariella Stgenega, Marlene Bardo, Principal Alice Cook, Superintendent George Kingsland, Sue Peters, Arlene Voss, and Diane Harris; (third row) John Ronkowski, Joe Congotelli, Ted Rietveld, Marion Wognum, Anne Gorndon, Nancy Gouwens, Jean Boer, Andrew Rietveld, James Vyerberg, and Porter Rodgers; (back row) Norman Polaskey, Jaems De Young, William Dienema, Fred Nuebert, James Veld, Henry Baker, Tom Walvoord, Earl Cummings, Peter Kickert, and Allan McClelland. (Photo courtesy of James Veld.)

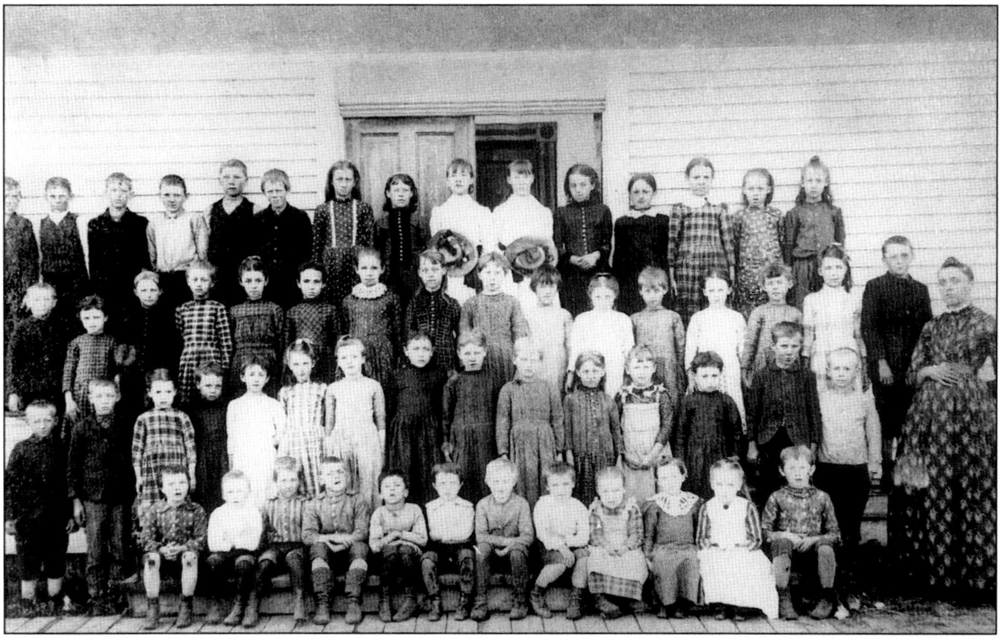

Teacher Johanna Gouwens (who married John Vinke and had children Louis, Annie, Harry, and Theodore) is pictured with her students at the early South Holland Public School, located on 167th Street. (Photo courtesy of South Holland Historical Society from the collection of Dr. Carl Walvoord.)

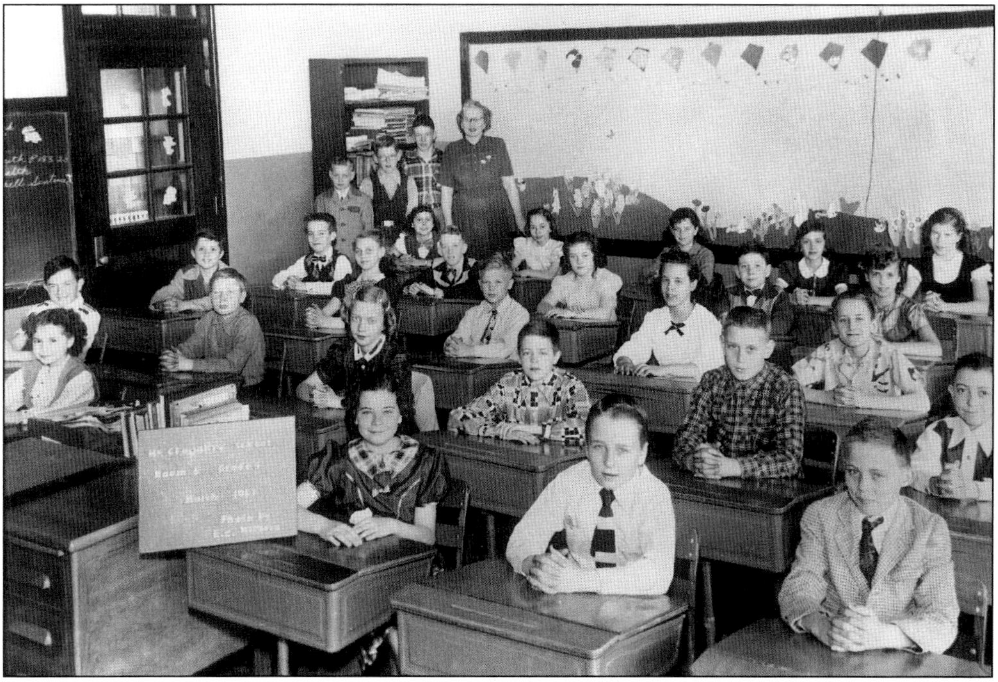

The 1953 third grade class of the McKinley School; Mrs. Jacobs is the teacher. (Photo courtesy of South Holland Historical Society from the collection of Dr. Carl Walvoord.)

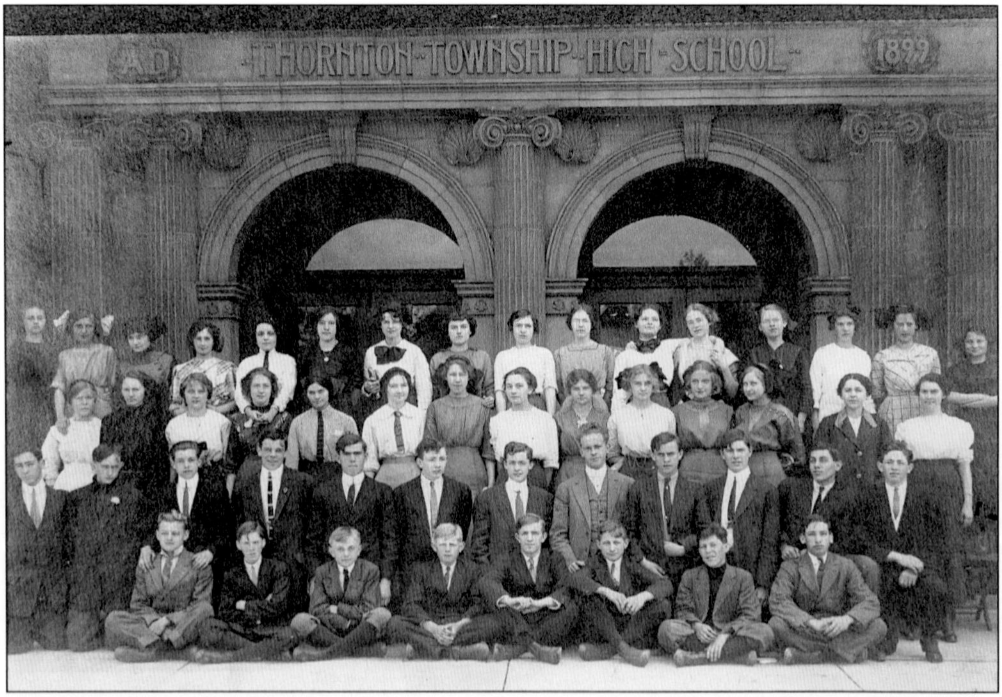

The 1914 graduating class of Thornton Township High School included: John Dalenberg (front row, third from left), George Gouwens (front row, sixth from left), Russel Gibson (front row, seventh from left), Margaret Gouwens (third row, second from left) and Cornelia Veld Gouwens (third row, twelfth from left). (Photo courtesy of South Holland Historical Society from the collection of Dr. Carl Walvoord.)

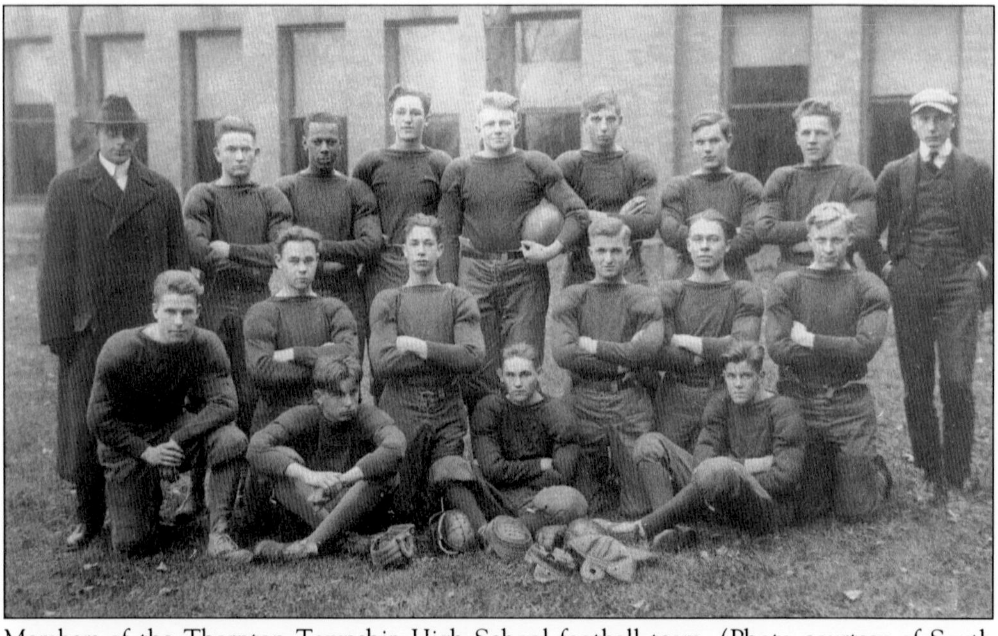

Members of the Thornton Township High School football team. (Photo courtesy of South Holland Historical Society from the collection of Dr. Carl Walvoord.)

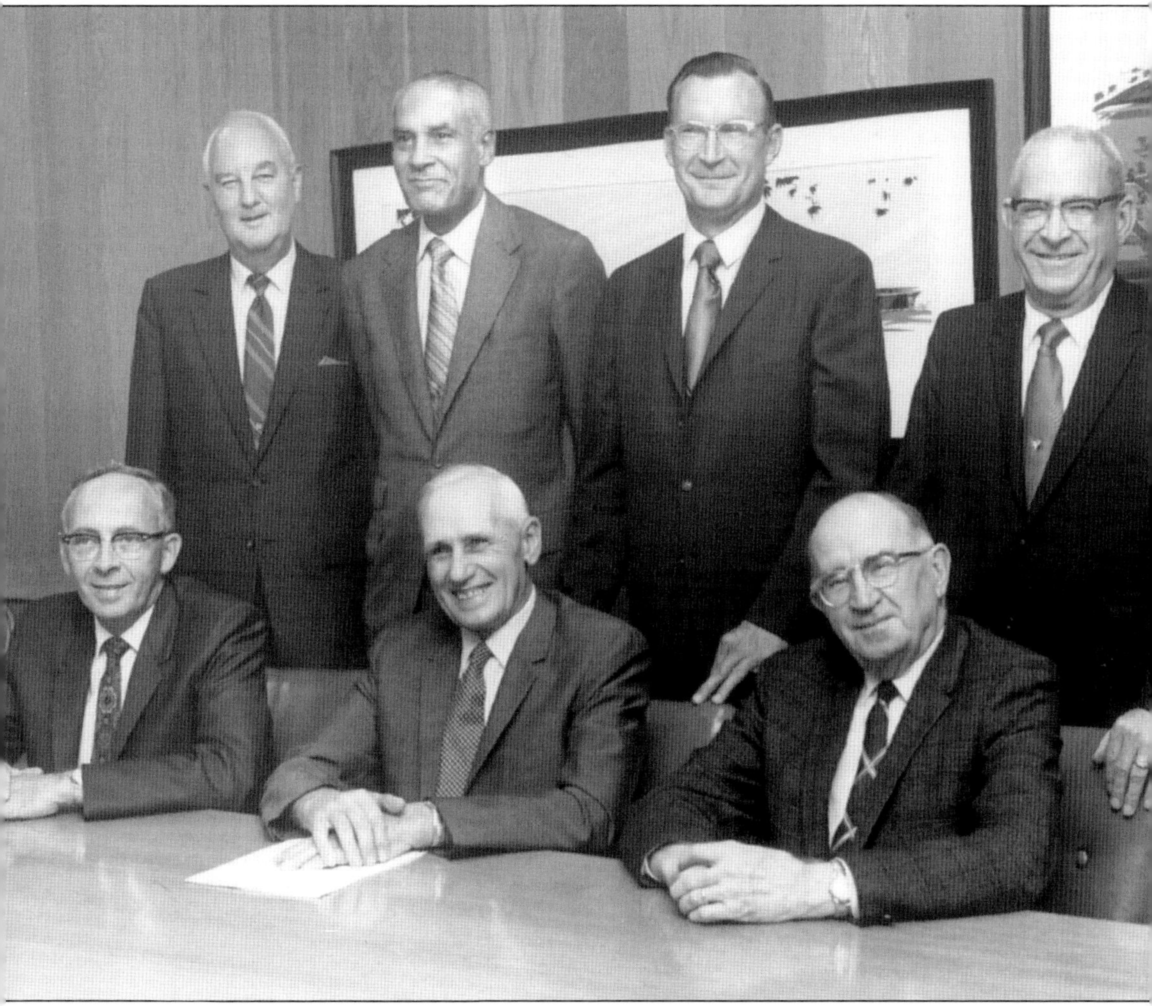

For many decades Thornton Township High School was the only public high school to serve residents of the district. Due to the massive growth in the area, Thornridge High School was later added in the 1960s and finally, Thornwood High School opened in 1972 for the second semester of the 1971-72 school year. Pictured here is the 1970 Board of Education, which was involved in the planning of Thornwood High School. From left to right are: (seated) Robert C. Evans, Henry Vandenberg (president), and Robert H. Reese; (standing) George E. Webb, Leo F. Piernas, Albert T. Krebs, and Fred R. Hennig. Henry Vandenberg served as a District 205 Board member for 30 years, retiring in 1983. Combined with the 25 years he served as a Board Member for District 149, Mr. Vandenberg is the longest serving board member in the state, with a total of 55 years of service. Each year, one member of the graduating class of each of the District 205 high schools receives an award named in honor of Mr. Vandenberg, based on academic excellence, character, leadership and service in the school and community. (Photo courtesy of Thornwood High School.)

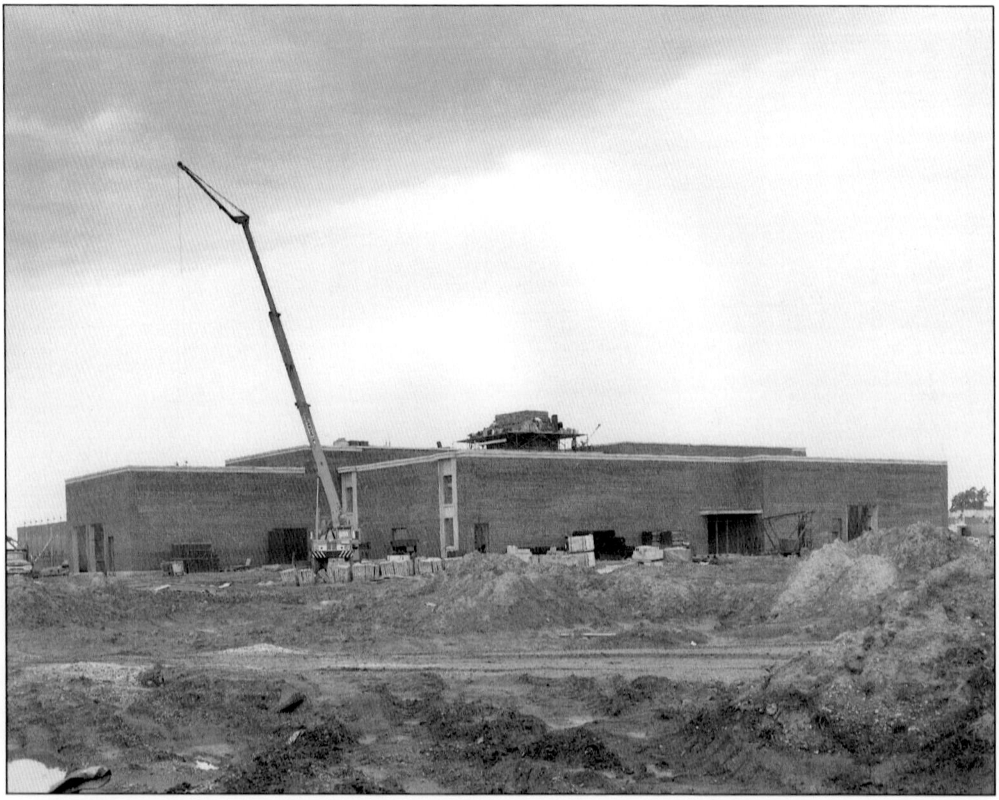

Construction is underway on the new high school building. (Photo courtesy of Thornwood High School.)

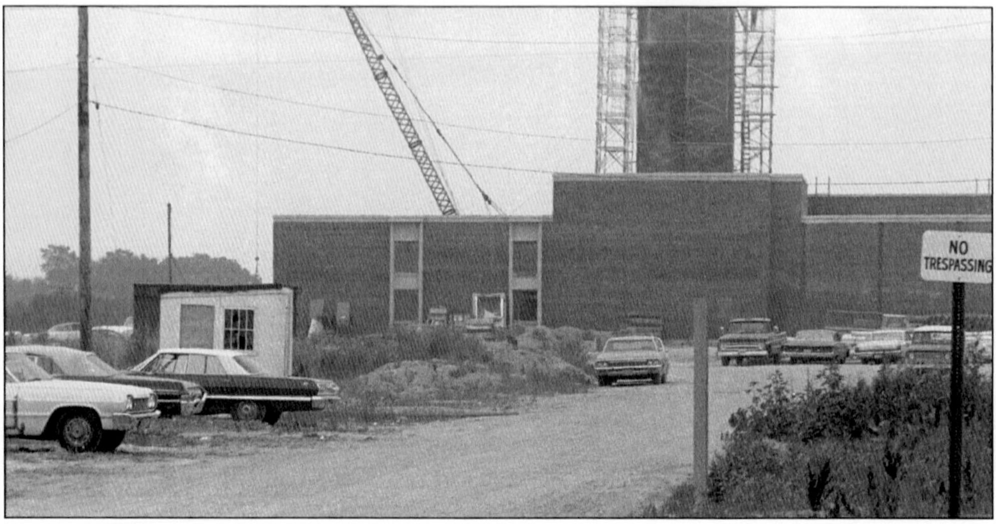

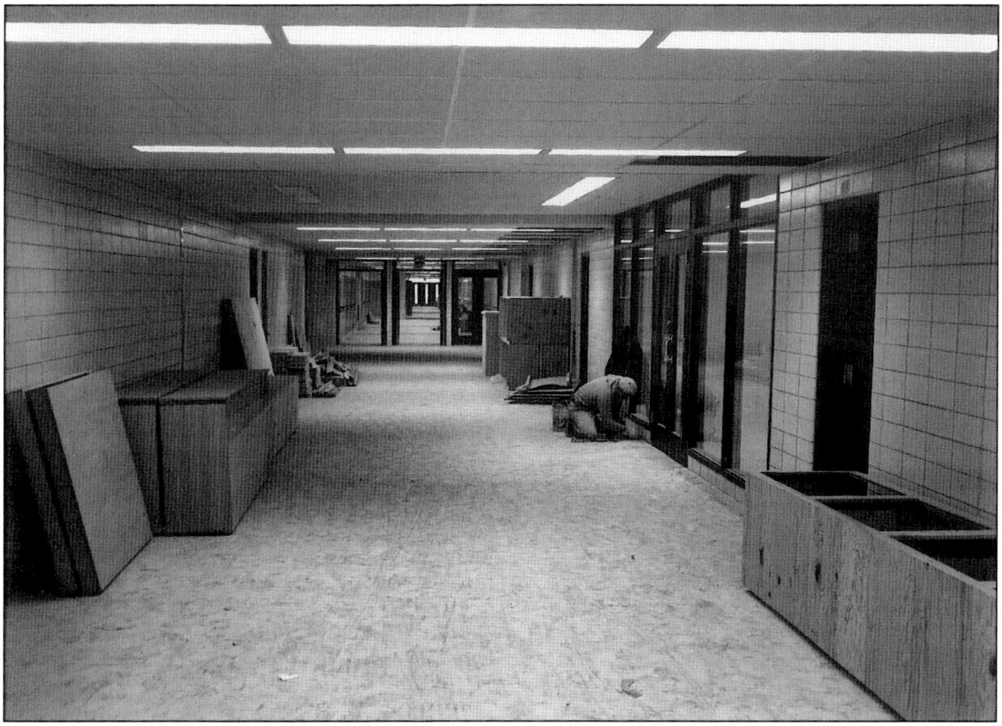

A worker puts finishing touches on the tile outside the main office as the interior work on the school nears completion. (Photo courtesy of Thornwood High School.)

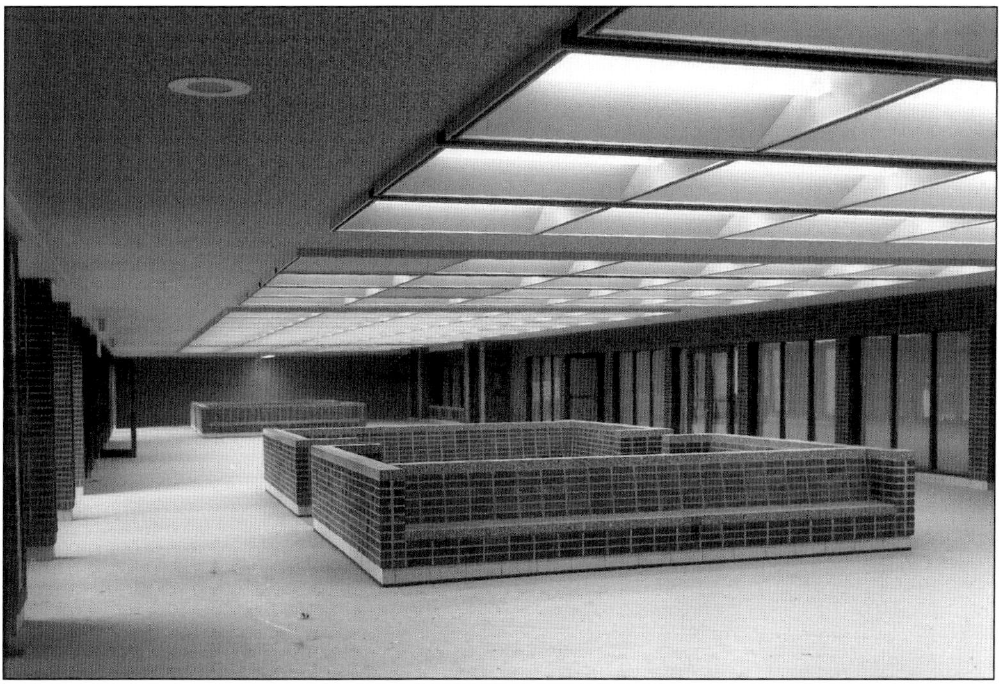

The commons area is yet to be tiled in this photo. This area has served as a social gathering place for many students before and after school. (Photo courtesy of Thornwood High School.)

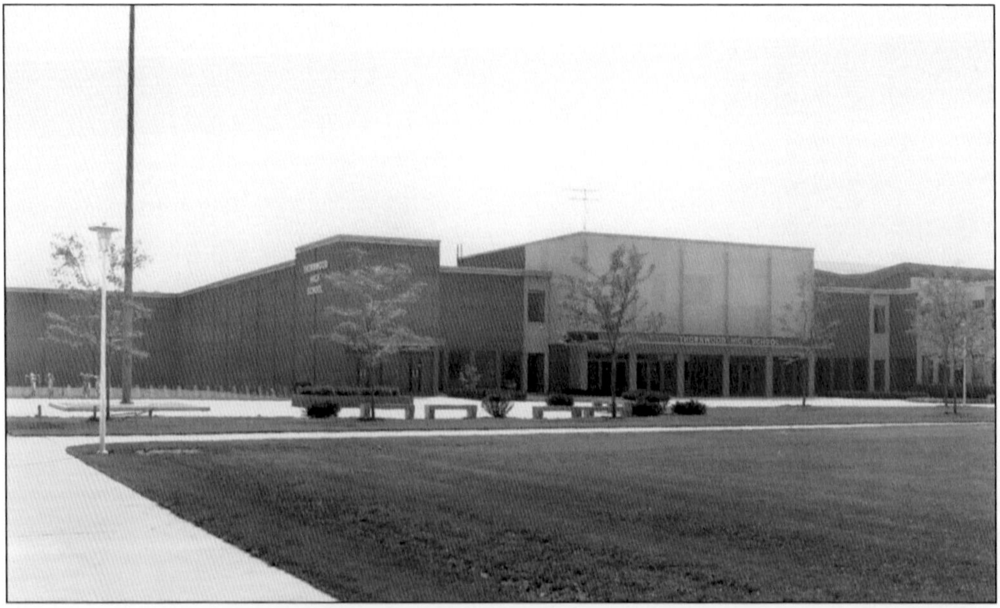

This is how the main entrance appeared after completion and how it still appears today. (Photo courtesy of Thornwood High School.)

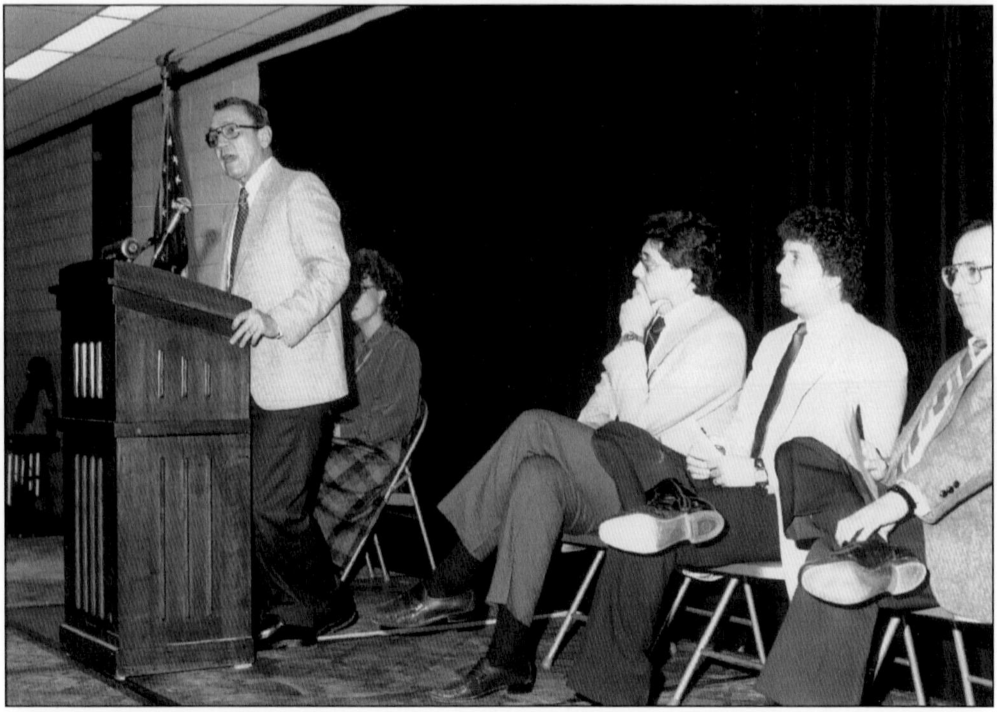

Dr. Robert C. Mitchell, the school's first principal, speaks to a group as Larry Corley, Eric Kennedy and Richard Bruno look on. Larry Corley retired from Thornwood High School as an assistant principal, Eric Kennedy served as an assistant principal and later retired as Director of Human Resources, and Mr. Bruno, now retired, became the school's second principal. (Photo courtesy of Thornwood High School.)

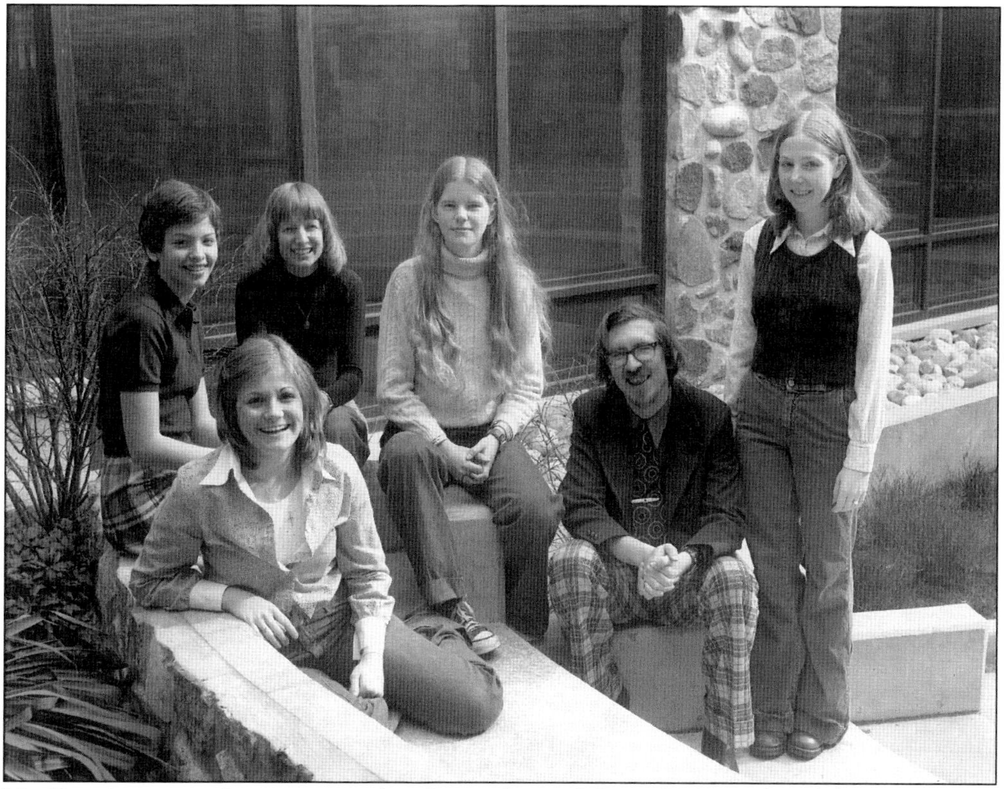

Mr. Brandon, a teacher, is pictured with members of the 1972-73 Tribe Club, a group that planned dances and social events. (Photo courtesy of Thornwood High School.)

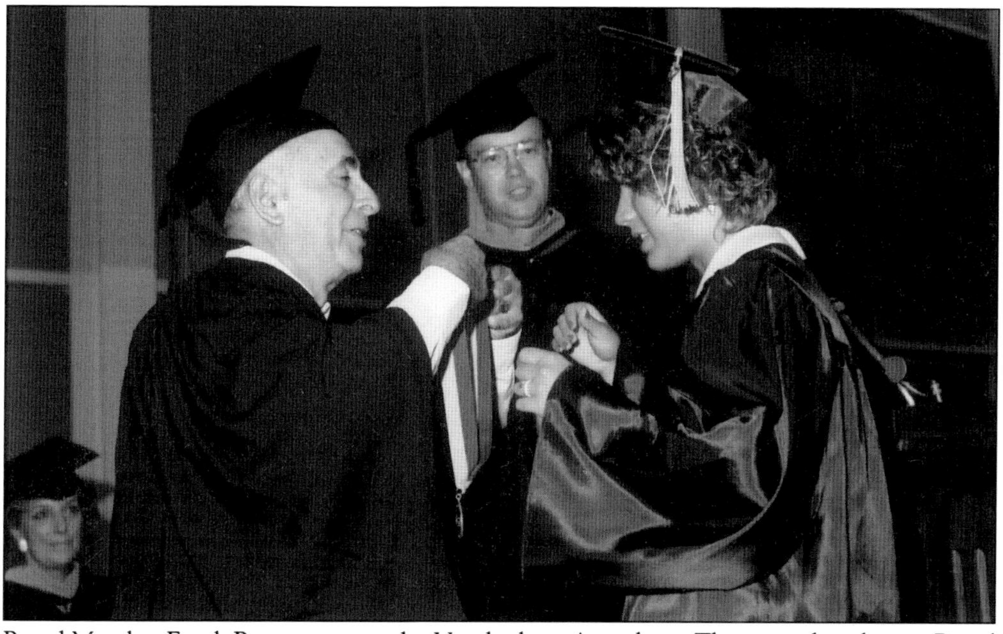

Board Member Frank Russo presents the Vandenberg Award to a Thornwood student as Board Member Jim Veld looks on. (Photo courtesy of Thornwood High School.)

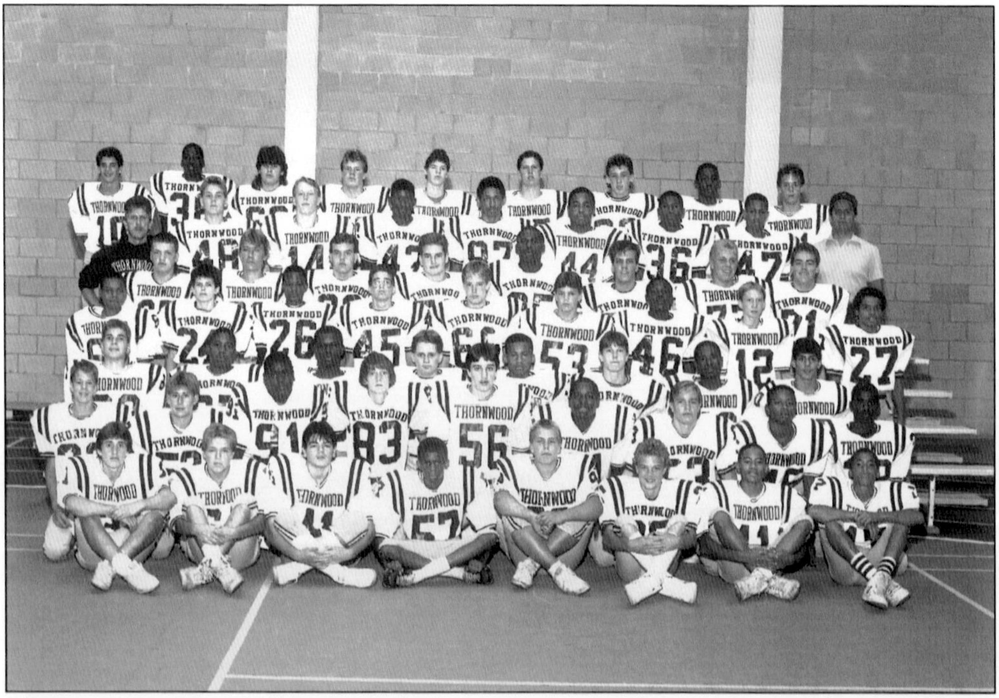

Thornwood's 1987 freshman football team is pictured here. (Photo courtesy of Thornwood High School.)

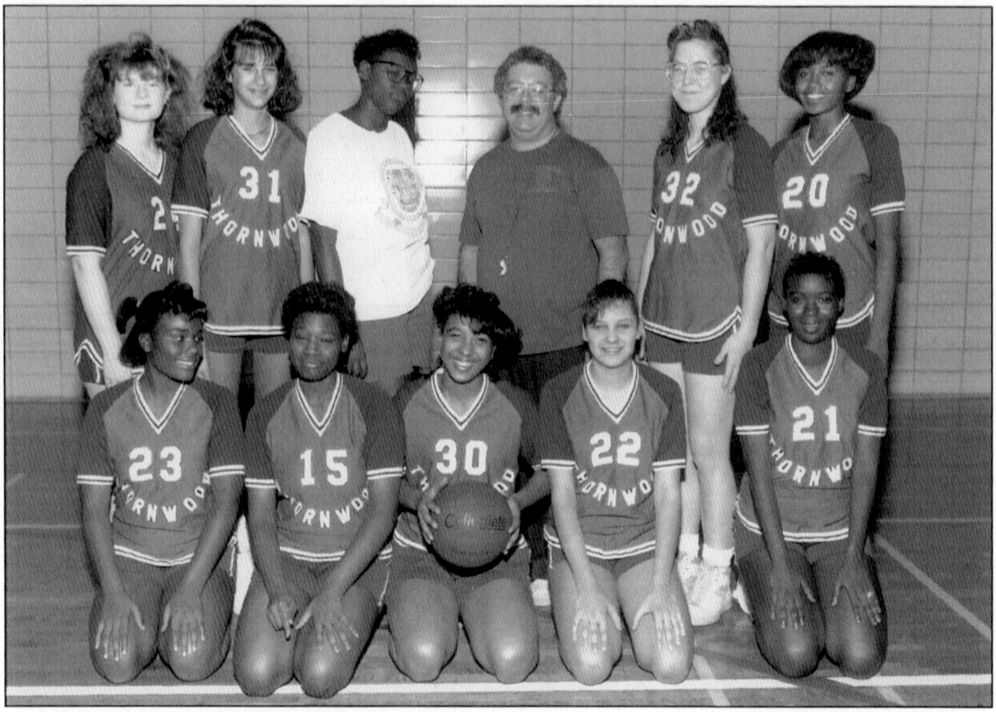

The Thornwood 1989-90 freshman girl's basketball team, coached by Robert "Skip" Considine. (Photo courtesy of Thornwood High School.)

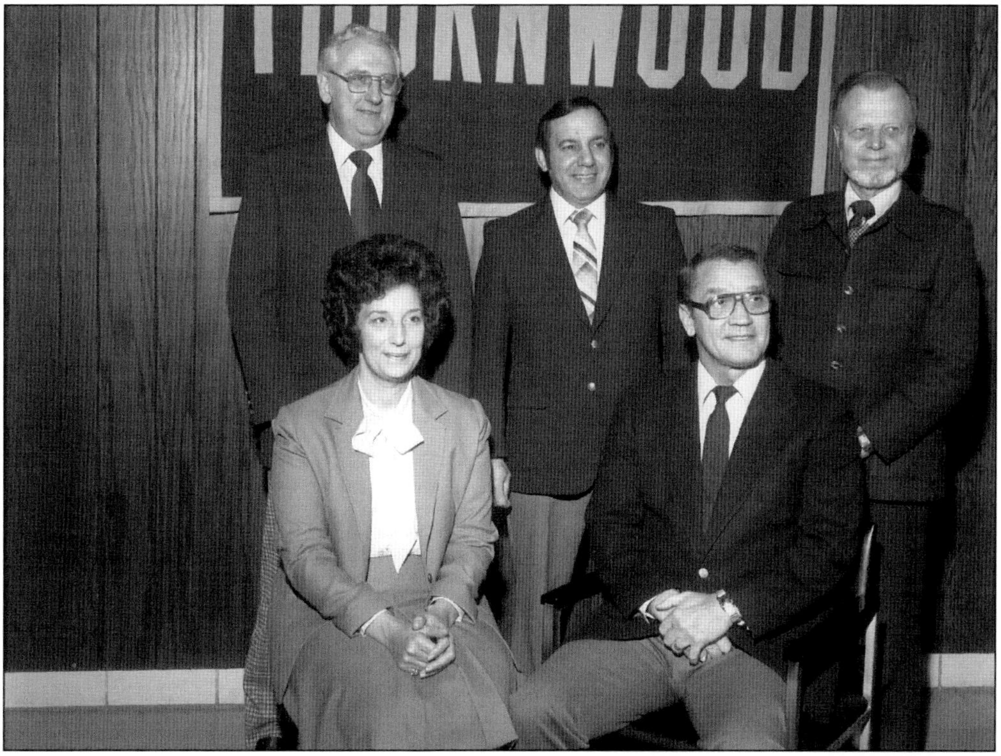

Thornwood Administrators: (seated) Marilyn Bauer and Dr. Robert Mitchell; (standing) Robert Anderson, Richard Bruno, and Ralph Rowe. (Photo courtesy of School District 205.)

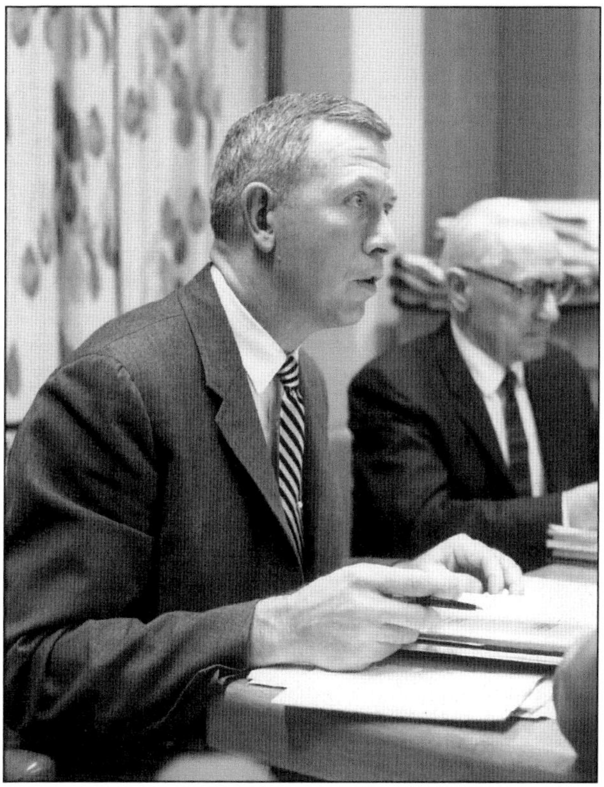

William Augustus served as the district superintendent starting in 1968 after serving as Principal of Thornridge High School in Dolton. He was superintendent at the time of Thornwood's planning and construction. (Photo courtesy of School District 205.)

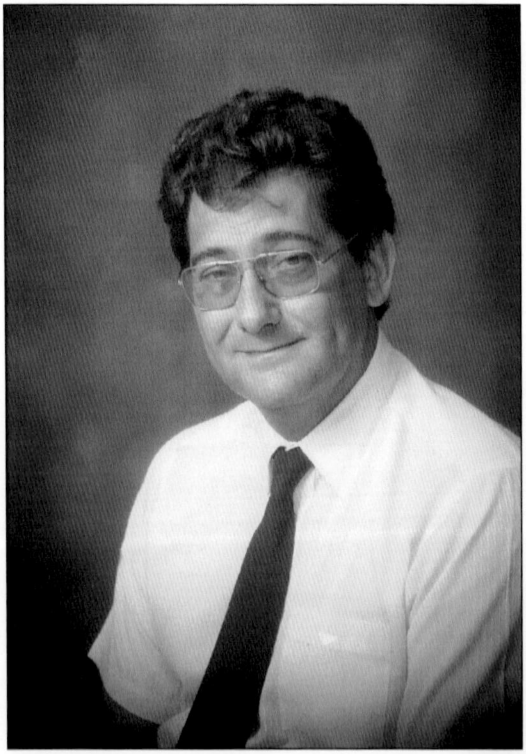

Larry Corley taught social studies in the school district before becoming a counselor, administrative assistant, and later an assistant principal. He retired from the school district in 1995. (Photo courtesy of School District 205.)

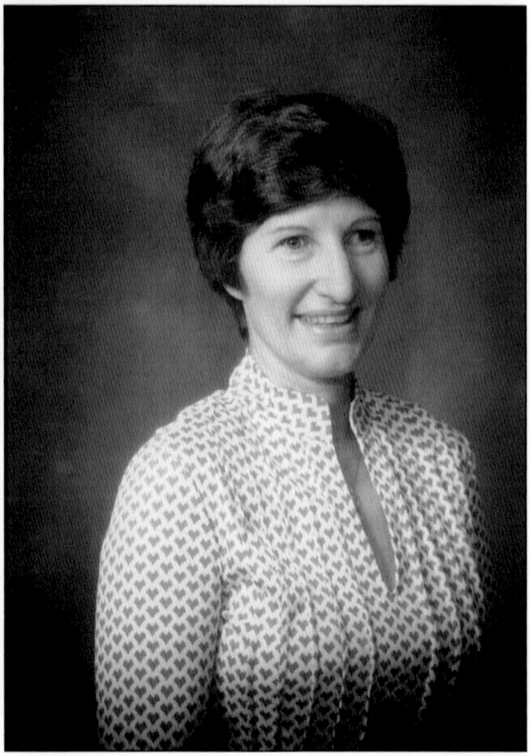

Johanna Crull was another assistant principal to serve at Thornwood High School after many years of teaching in the district as a foreign language teacher. (Photo courtesy of School District 205.)

Eric Kennedy began his teaching career at Thornridge High School in Dolton in the science department in 1969. When Thornwood opened, he transferred there and taught chemistry and served as the Student Activities Director. He later became an assistant principal and eventually moved to the district office in 1993, where he held the position of Director of Human Resources until his retirement in 2002. (Photo courtesy of School District 205.)

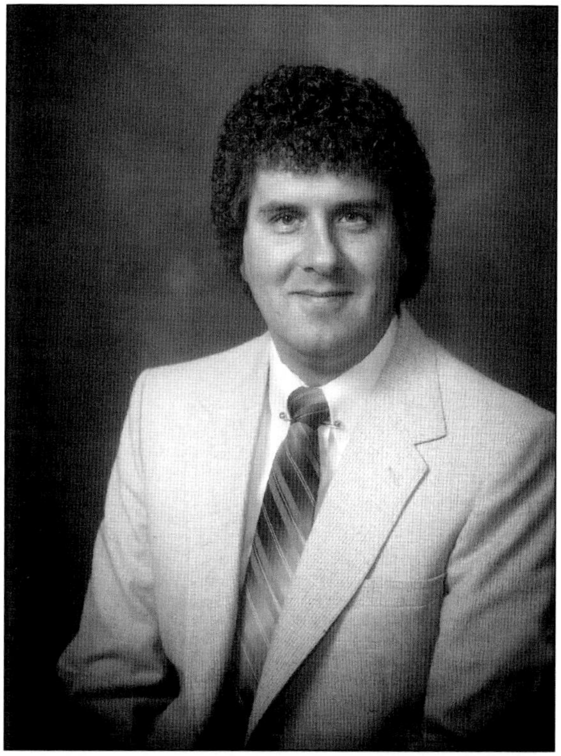

Band director Paul Jankowski (far left) is pictured with band members in the late 1980s. (Photo courtesy of Thornwood High School.)

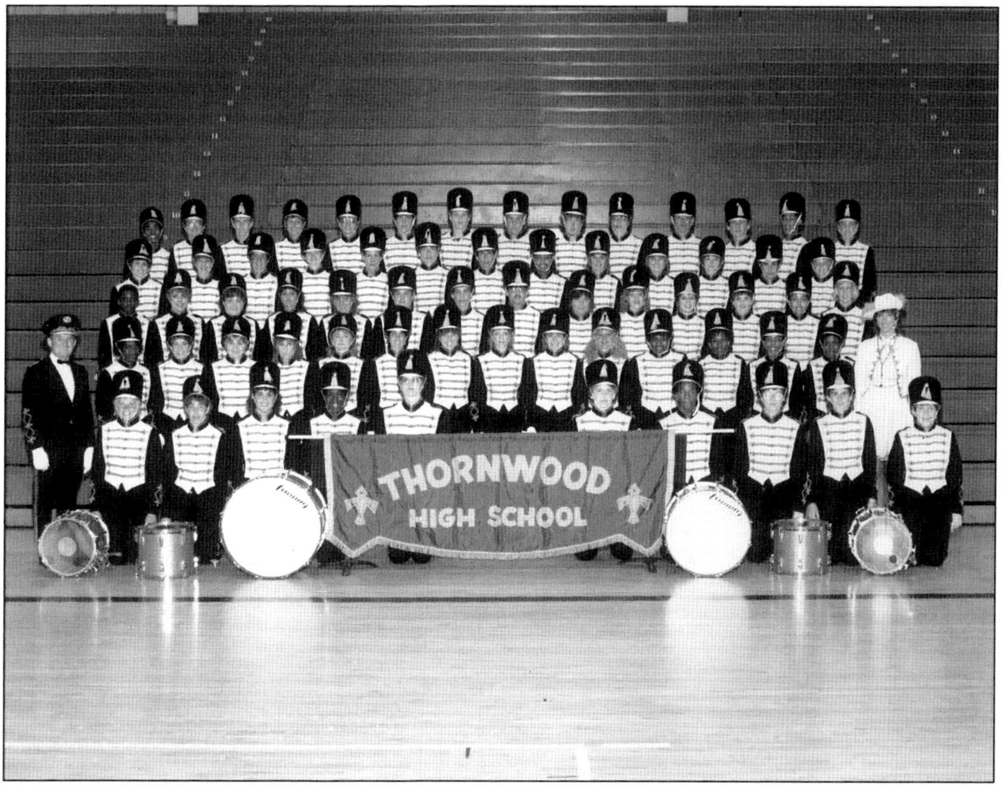

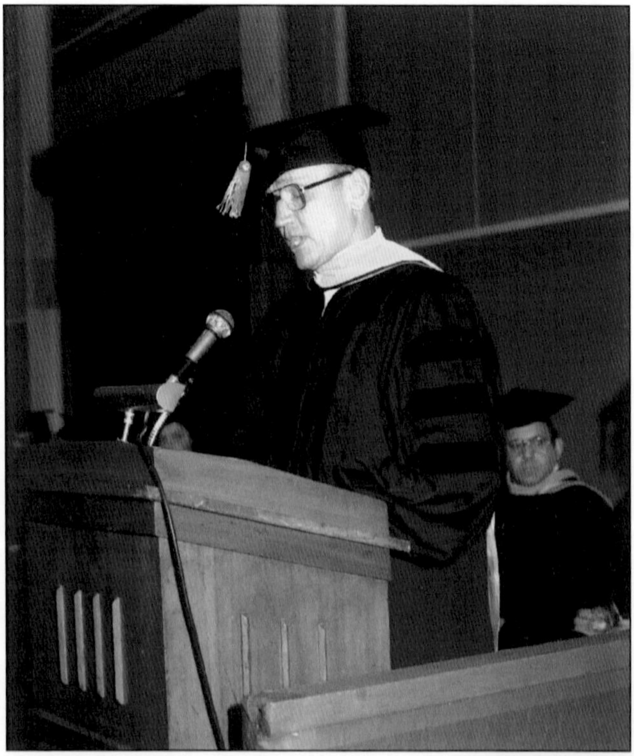

Thornwood High School has had five principals since its opening. Dr. Robert C. Mitchell was the first. He served from 1971 through 1987. He is pictured here speaking at a graduation ceremony. (Photo courtesy of Thornwood High School.)

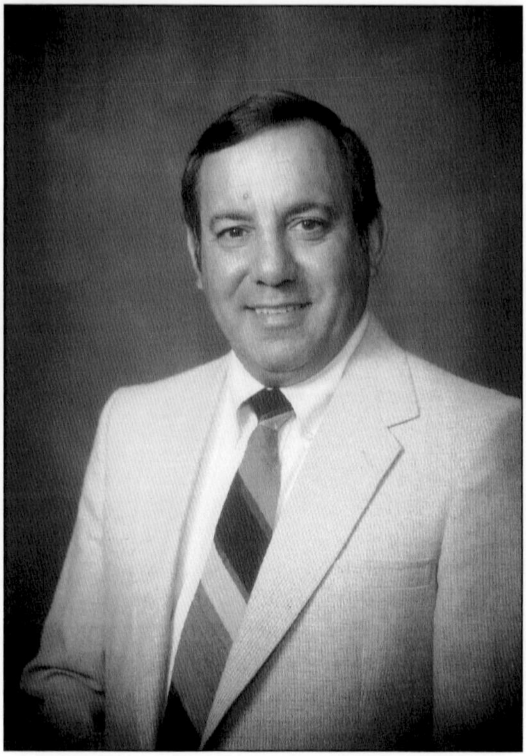

Richard Bruno became principal in 1987 after teaching in the English department at Thornton High School in Harvey. He later served as a counselor and the Dean of Boys at Thornwood and as an administrative assistant and assistant principal. He retired from the position of principal in 1991. (Photo courtesy of School District 205.)

Thornwood's third principal was Dr. Gary T. Catalani. He spent four years as principal, from 1991–1995, until becoming district superintendent. In 1999 he left the district after accepting a superintendent position in another school district. (Photo courtesy of School District 205.)

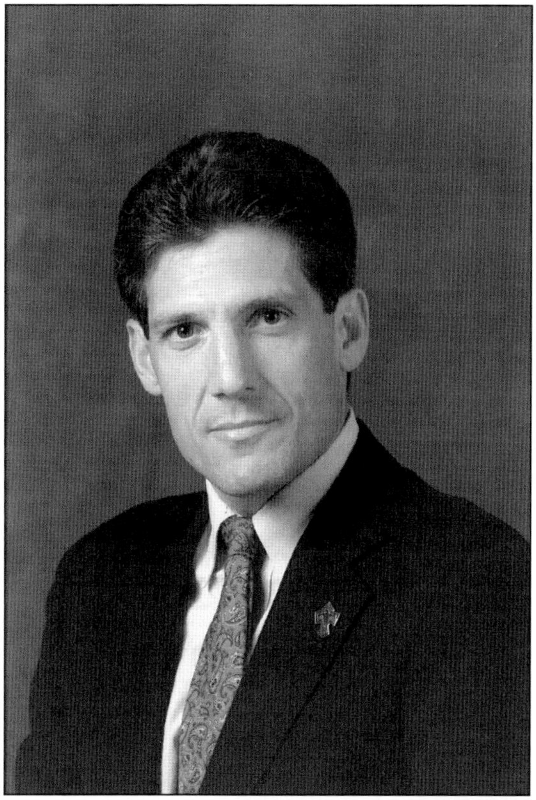

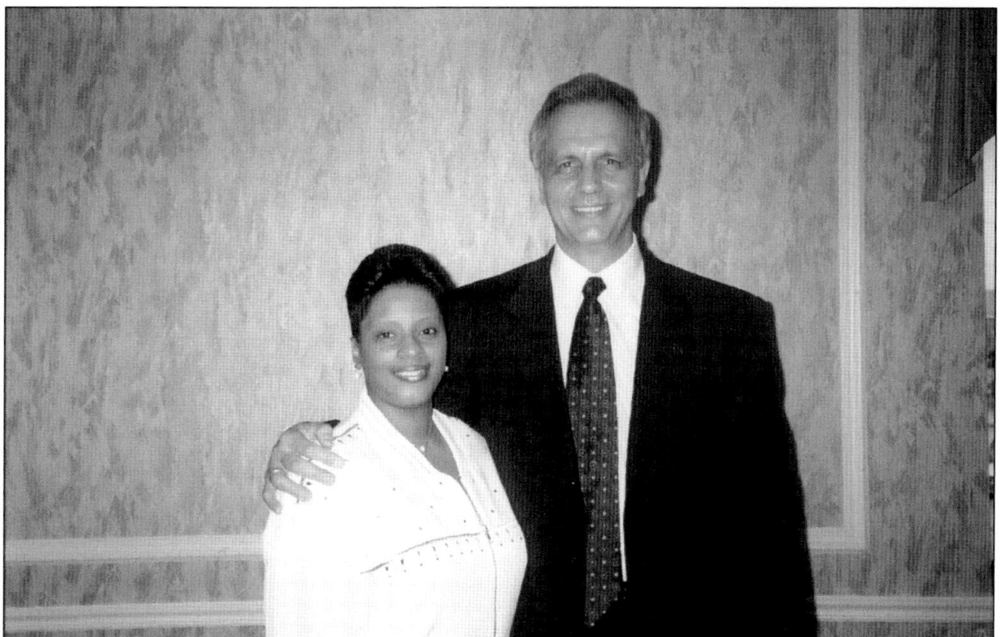

Dr. Gregory Fantozzi, pictured with Dana Thigpen (currently principal's secretary), was principal from 1995 until 2000, when he left the district after accepting a position in another school district. (Photo courtesy of Dana Thigpen.)

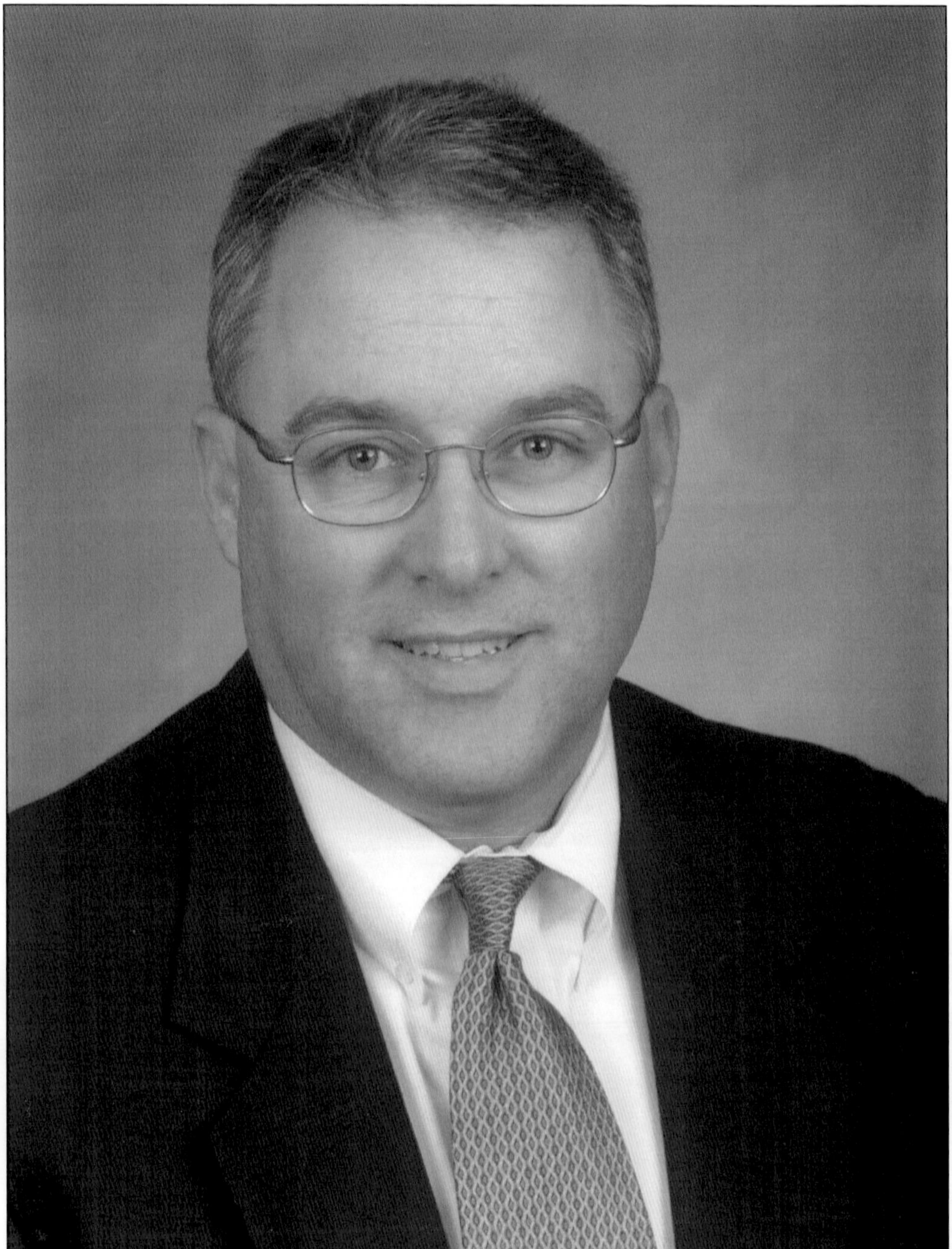

Mr. Gary Lester, the current principal, has spent most of his life in the institutions of School District 205, first as a Thornridge student, where he served on a student planning committee for Thornwood High School. He first entered Thornwood's doors when he interviewed for a teaching position in 1975. That year he began his teaching career in the social studies department. He later held the positions of dean, assistant athletic director, administrative intern and assistant principal before becoming principal in 2000. He has also coached several sports over the years. (Photo courtesy of Gary Lester.)

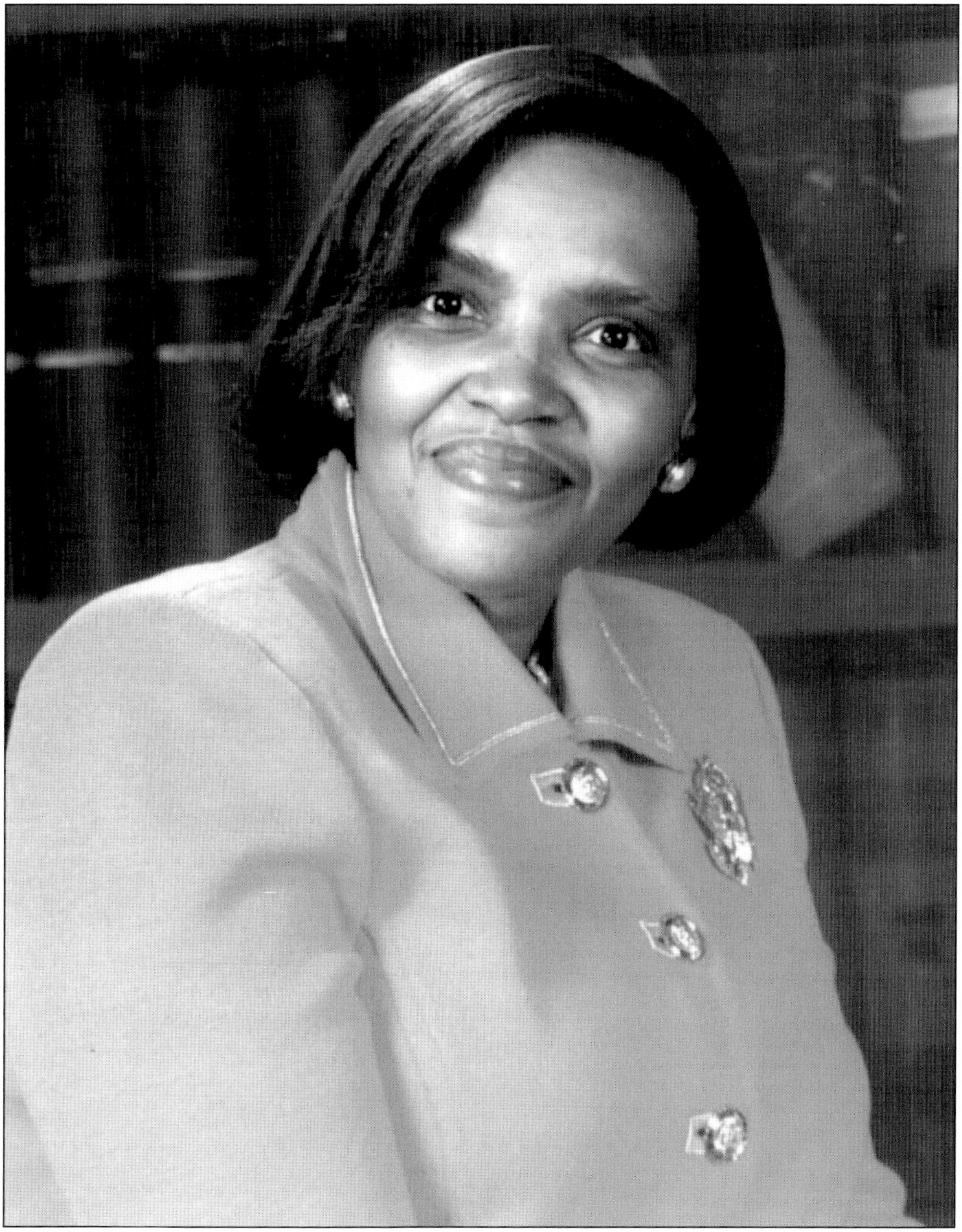

In 1999, J. Kamala Buckner became School District 205's first female superintendent, as well as the district's first African-American superintendent. She is one of a small number of African-American female superintendents in the state. Buckner graduated from Thornridge High School in Dolton (as did her brother, Quinn Buckner, who went on to play professional basketball). Buckner started in the district as a special education teacher and then served as a district administrator for several years before becoming superintendent. (Photo courtesy of J. Kamala Buckner.)

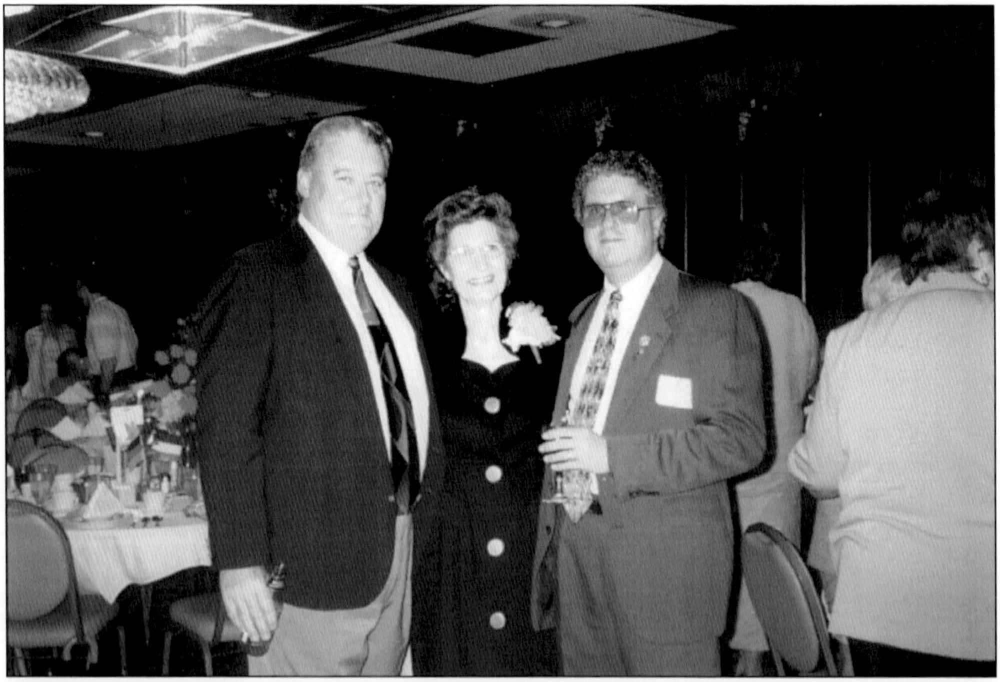

Fellow administrators Harold Olson (left) and Eric Kennedy (right) celebrate with Johanna Crull at her June 2000 retirement party. (Photo courtesy of Gary Lester.)

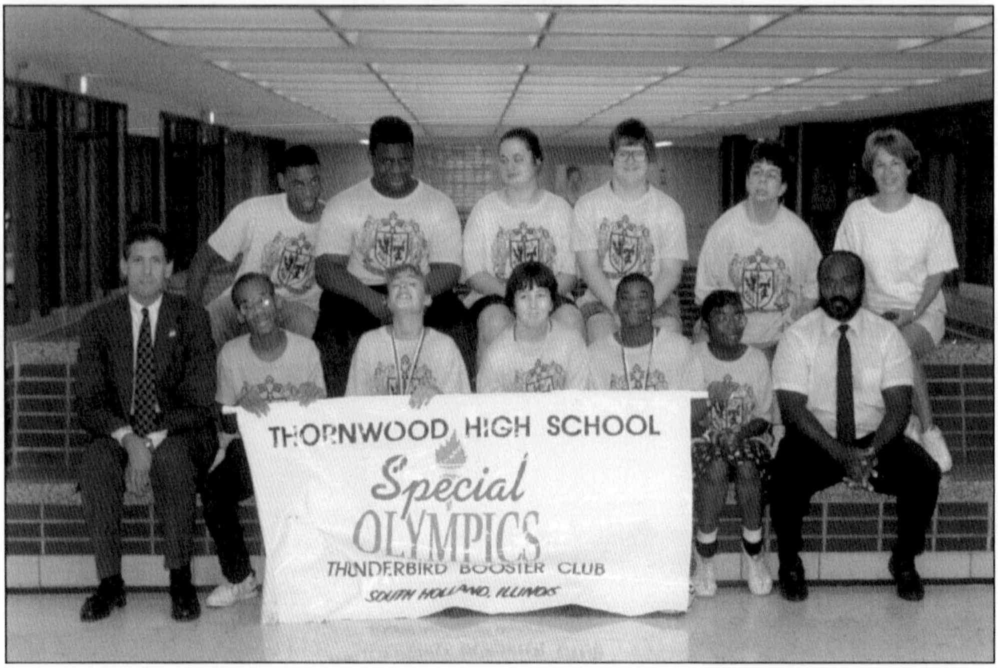

Principal Dr. Gary Catlani (seated, front row, left), Assistant Principal Leroy Coleman (seated, far right) and physical education teacher Judith Peters sit with students participating in the Special Olympics in the early 1990s for a photograph. The Special Olympics is an annual event that has often been hosted by Thornwood High School. (Photo courtesy of Thornwood High School.)

Enid Scott straightens the cap of a fellow graduate in this photo, which was taken around 1988. (Photo courtesy of Thornwood High School.)

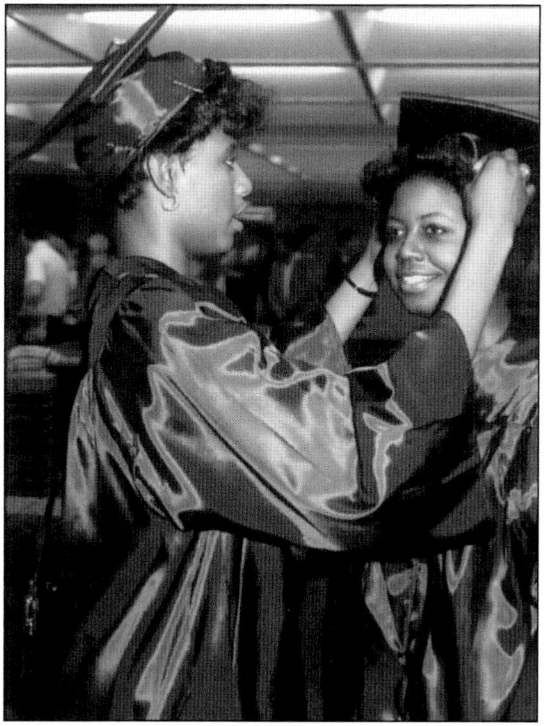

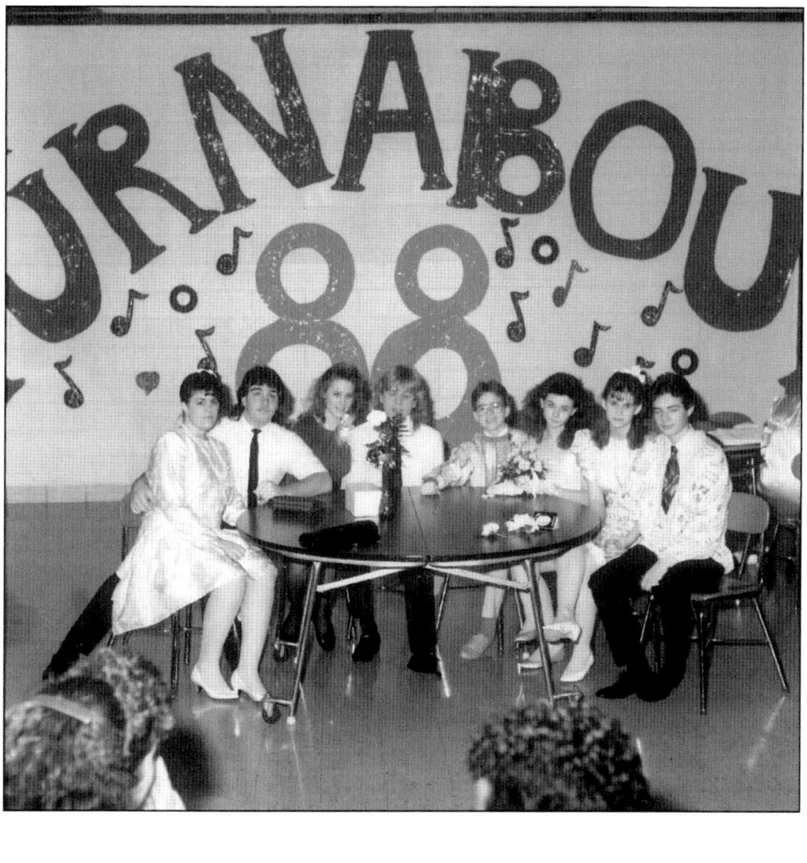

A group of students gather for a photograph at the 1988 Thornwood Turnabout Dance. (Photo courtesy of Thornwood High School.)

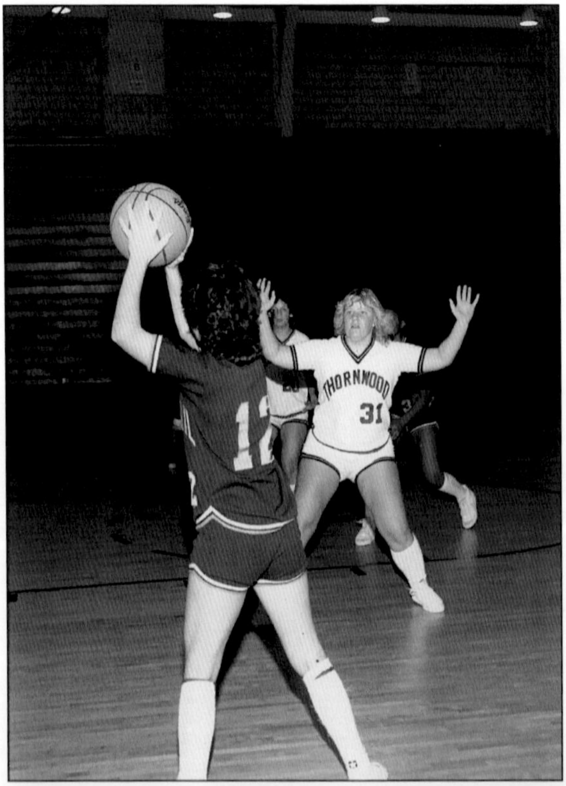

Kris Johansen, a 1985 graduate and a member of the girl's basketball team, participates in a game. (Photo courtesy of Thornwood High School.)

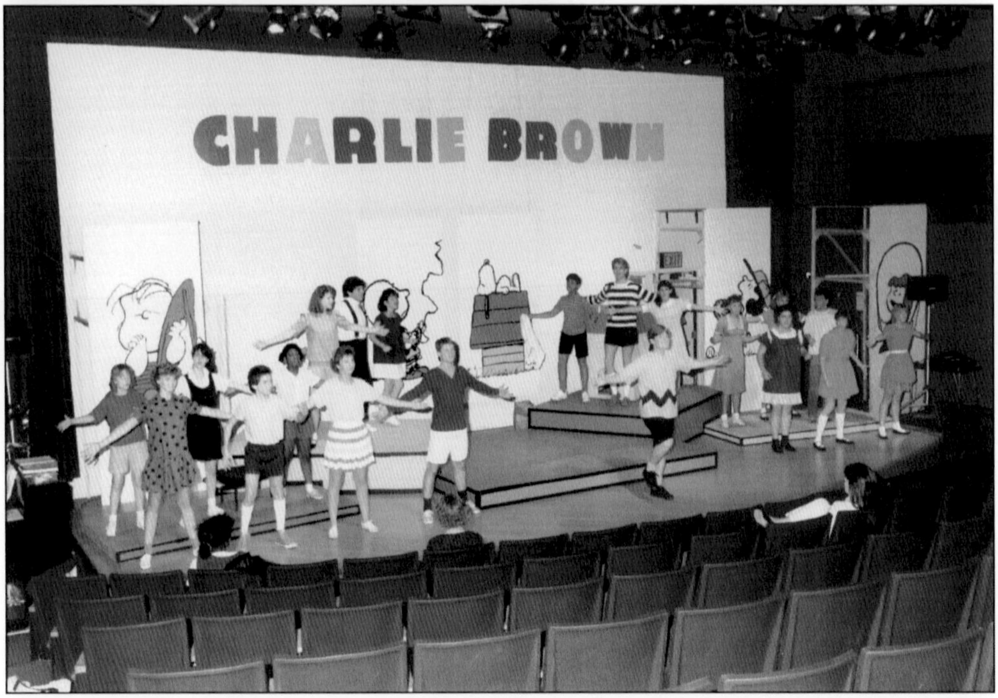

Drama students rehearse for an upcoming school play. (Photo courtesy of Thornwood High School.)

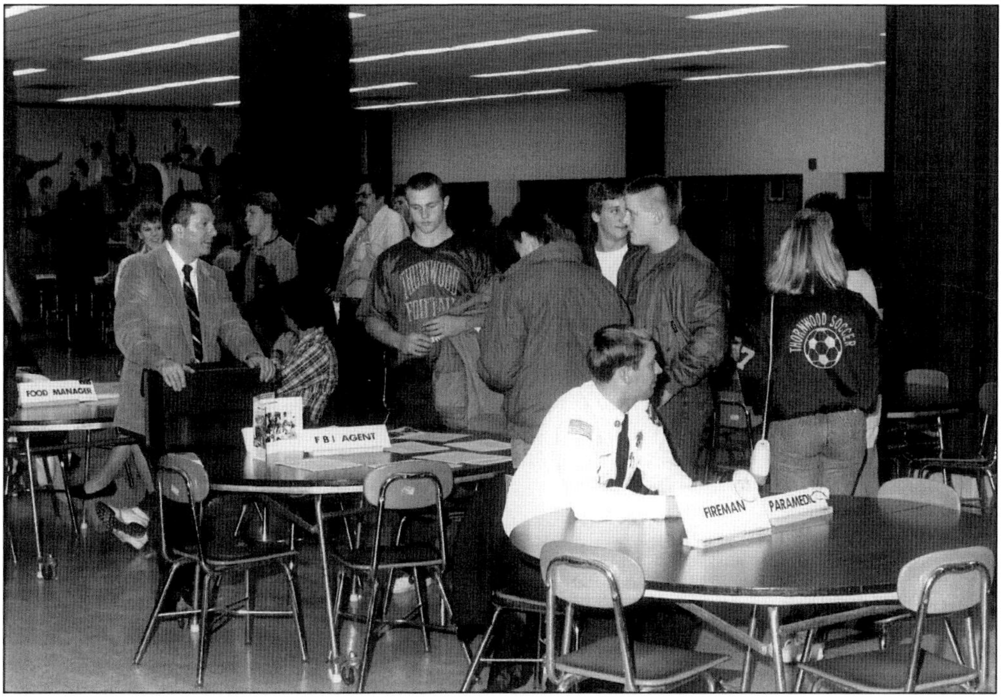

A career day at Thornwood High School in the 1980s. (Photo courtesy of Thornwood High School.)

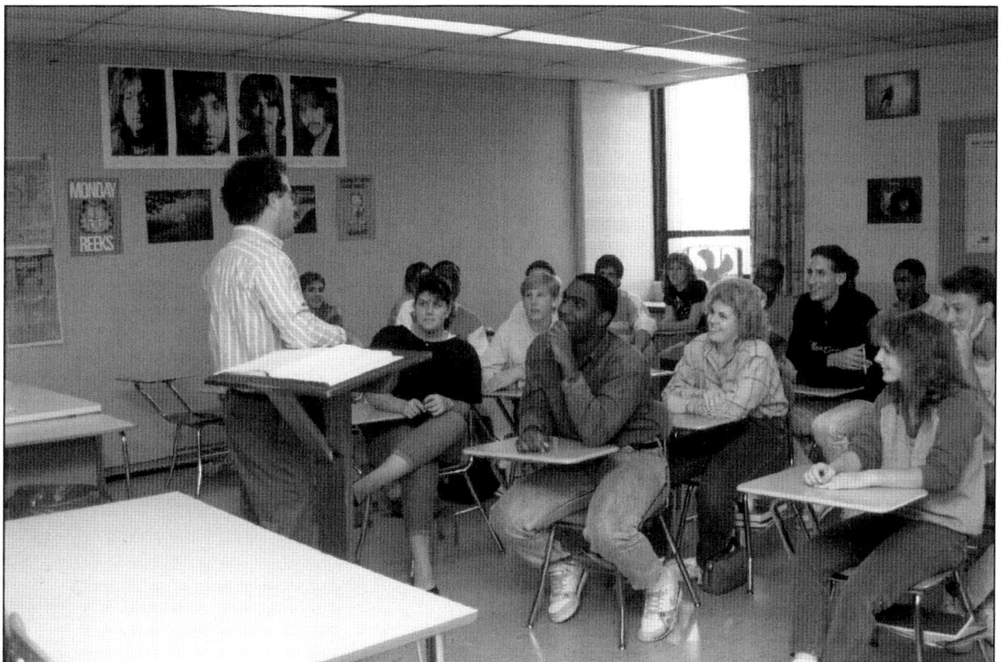

Gary Lester (current principal) has a discussion with students in his social studies class in the mid to late 1980s. (Photo courtesy of Thornwood High School.)

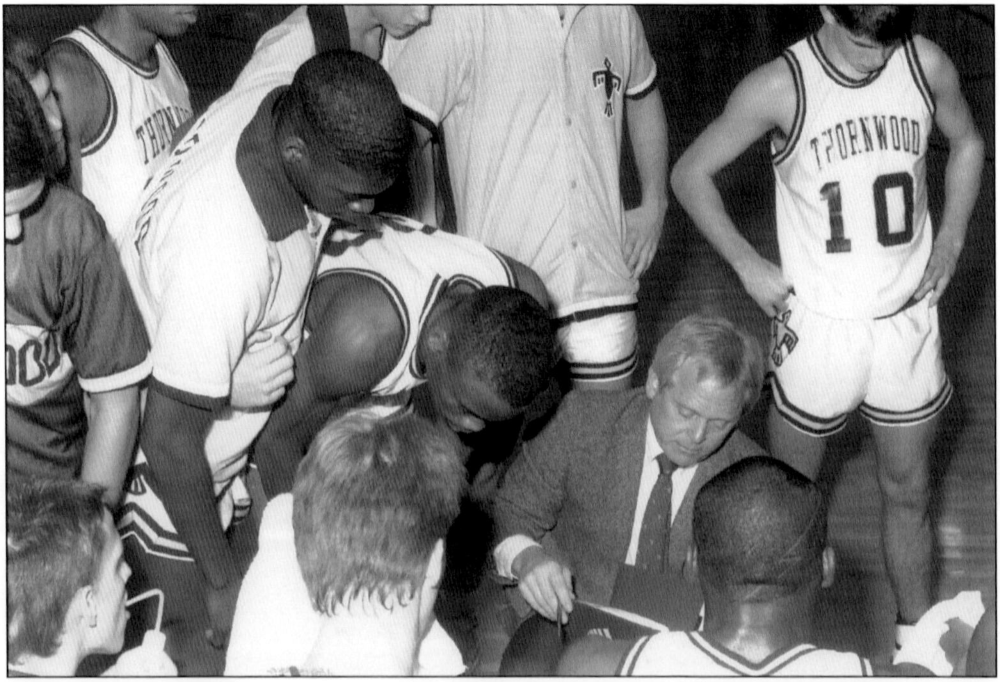

Head coach Al Holverson talks to players before a game during the 1989-1990 season. Mr. Holverson later became the chairman of the school's math department. (Photo courtesy of Thornwood High School.)

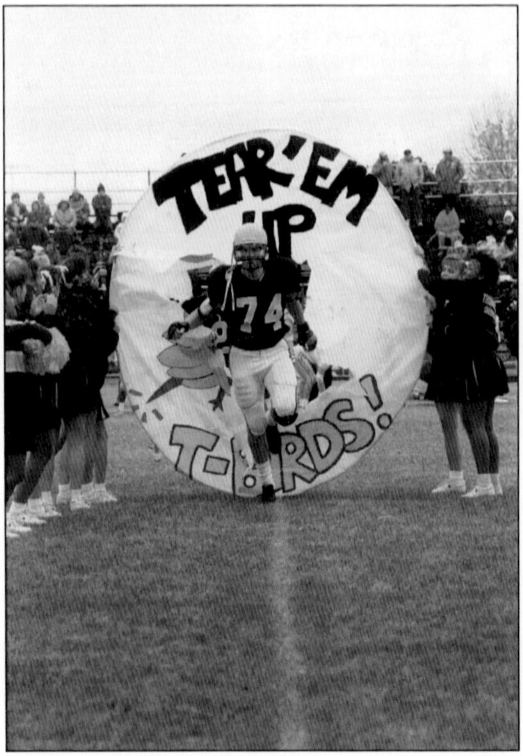

A player hits the field for a homecoming game in the mid 1980s. (Photo courtesy of Thornwood High School.)

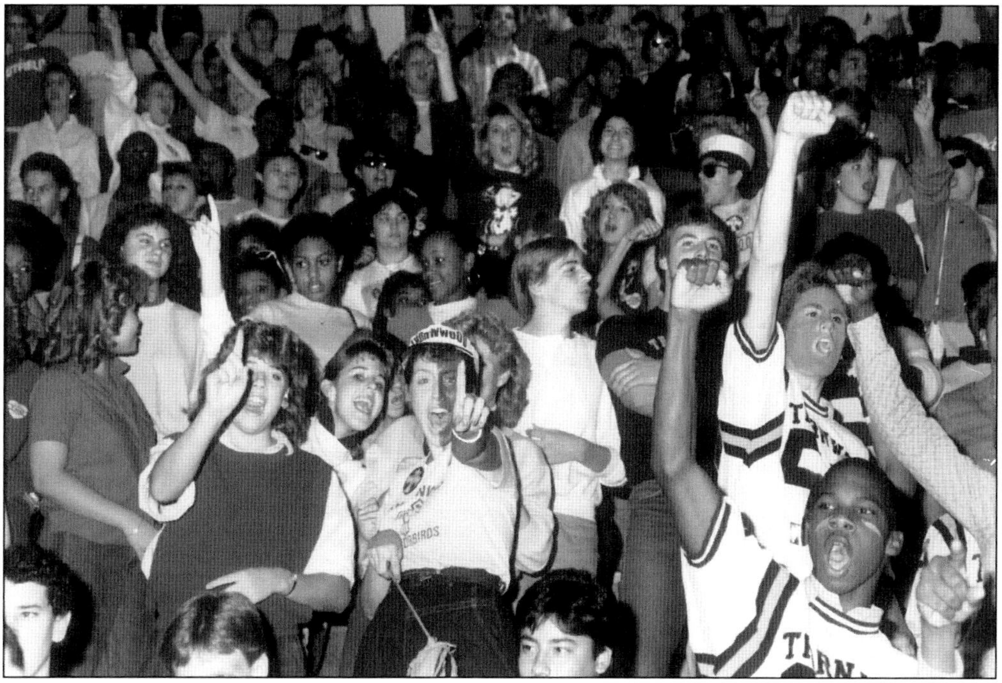

Students show off their school spirit at a homecoming assembly in the mid 1980s. (Photo courtesy of Thornwood High School.)

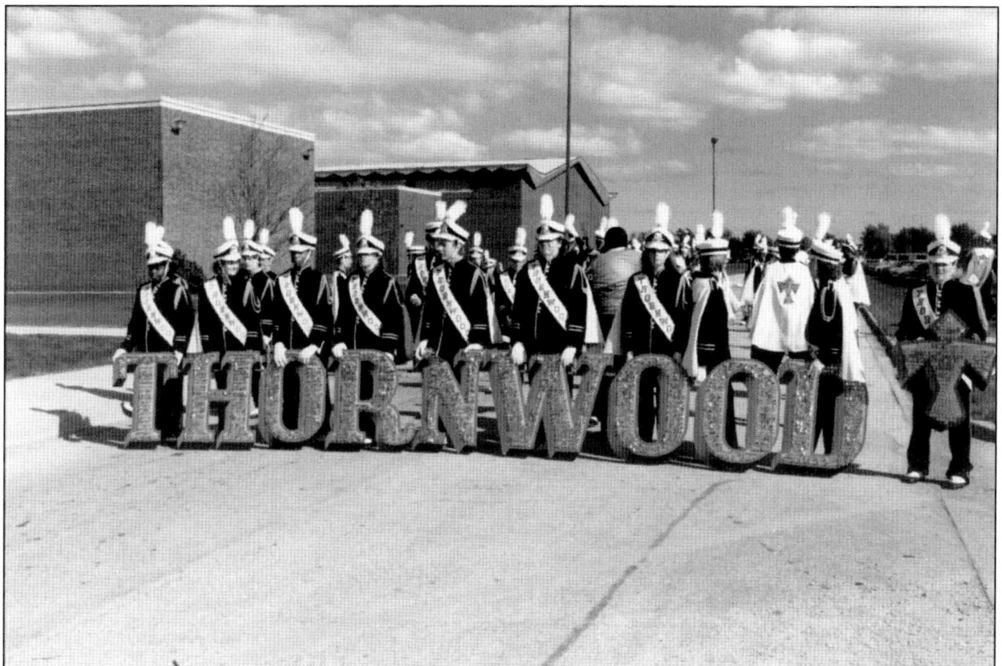

Members of the school band line up at a homecoming parade in the mid 1980s. (Photo courtesy of Thornwood High School.)

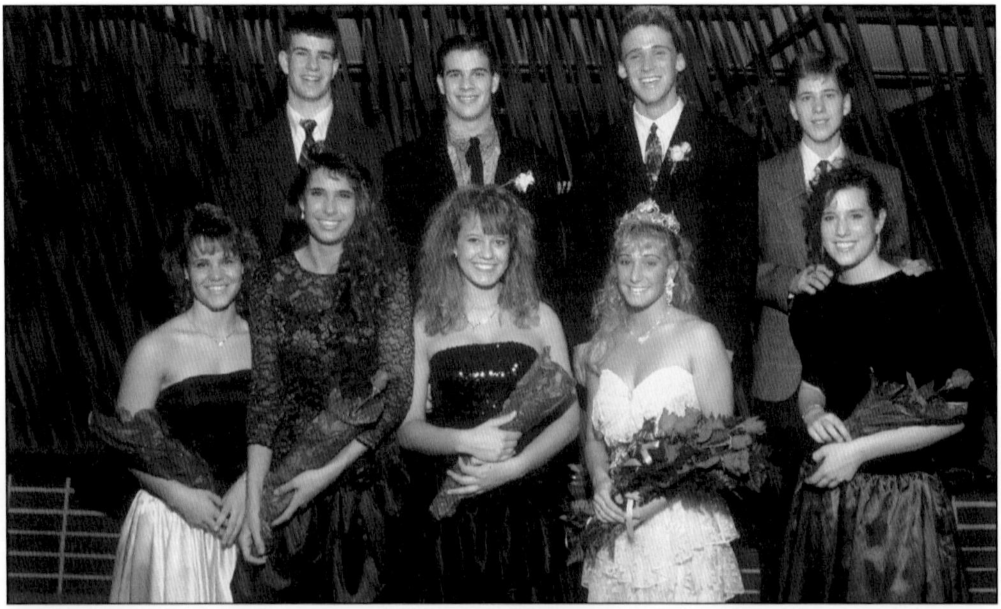

This photo of the Homecoming Court includes Michelle Venturella, who won a gold medal in the 2000 Olympics in women's softball. (Photo courtesy of Thornwood High School.)

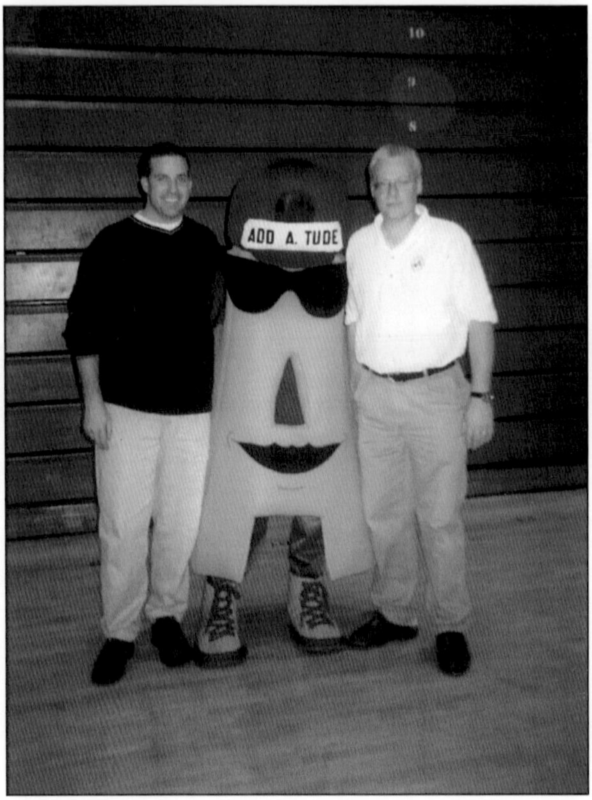

Assistant Athletic Director Kevin Connor (left) and Athletic Director Gary Lagesse (right) are photographed with the IHSA Sportsmanship mascot. Thornwood High School won the sportsmanship award from the IHSA three years in a row (2001–2003). No other school in the state has ever won the award three years in a row. (Photo courtesy of Thornwood High School.)

Thornwood has graduated many star athletes who have gone on to play professional sports. One of those athletes was Cliff Floyd, from the class of 1991, who appears on this Topps' baseball card wearing his Thornwood jersey and his state championship baseball medal. He went on to play for the Florida Marlins and currently plays for the New York Mets. (Courtesy of Gary Lester.)

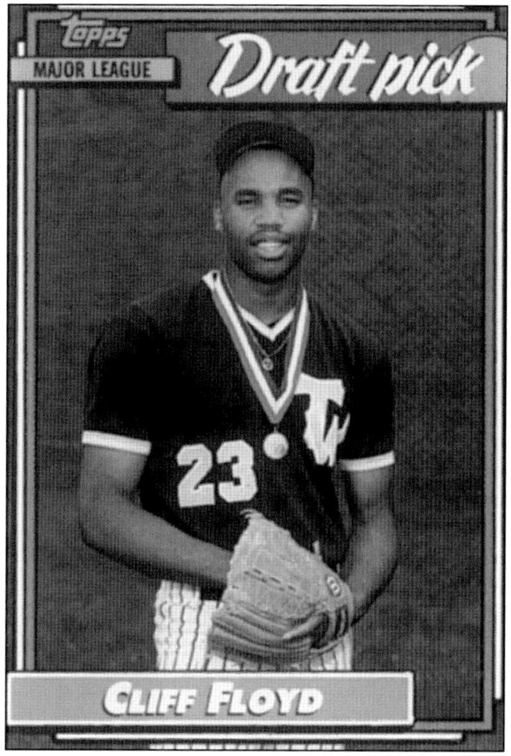

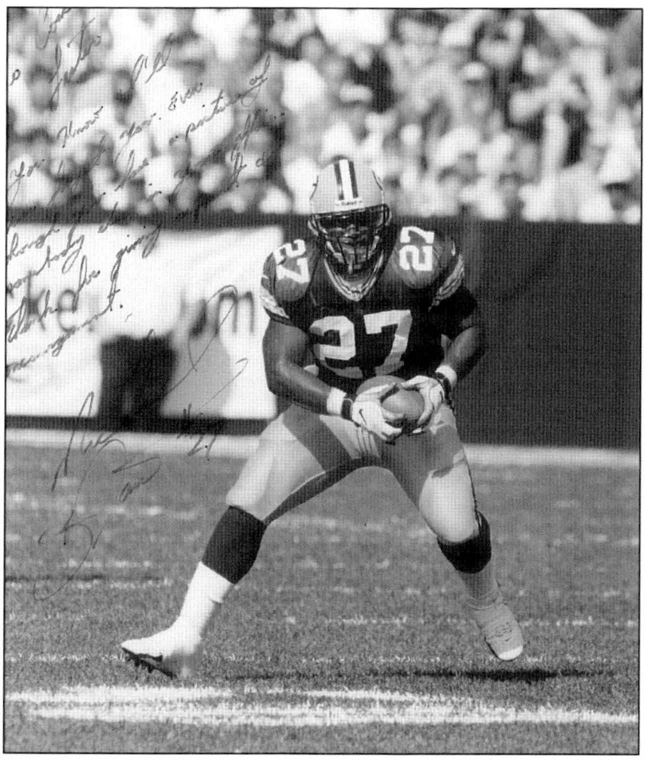

Michael Blair, from the class of 1992, went on to play professional football for the Green Bay Packers. (Courtesy of Gary Lester.)

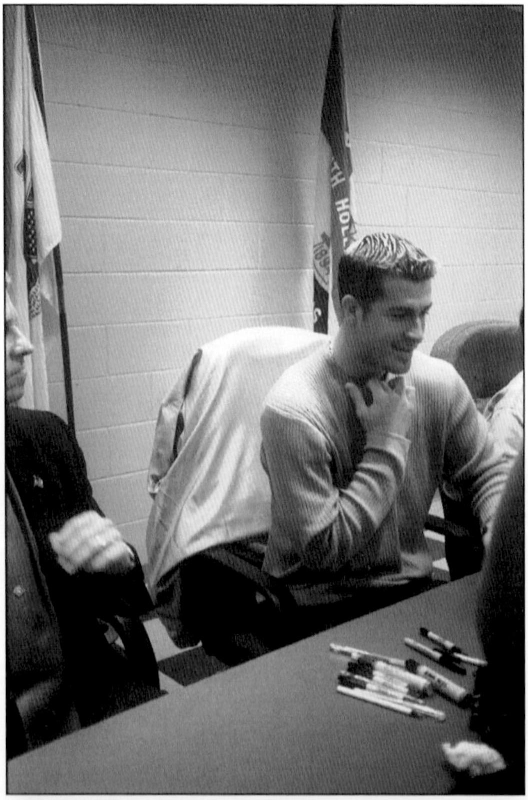

Mark Mulder, from the class of 1995, went on to play professional baseball and pitches for the Oakland A's. (Photo courtesy of Luella Bader.)

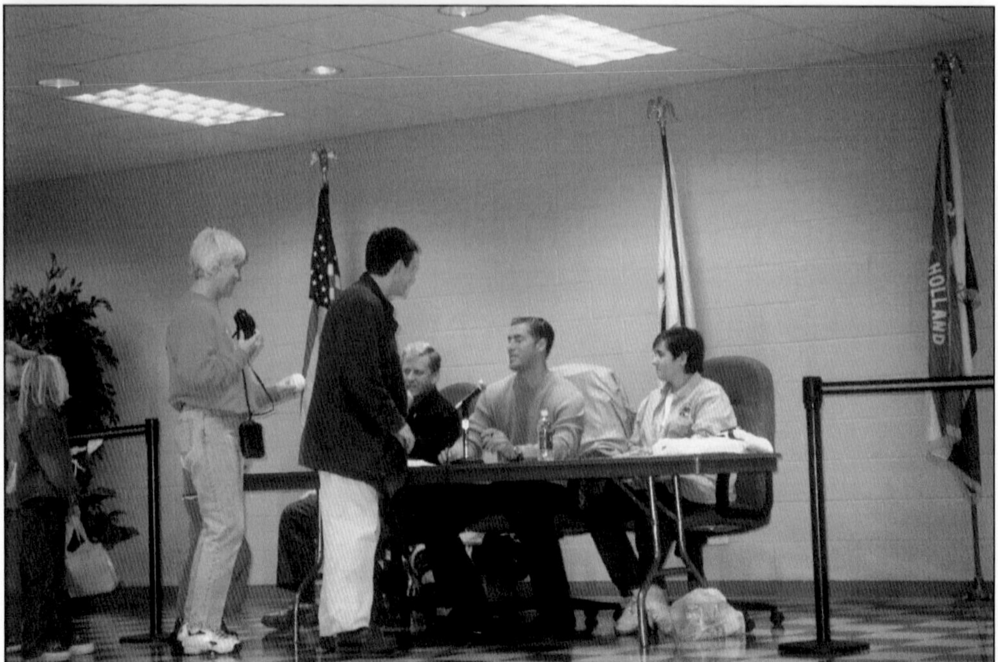

Mark Mulder talks to fans and signs autographs at a 2002 appearance at the South Holland Community Center. (Photo courtesy of Luella Bader.)

As a senior at Thornwood, Eddy Curry and his teammates took their team downstate where they lost the final game to Shaumburg. Prior to the final game, the team only had one loss for the season. (Photo courtesy of Luella Bader.)

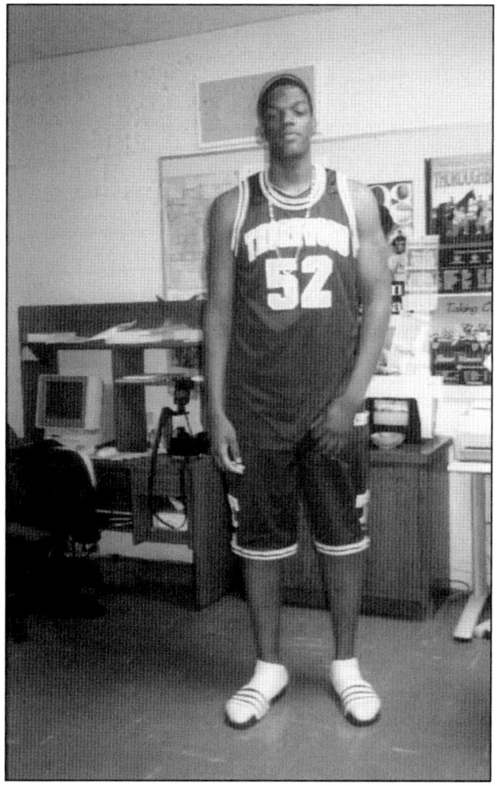

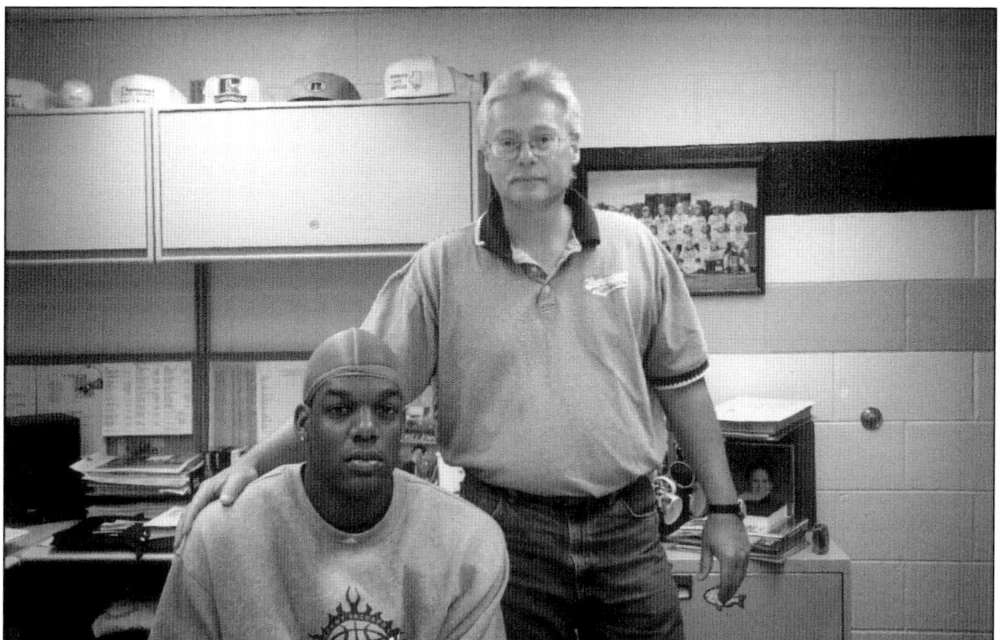

Eddy Curry is pictured with Thornwood Athletic Director Gary Lagesse. (Photo courtesy of Luella Bader.)

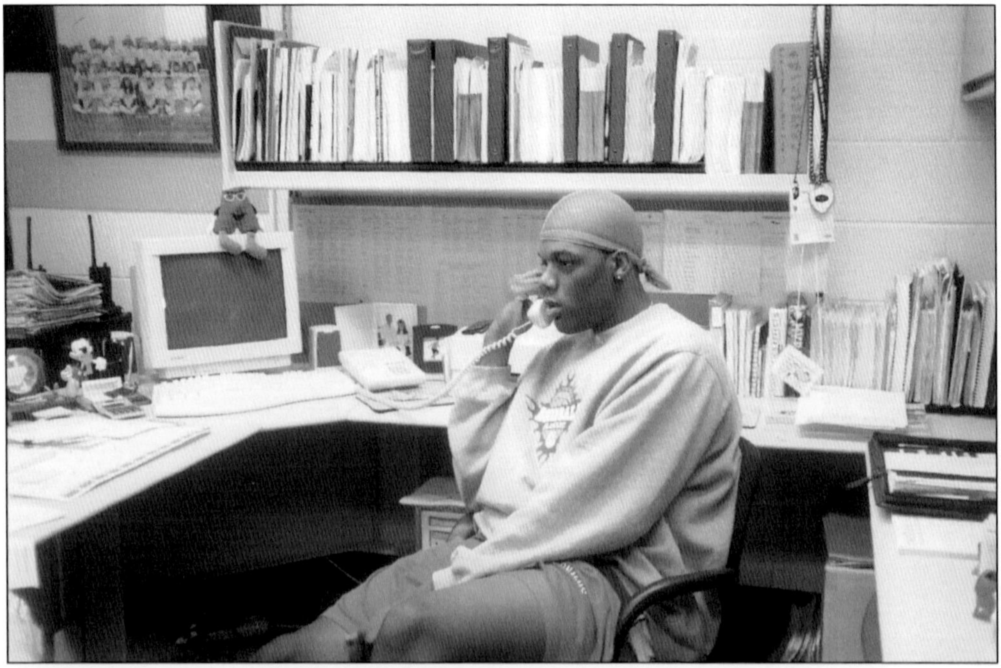

Before graduating from Thornwood, Eddy Curry had already signed to play for the Chicago Bulls. Here Curry does a phone interview in the athletic office about becoming a member of the Bulls. (Photo courtesy of Luella Bader.)

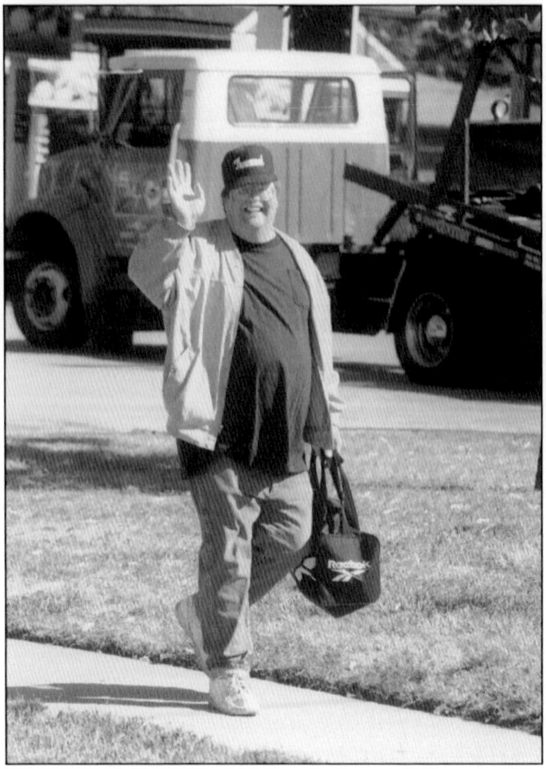

South Holland resident Dave Brown has become known as the "Thornwood Superfan." Walking from his nearby home, Brown has been present at countless school events. Here he is pictured on South Park Avenue, watching the Homecoming Parade pass by in 1999. (Photo courtesy of Gary Lester.)

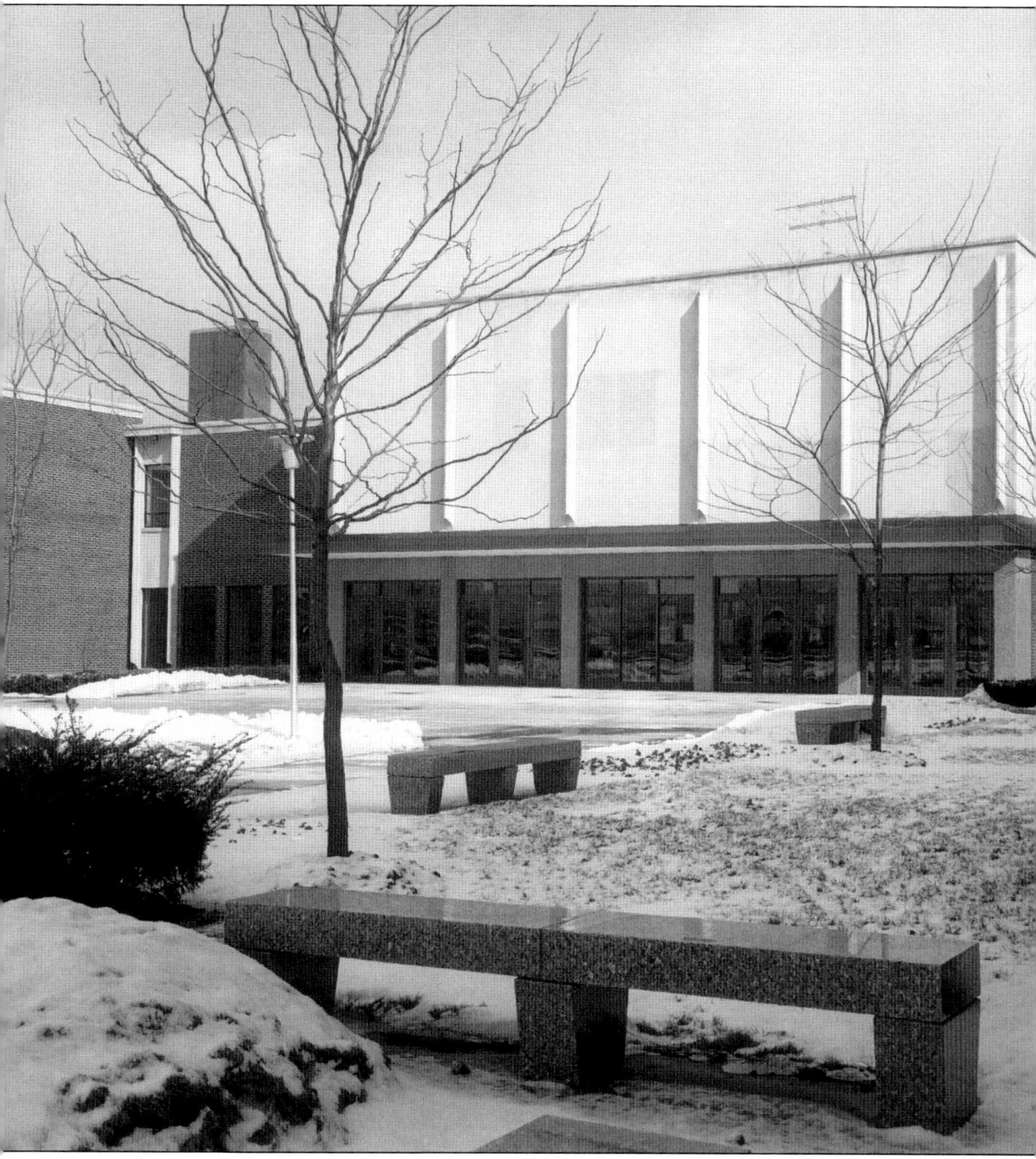

Thornwood's main entrance on a winter day. (Photo courtesy of Thornwood High School.)

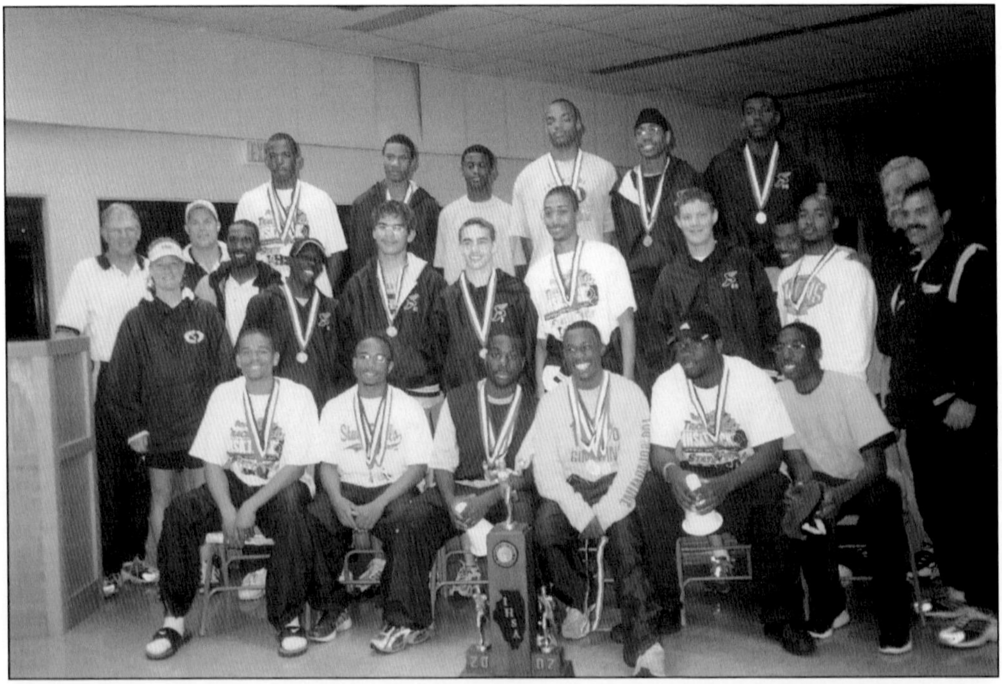

Thornwood's 2002 State Championship Track Team. (Photo courtesy of Gary Lester.)

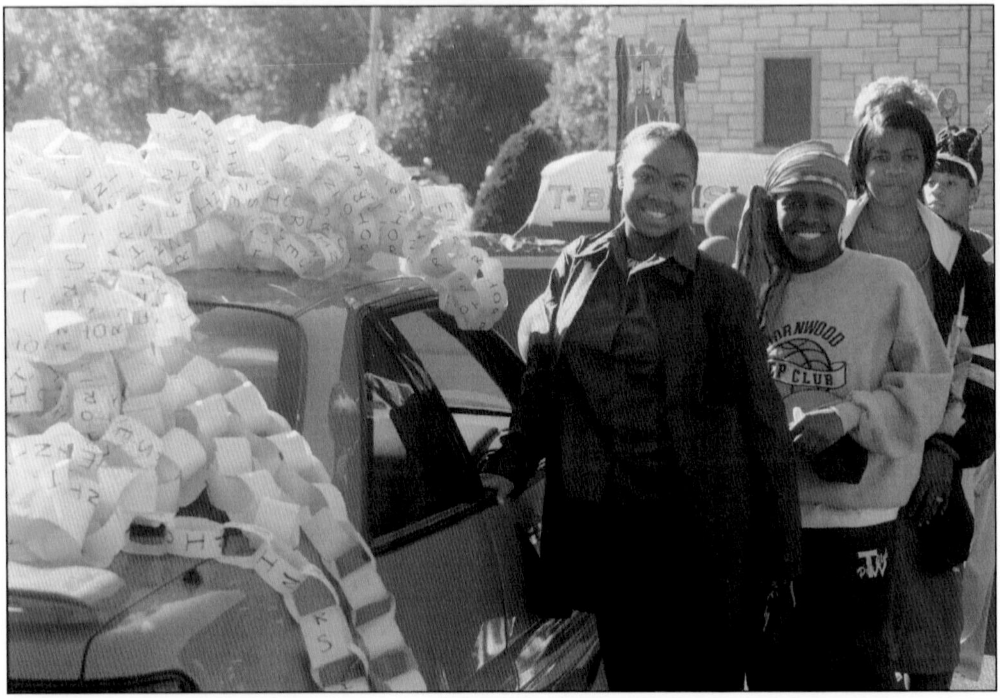

Students prepare for the 1999 Homecoming Parade. (Photo courtesy of Gary Lester.)

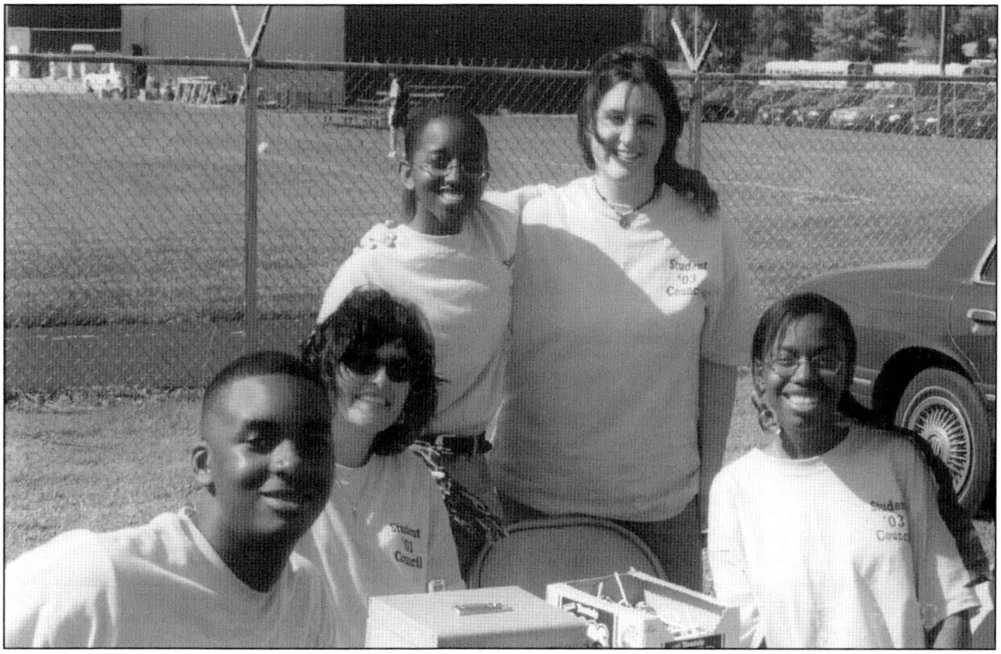

The class of 2003 student council members sell snacks at the homecoming game. (Photo courtesy of Gary Lester.)

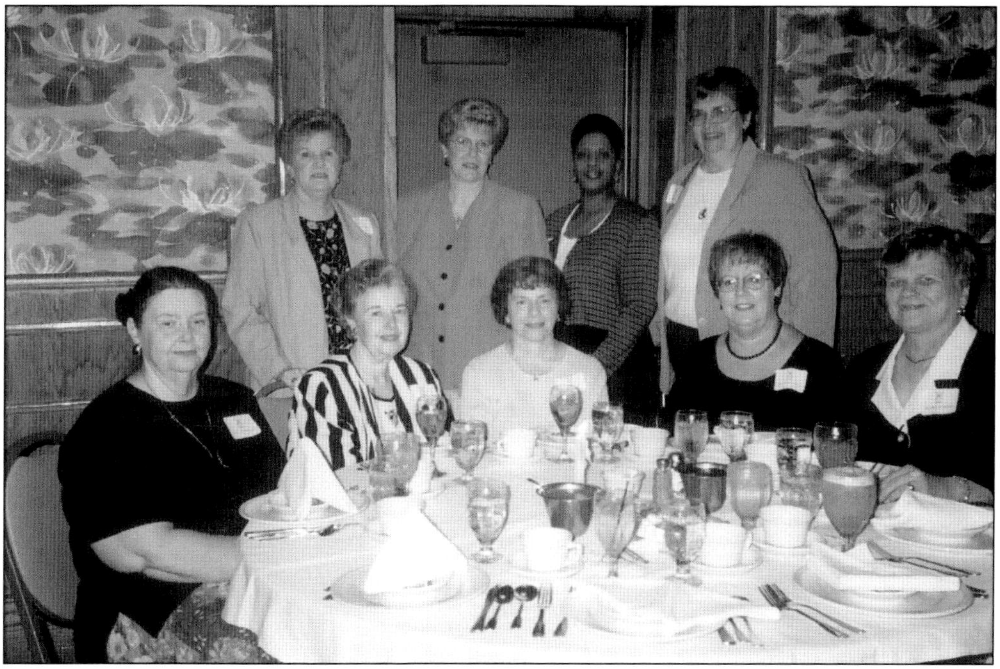

Some of the Thornwood secretaries gather for a photo at a retirement party. Pictured from left to right are: (front row) Glenda Schowalter (registrar, still working at school, employed in district over 40 years), Arlene Mokate (retired principal's secretary), Orie Matyasik, Mary Jane Scanlon, and Beverly Petrovic; (back row) Marilyn Anderson, Jo Kuzniewski, Dana Thigpen (current principal's secretary), and Gail Silzer. (Photo courtesy of Gary Lester.)

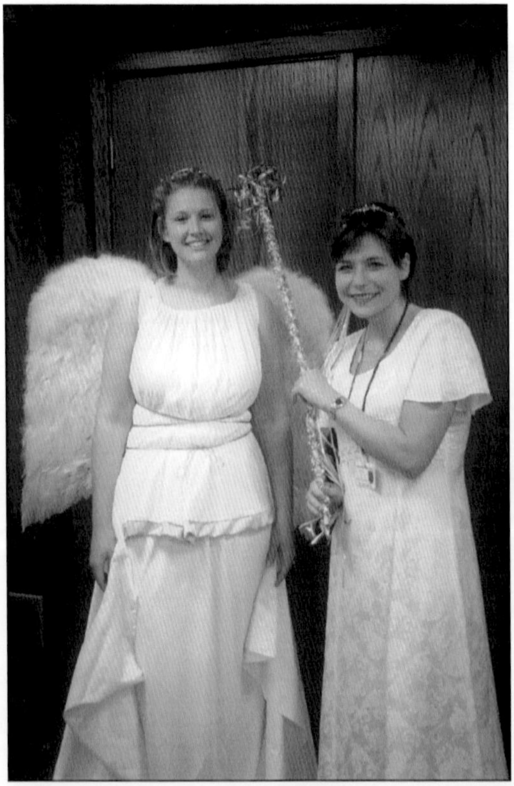

Thornwood Staff members Heather Beaver and Dee Gozder dress up for Halloween in 2000. (Photo courtesy of Gary Lester.)

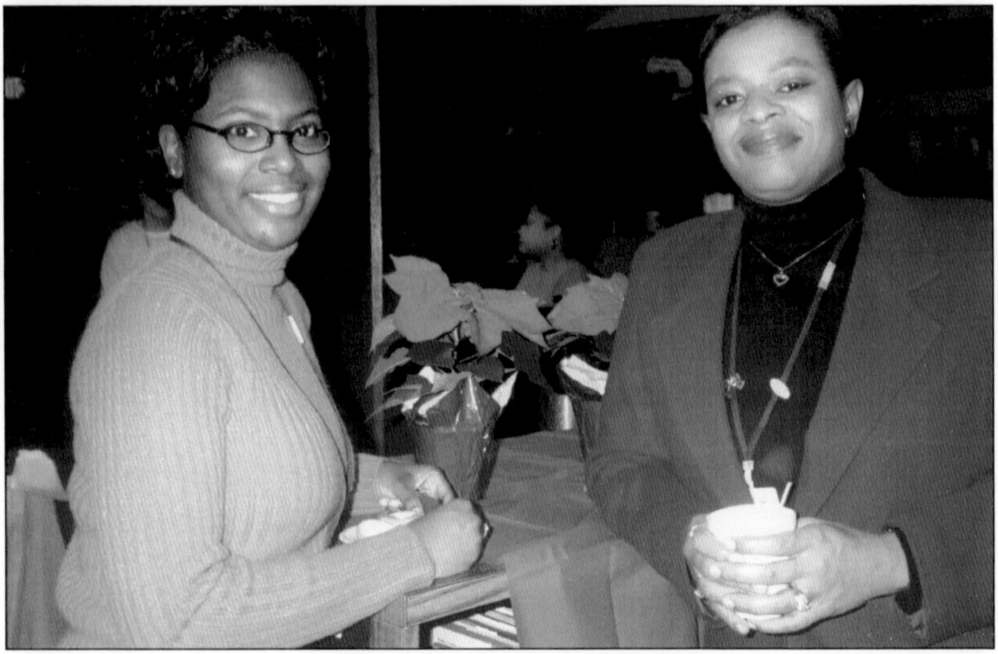

Laura Alexander-Flaherty and Benita Anderson, both Thornwood teachers, socialize at a Christmas luncheon. (Photo courtesy of Gary Lester.)

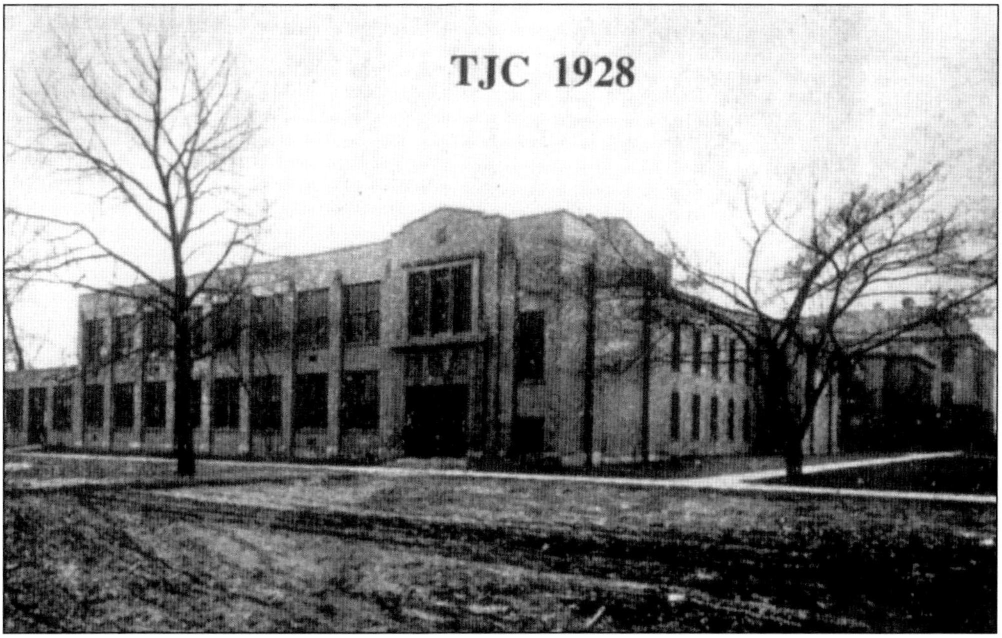

Thornton Junior College was founded on September 19, 1927 and was first located within the Thornton Township High School building in Harvey. It was the fifth junior college established in Illinois and for the first nine years of operation students living within School District 205 boundaries could attend the school free of charge. Here is the college as it appeared in 1928. (Photo courtesy of South Suburban College.)

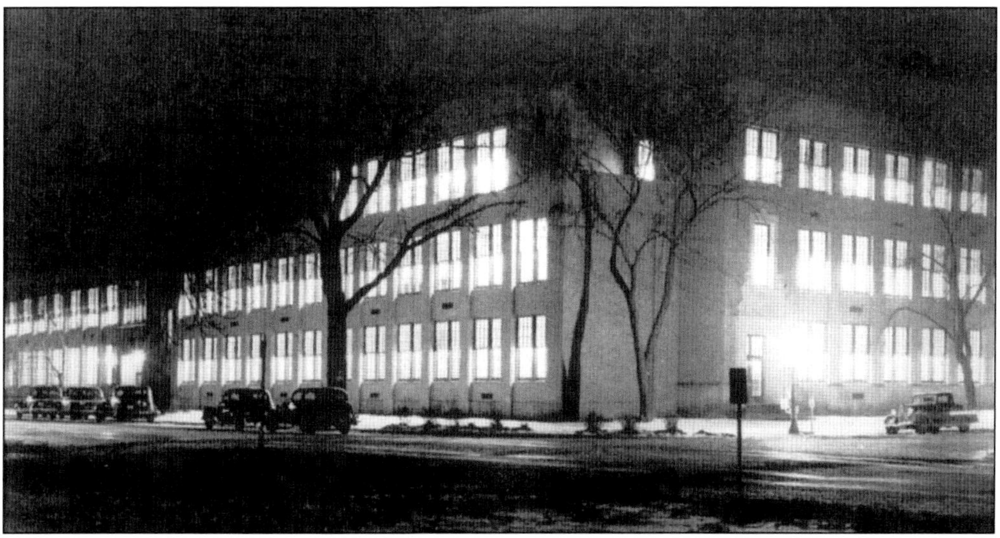

By the 1940s, Thornton Township High School and Thornton Junior College had seen the addition of several classrooms. College classes were held on the second and third floors of the north end of the building. The college still shared gymnasium facilities with the high school until a new gym and field house were later added. In October 1946, *Look Magazine* ranked TJC as one of the top 13 junior colleges in the country, placing it on the "Honor Roll of American Public Schools." It was the only Illinois junior college on the list. The photo shows the school at night in 1946. (Photo courtesy of South Suburban College.)

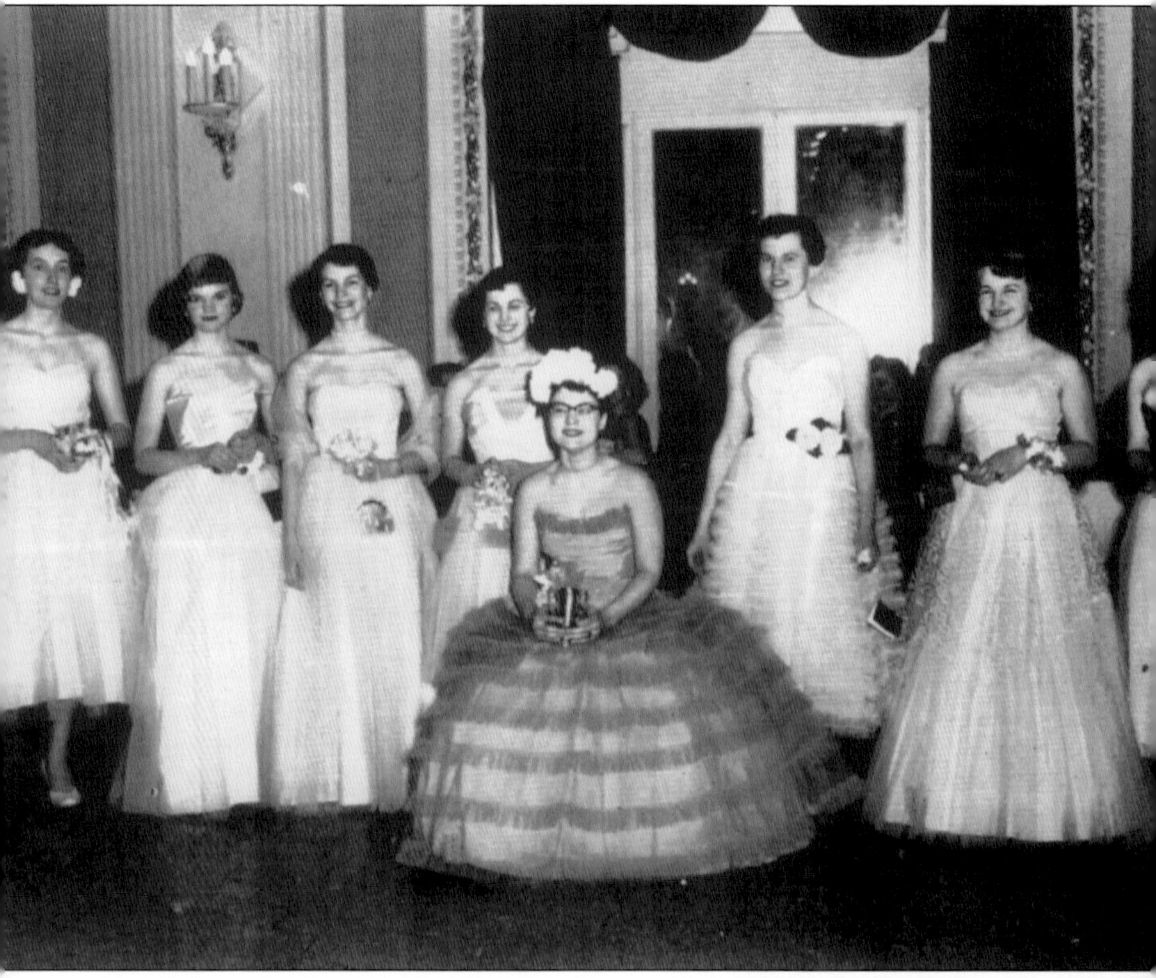

The TJC Stagette Court in the 1950s. (Photo courtesy of South Suburban College.)

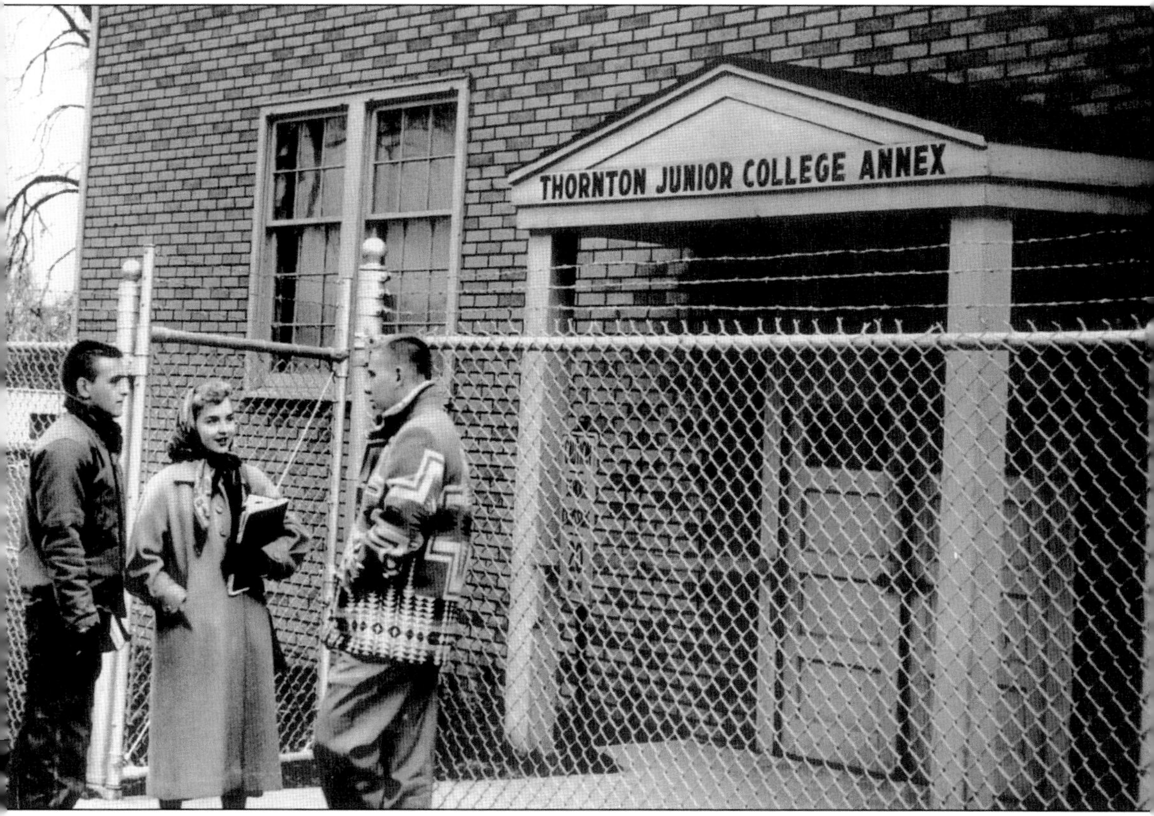

A 1950s photo of students outside the Annex. (Photo courtesy of South Suburban College.)

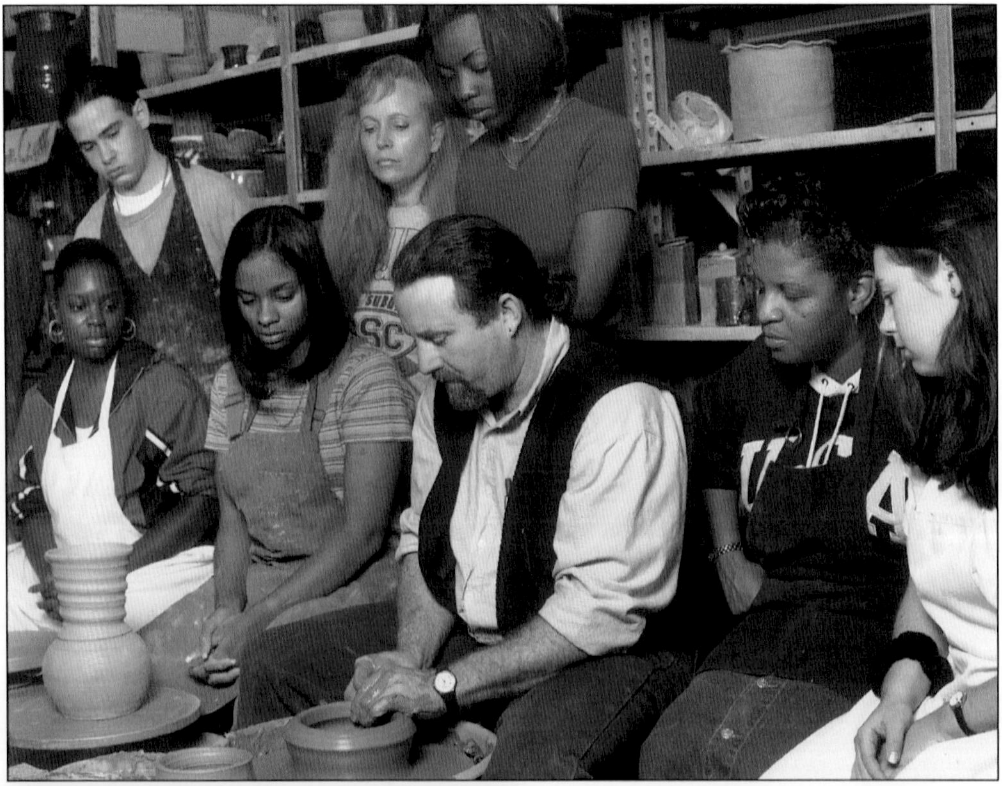

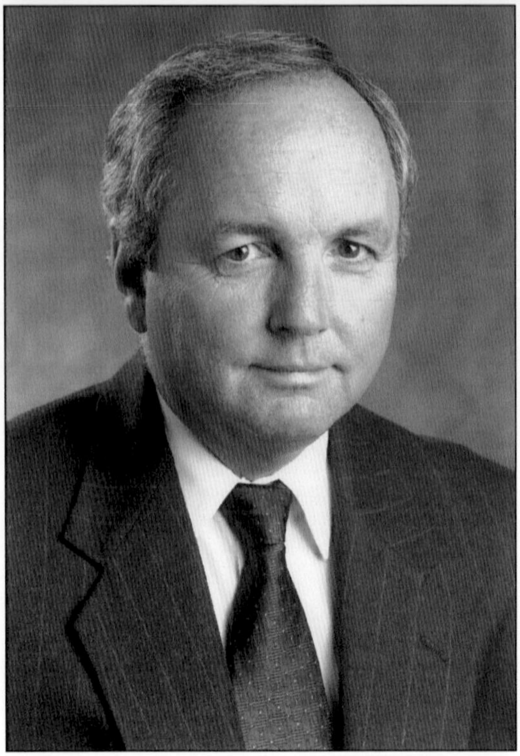

In 1969, TJC changed its name to Thornton Community College and in 1971, the campus was moved to a 103-acre site in South Holland that was formerly an onion farm. In 1988, the school name was changed to South Suburban College. In this 2000 photo, SSC students watch a ceramics demonstration by instructor Jack Kirkpatrick. (Photo courtesy of South Suburban College.)

South Suburban College, which celebrated its 75th anniversary in 2002, has had 17 individuals serve as president. Pictured is George Dammer, the current president of the college. (Photo courtesy of South Suburban College.)

Five

Serving the Community

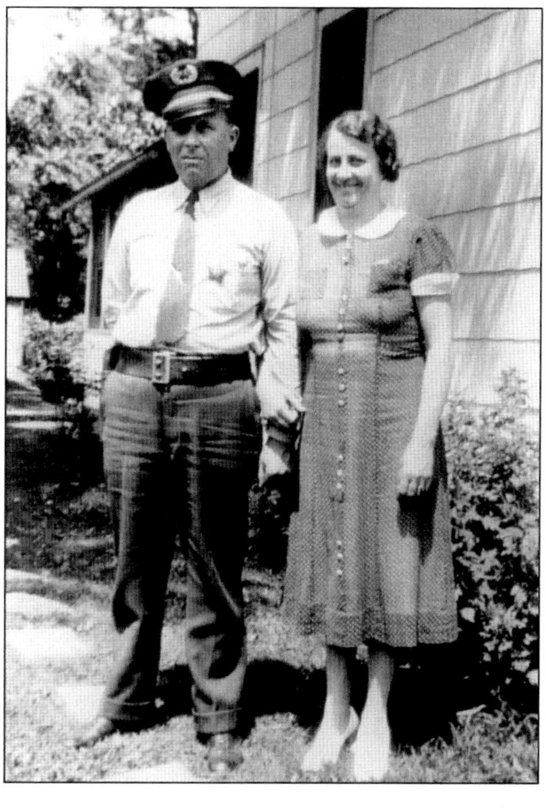

Mr. Westly Diekman, a policeman in South Holland in the 1920s and 1930s, and Mrs. Josephine De Young Diekman. (Photo courtesy of South Holland Historical Society from the collection of Dr. Carl Walvoord.)

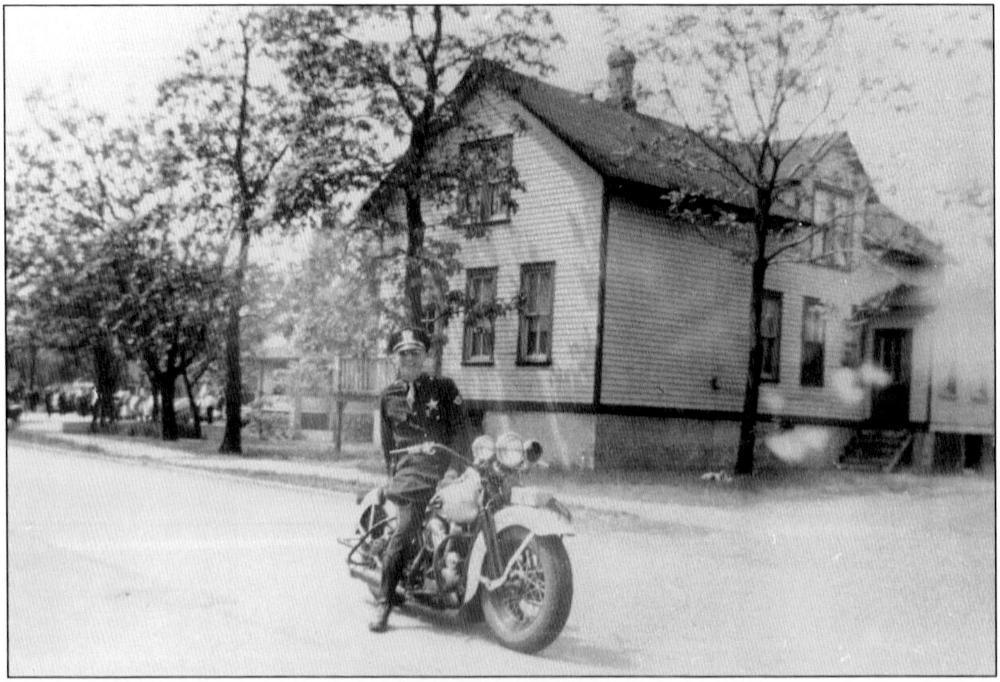

Hiram Vanderbilt was South Holland's first motorcycle policeman. (Photo courtesy of South Holland Historical Society from the collection of Dr. Carl Walvoord.)

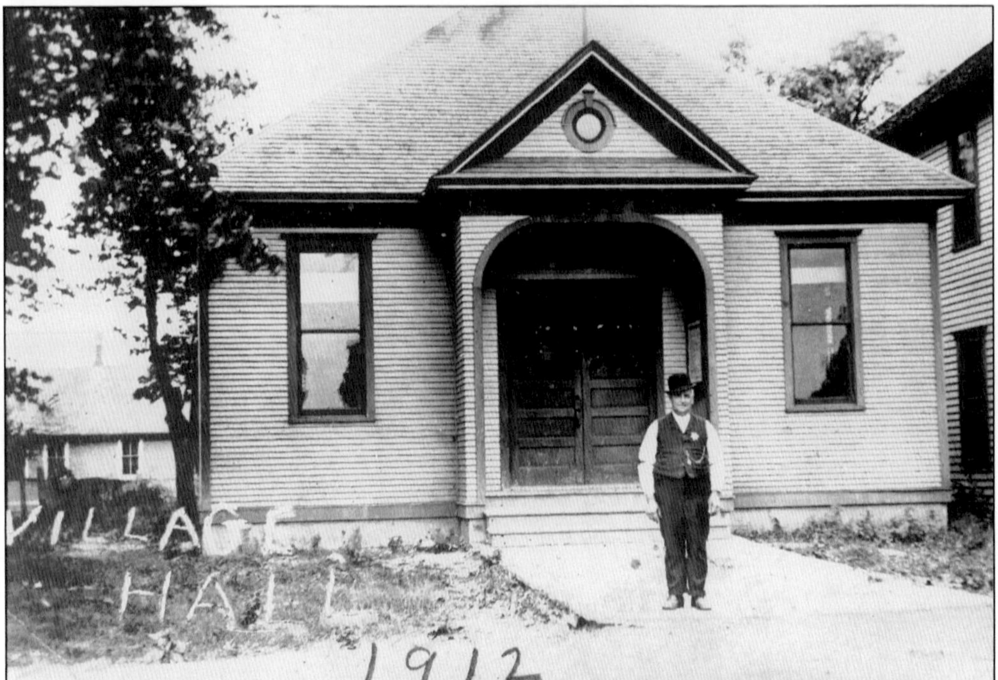

Michael Van Der Aa stands in front of Village Hall (which was located on South Park Avenue) in this 1912 photo. He was a civil war veteran and father of Teddy Van Der Aa. (Photo courtesy of South Holland Historical Society from the collection of Dr. Carl Walvoord.)

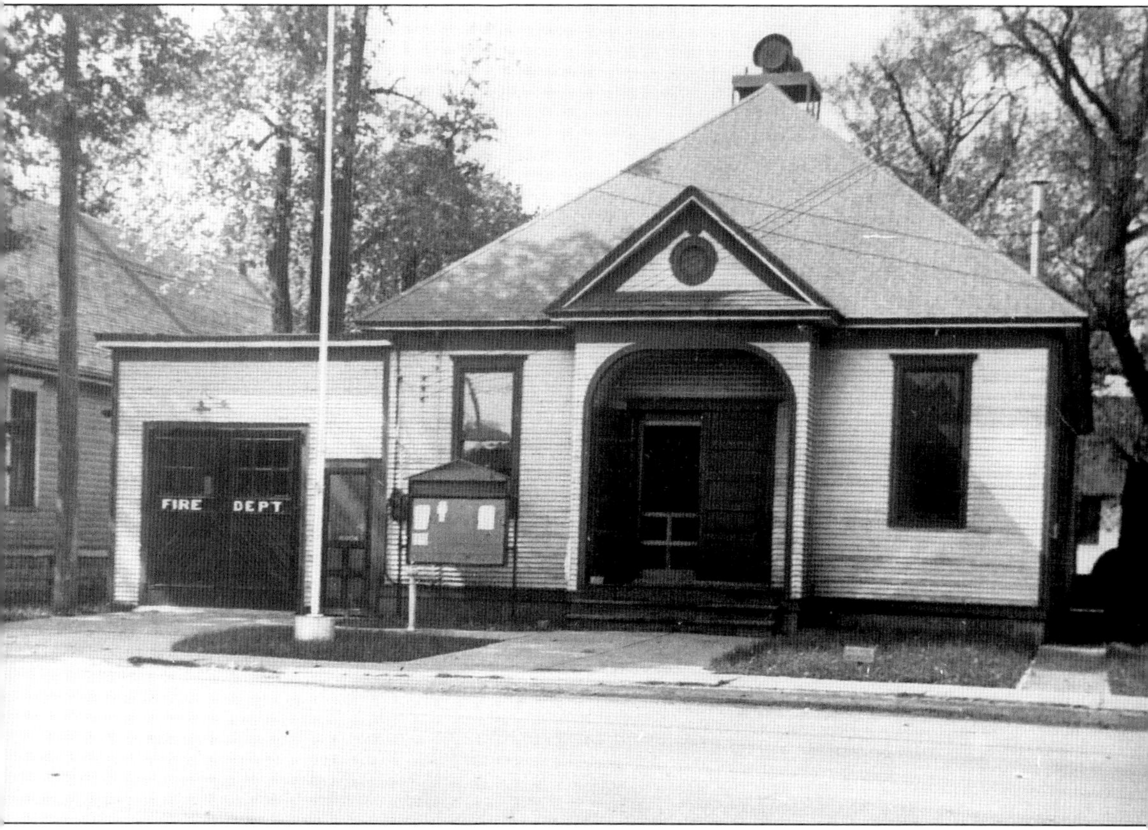

A later photo of the Village Hall with the fire department addition, which was added in 1920. (Photo courtesy of South Holland Historical Society from the collection of Dr. Carl Walvoord.)

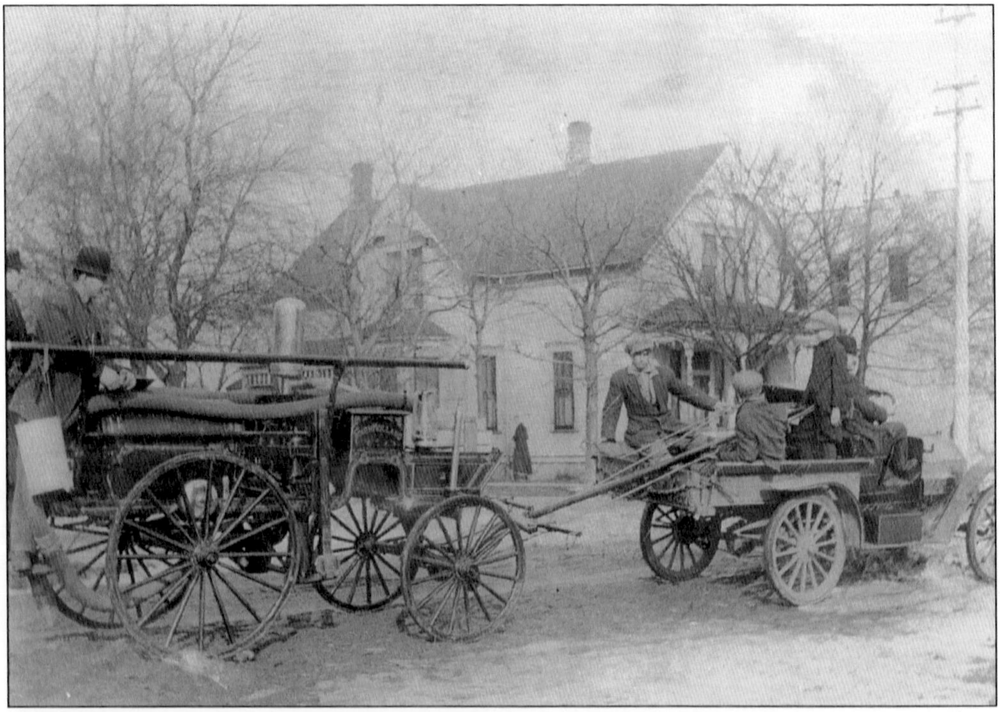

South Holland's first "fire engine" was a hand pumper, seen here being pulled by a small pick-up truck. (Photo courtesy of South Holland Fire Department.)

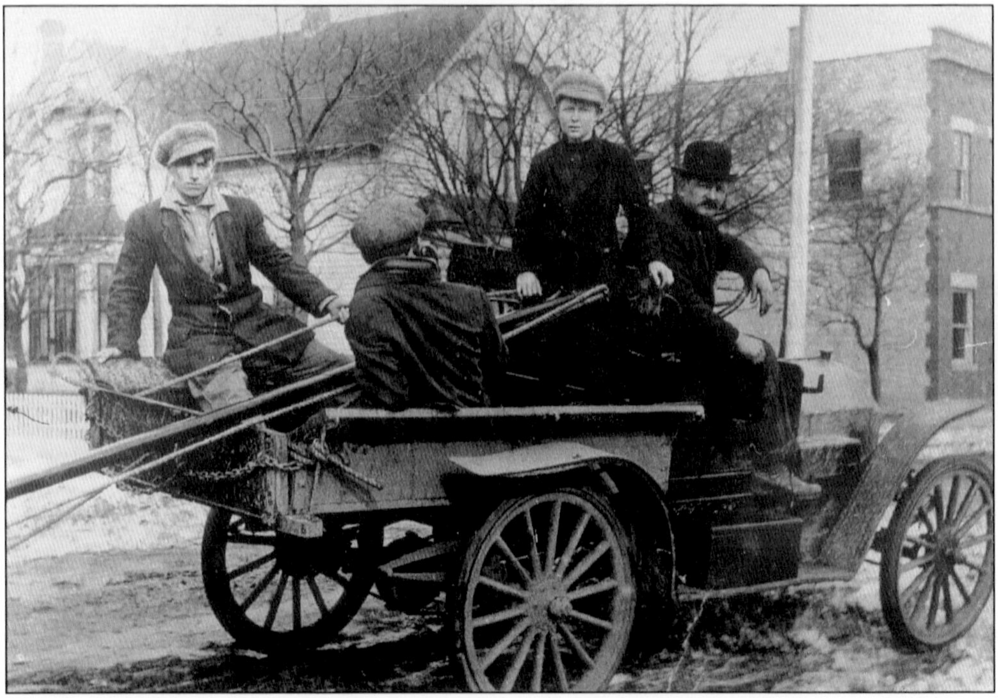

A closer look at the men pulling the hand pumper, with Mr. Kickert in the driver's seat. (Photo courtesy of the South Holland Fire Department.)

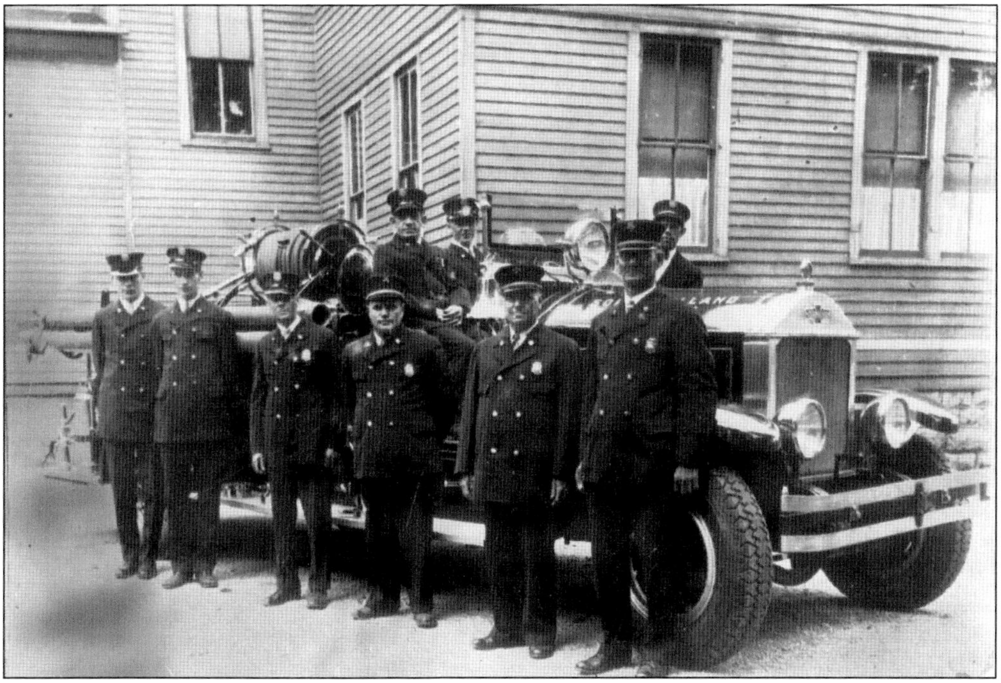

The third South Holland Fire Engine and firemen George Bogerschnieder, Mike Van Der Aa, Jacob Triemstra, Harold De Young, Jacob De Young, Jeff Van Der Aa, Teddy Van Der Aa, and Morris Van Der Aa. The photo was taken in front of the Roosevelt School. (Photo courtesy of South Holland Historical Society from the collection of Dr. Carl Walvoord.)

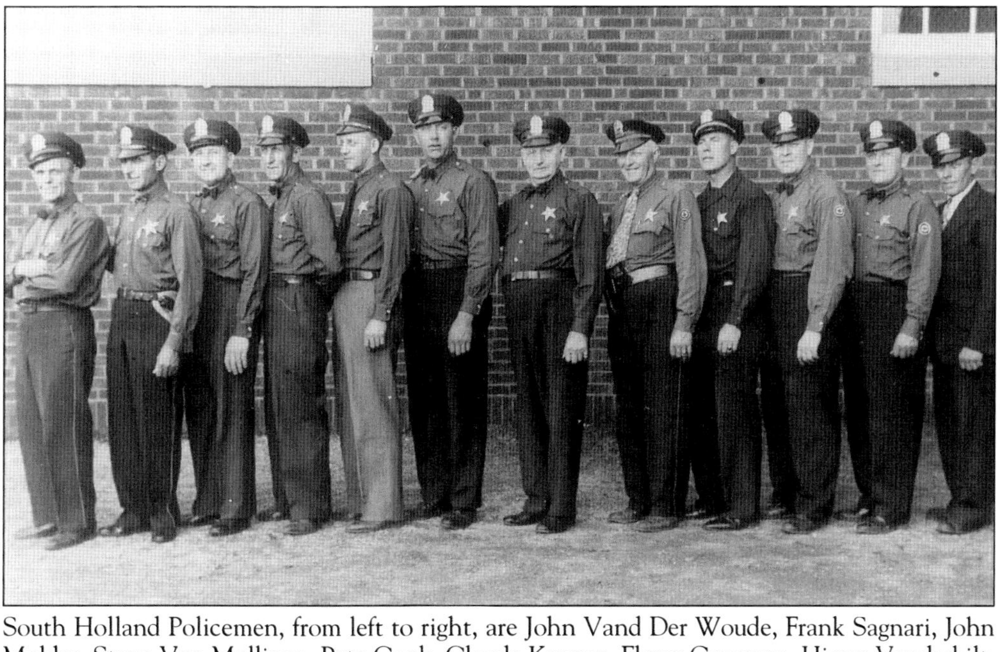

South Holland Policemen, from left to right, are John Vand Der Woude, Frank Sagnari, John Mulder, Steve Van Mulligan, Pete Cook, Claude Kramer, Flores Gouwens, Hiram Vanderbilt, Doug Gouwens, T. Huizenga, Niel Van Kanagen, and Toney Bultema. (Photo courtesy of South Holland Historical Society from the collection of Dr. Carl Walvoord.)

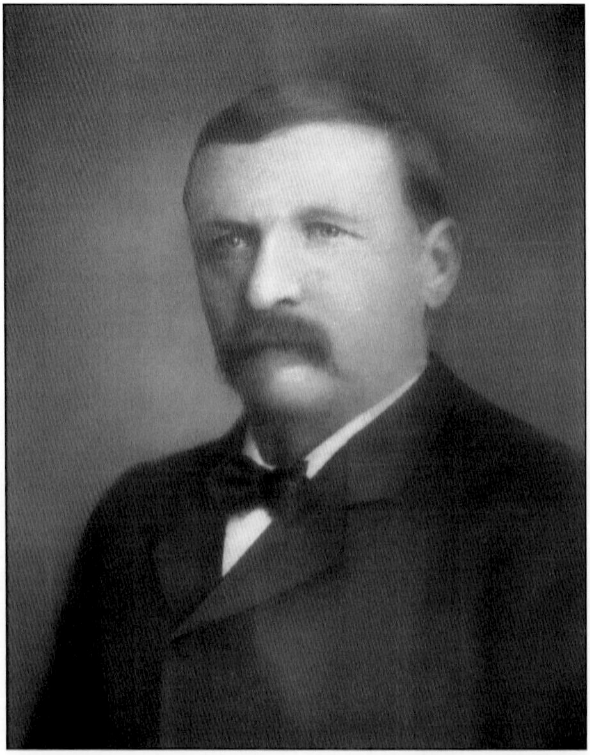

John Shilling, Sr. was the first mayor of South Holland, serving from 1894 to 1896. He lived on South Park Avenue and ran a meat market. His residence was later purchased by the De Young family and the structure later became De Young's Funeral Home. The funeral home was later combined with a furniture business. The building still stands today and is still occupied by De Young & Sons Furniture. (Photo courtesy of the Village of South Holland.)

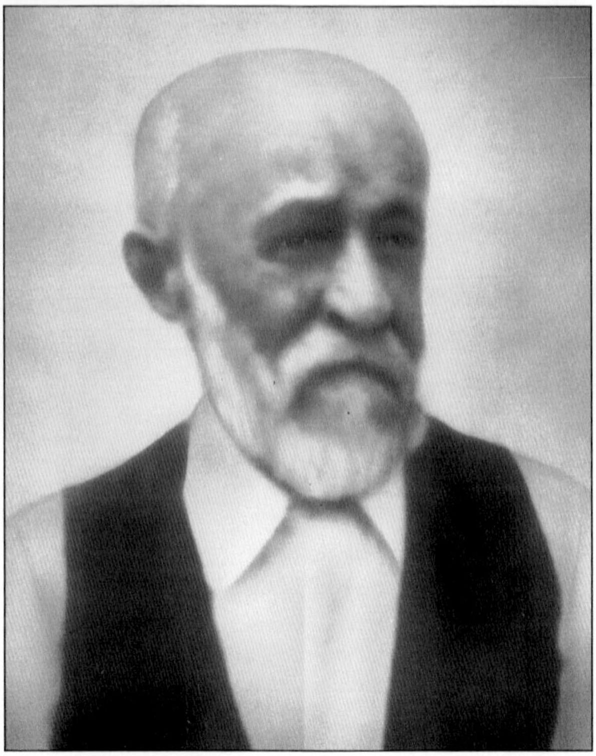

Gerrit Van Oostenberg was the second mayor, serving a two-year term from 1896–1898. (Photo courtesy of the Village of South Holland.)

Peter A. Anker was mayor from 1898–1908 and then again from 1910 until 1930. (Photo courtesy of the Village of South Holland.)

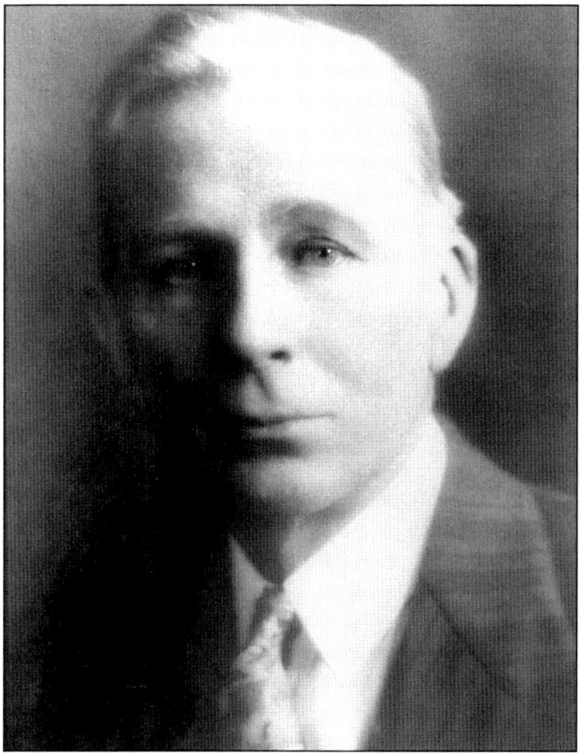

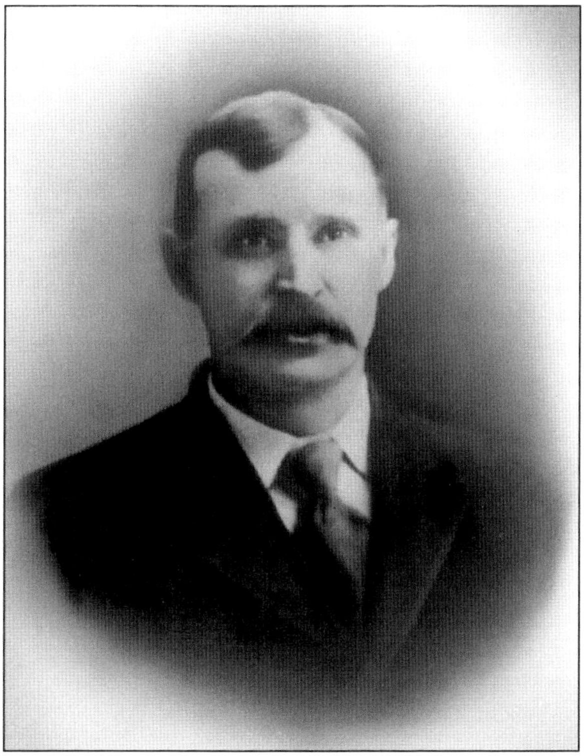

John Bardwick served for two years from 1908 until 1910. (Photo courtesy of the Village of South Holland.)

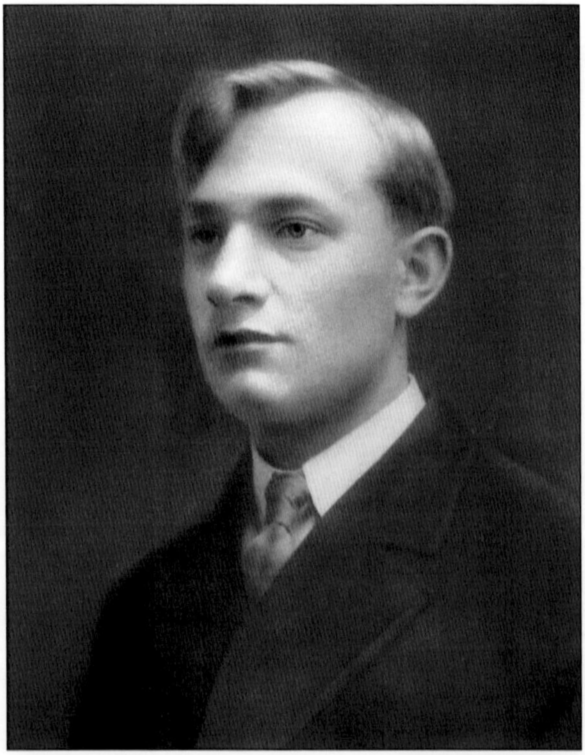

Joseph Fisher was mayor from 1930 until 1933. (Photo courtesy of the Village of South Holland.)

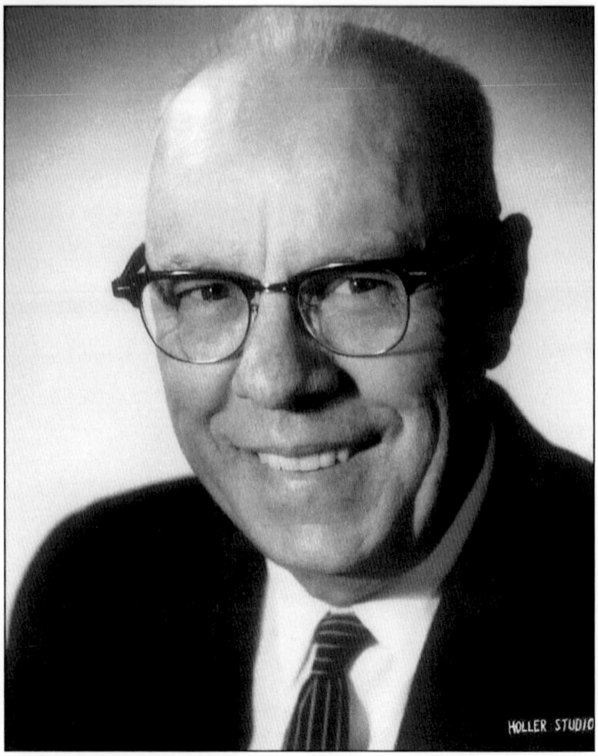

Gerrit H. Pals, who marketed onion sets, served as mayor from 1933 until 1935. (Photo courtesy of the Village of South Holland.)

James Gouwens served as mayor for 22 years, from 1935 until 1957. He was an uncle of the later mayor, Harold Gouwens, and sold farm equipment. (Photo courtesy of the Village of South Holland.)

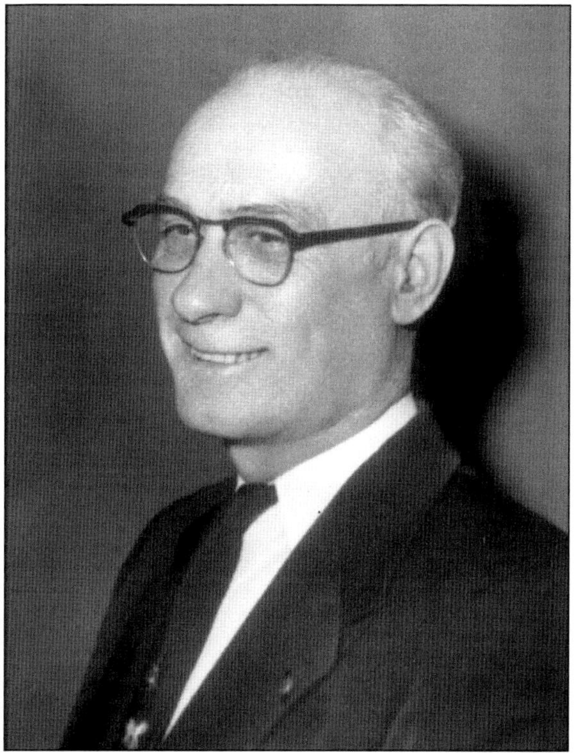

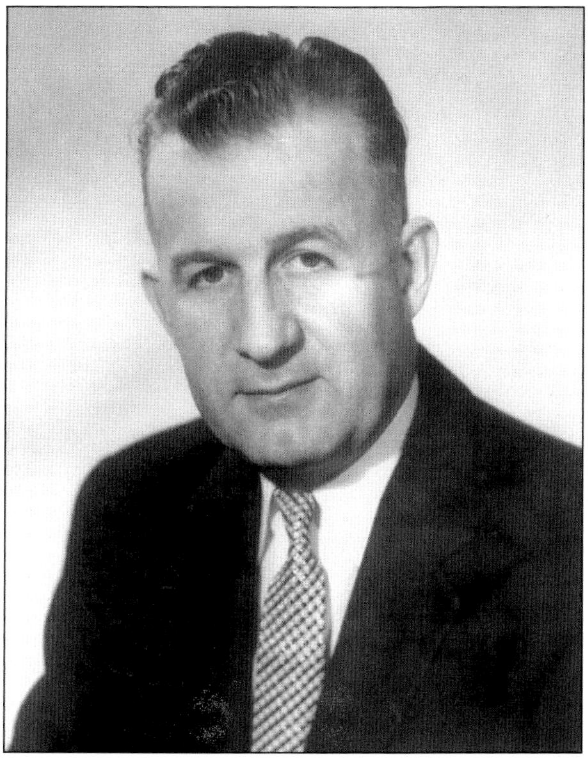

Henry Van Der Giessen served as mayor from 1957 until 1960. (Photo courtesy of the Village of South Holland.)

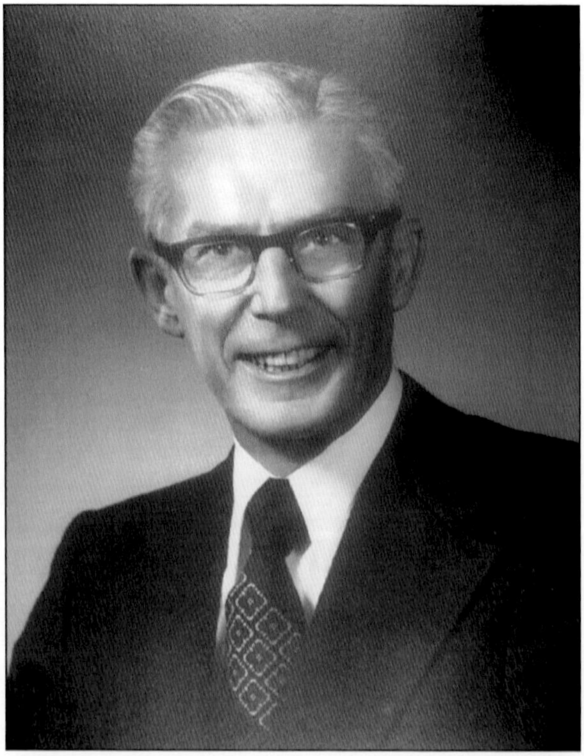

Harold J. Gouwens, the nephew of former mayor James Gouwens, was elected in 1960. He was a banker by profession and was president of the First National Bank in Dolton for many years. He was the village's longest serving mayor, serving for 34 years until 1994. (Photo courtesy of the Village of South Holland.)

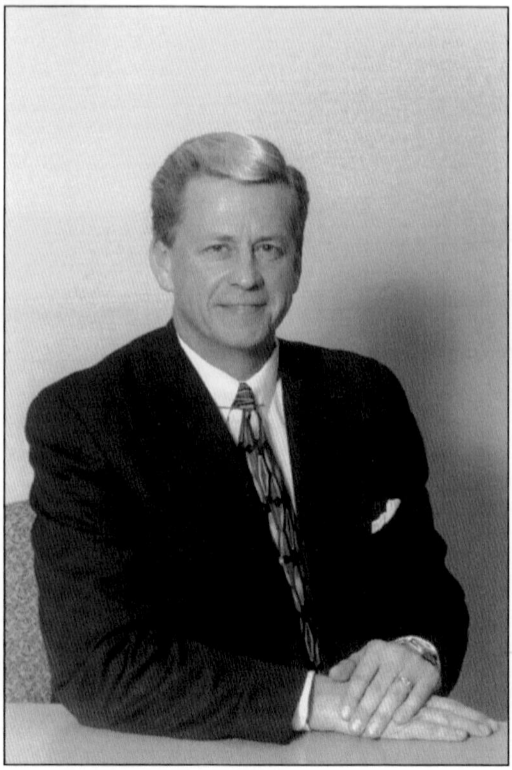

Don A DeGraff is South Holland's current mayor, serving since 1995. (Photo courtesy of the Village of South Holland.)

The growth in the village in recent years is apparent by this 1961 election flyer that shows just a handful of polling places. (Photo courtesy of the Village of South Holland.)

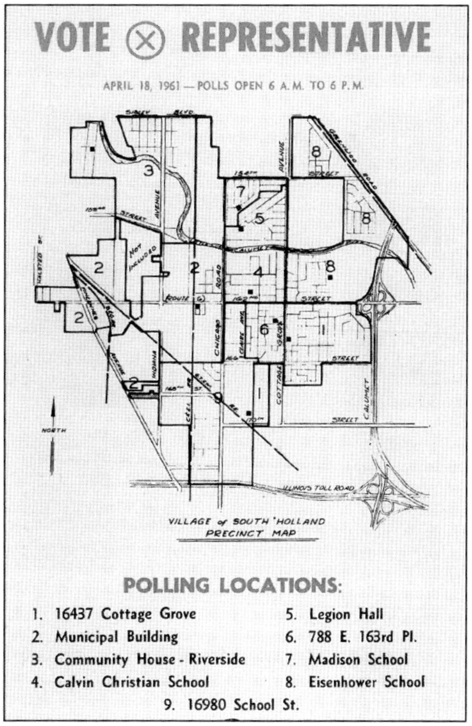

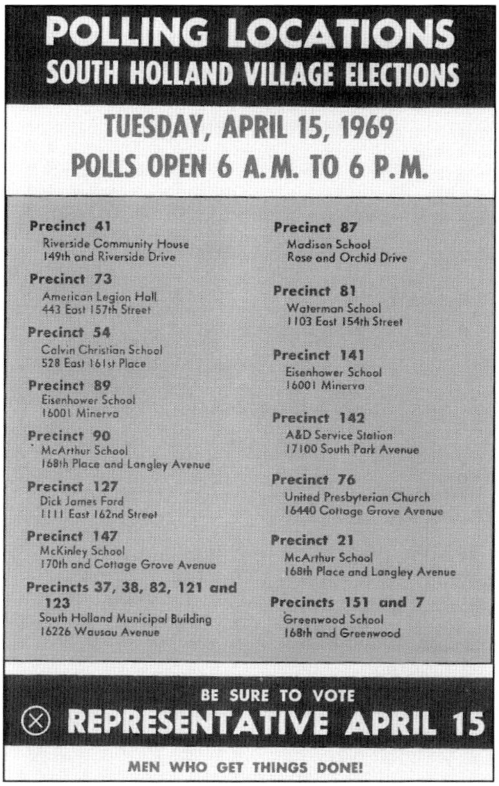

POLLING LOCATIONS
SOUTH HOLLAND VILLAGE ELECTIONS

TUESDAY, APRIL 15, 1969
POLLS OPEN 6 A.M. TO 6 P.M.

Precinct 41
Riverside Community House
149th and Riverside Drive

Precinct 73
American Legion Hall
443 East 157th Street

Precinct 54
Calvin Christian School
528 East 161st Place

Precinct 89
Eisenhower School
16001 Minerva

Precinct 90
McArthur School
168th Place and Langley Avenue

Precinct 127
Dick James Ford
1111 East 162nd Street

Precinct 147
McKinley School
170th and Cottage Grove Avenue

Precincts 37, 38, 82, 121 and 123
South Holland Municipal Building
16226 Wausau Avenue

Precinct 87
Madison School
Rose and Orchid Drive

Precinct 81
Waterman School
1103 East 154th Street

Precinct 141
Eisenhower School
16001 Minerva

Precinct 142
A&D Service Station
17100 South Park Avenue

Precinct 76
United Presbyterian Church
16440 Cottage Grove Avenue

Precinct 21
McArthur School
168th Place and Langley Avenue

Precincts 151 and 7
Greenwood School
168th and Greenwood

BE SURE TO VOTE
⊗ REPRESENTATIVE APRIL 15
MEN WHO GET THINGS DONE!

By 1969, the number of polling places had tripled. (Photo courtesy of the Village of South Holland.)

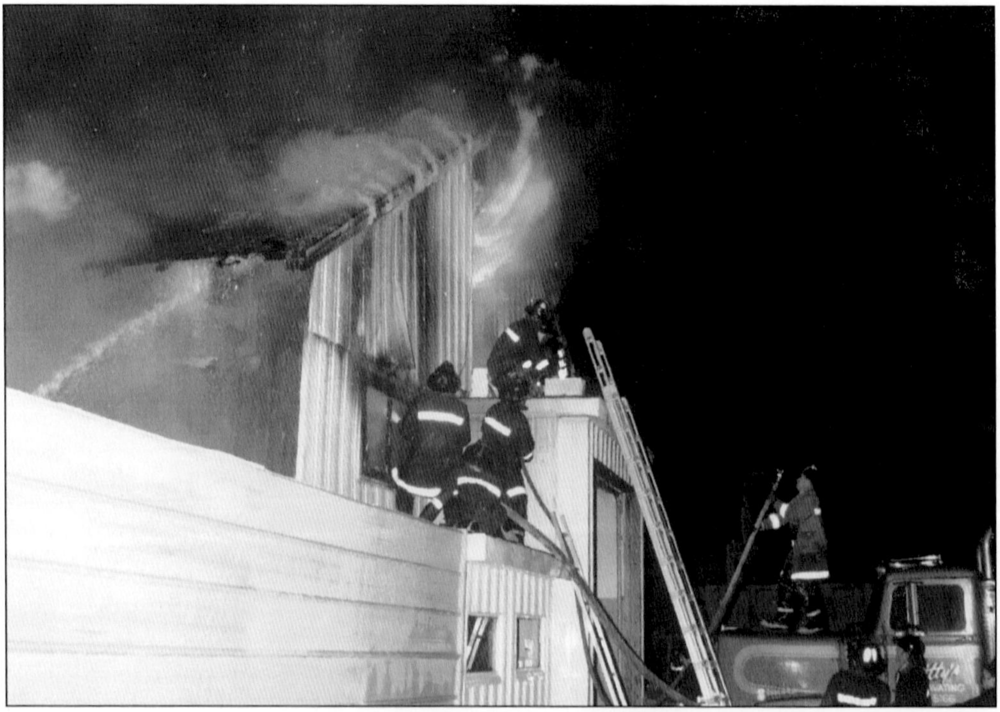

South Holland firefighters work to extinguish a fire at Smitty's barn at 172nd and South Park in the early 1980s. (Photos courtesy of the South Holland Fire Department.)

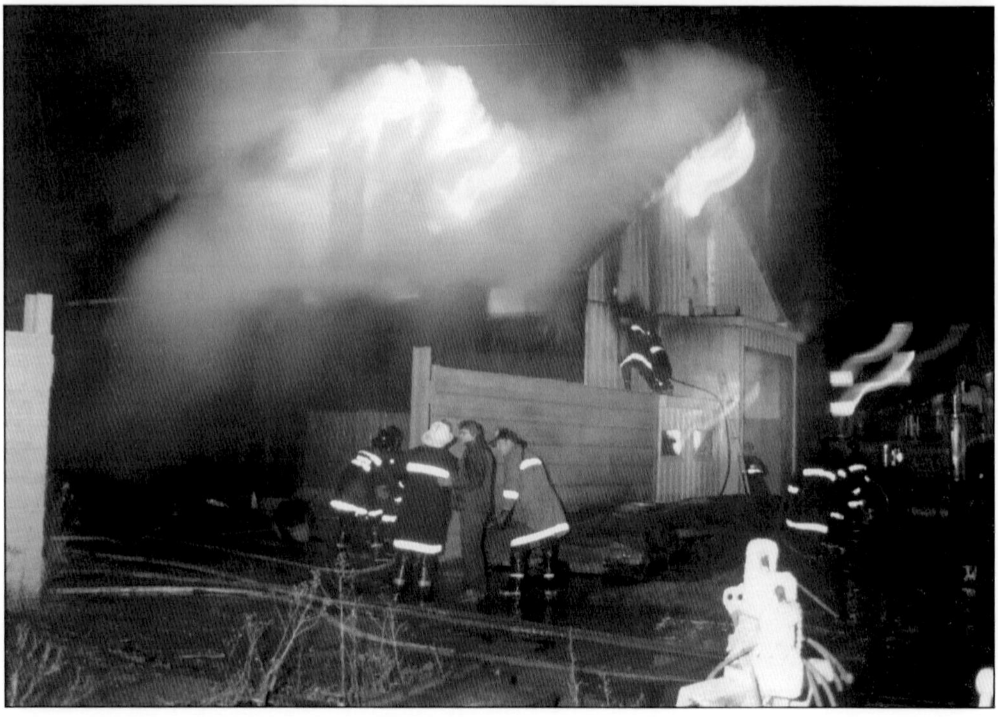

Six

FACES, PLACES, EVENTS, AND ACTIVITIES

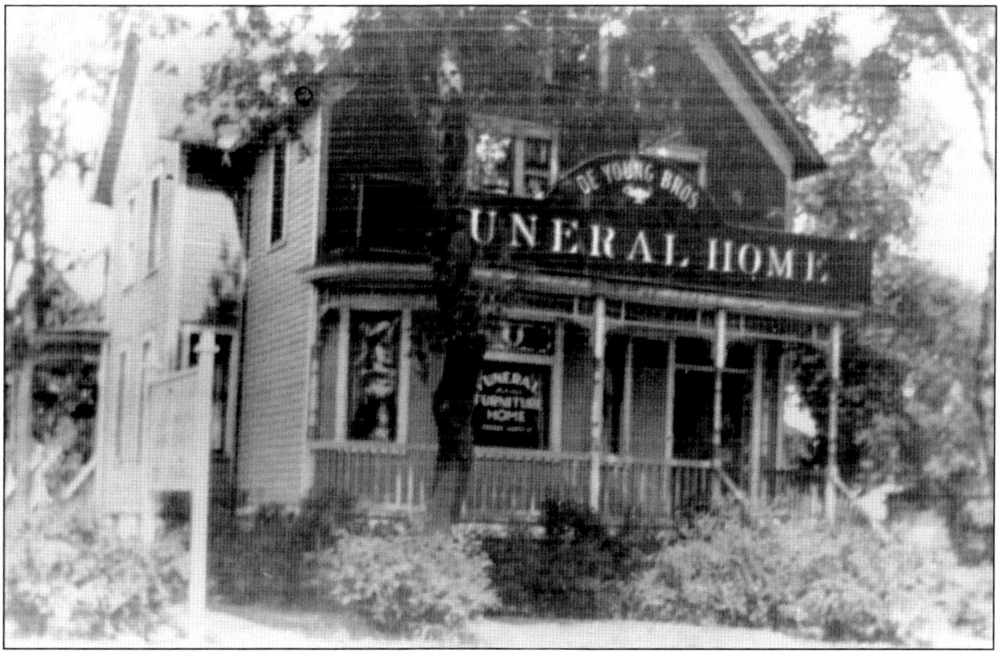

Originally the residence of the first mayor, John Shilling, this home was purchased by the De Young family and converted into the village's first funeral home. Later, the business was combined with a furniture store. Today it is De Young Furniture. (Photo courtesy of South Holland Historical Society from the collection of Dr. Carl Walvoord.)

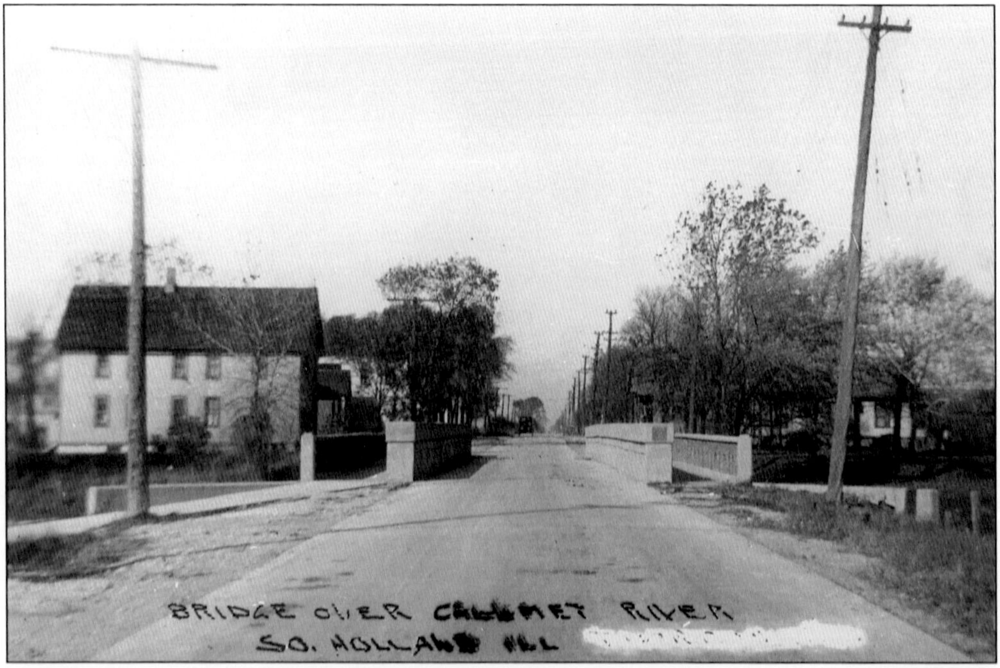

This is what the bridge on South Park Avenue once looked like. (Photo courtesy of South Holland Historical Society from the collection of Dr. Carl Walvoord.)

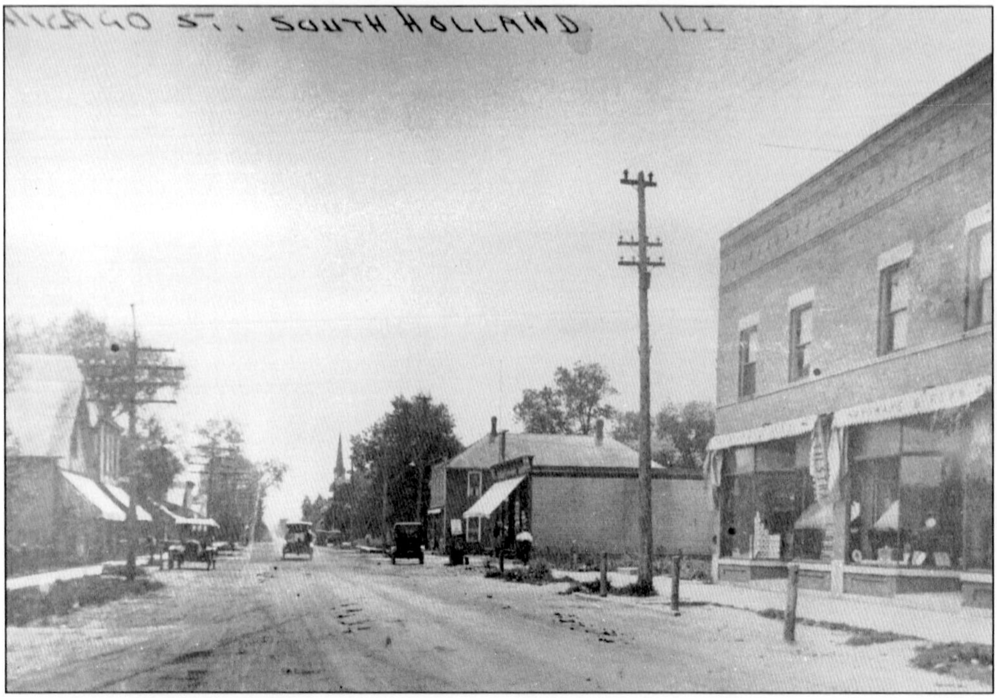

This photo of Chicago Street was taken prior to 1920. It is now called South Park Avenue, and this view is looking south. (Photo courtesy of South Holland Historical Society from the collection of Dr. Carl Walvoord.)

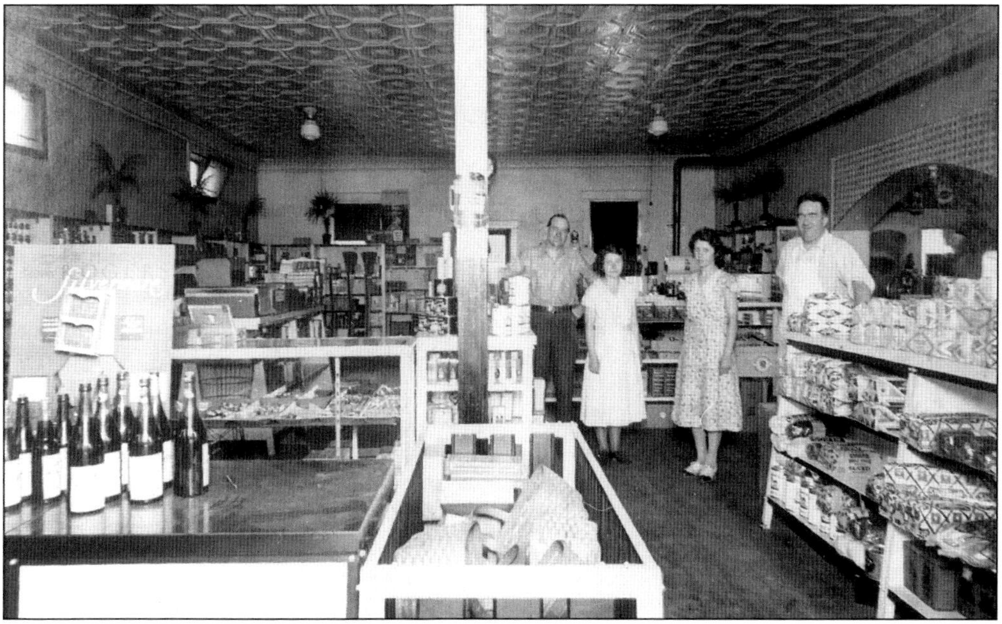

Pictured here are John Rinkema, Sophie Barwagon, Goldie Gowenhoven and Pete Rinkema inside the Rinkema Bros. Meat Market and Grocery Store, which was on South Park Avenue, north of the river on the east side of the street. (Photo courtesy of South Holland Historical Society from the collection of Dr. Carl Walvoord.)

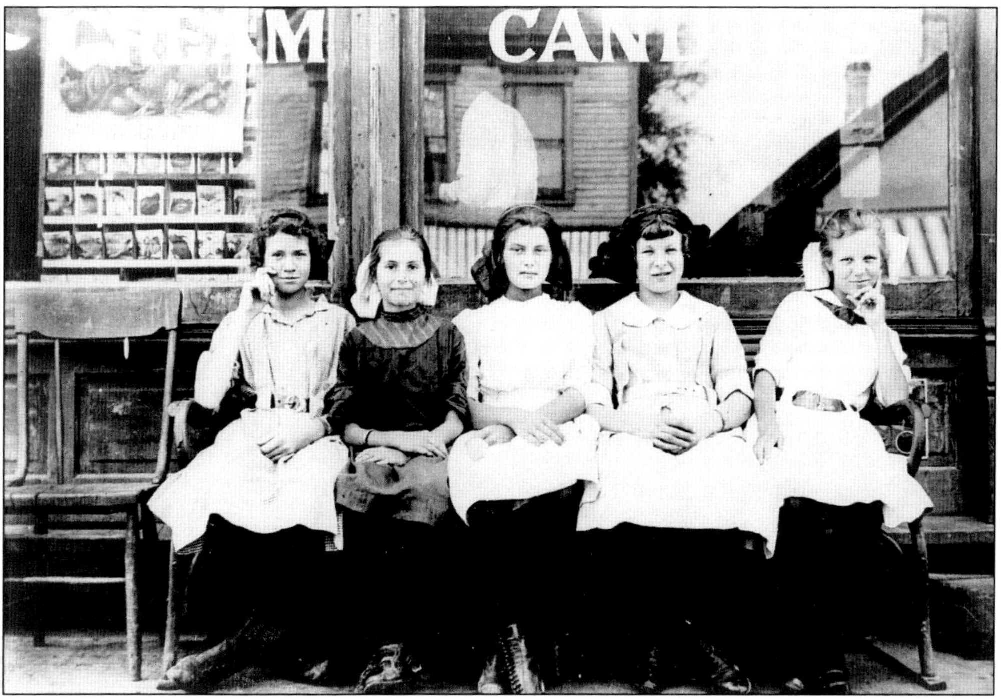

Pictured here, from left to right, are Agnes Rinkema, Annie De Young, Josey Van Der Aa, Esther De Graff, and Minnie Bardwick in front of Teddy Van Der Aa's store. (Photo courtesy of South Holland Historical Society from the collection of Dr. Carl Walvoord.)

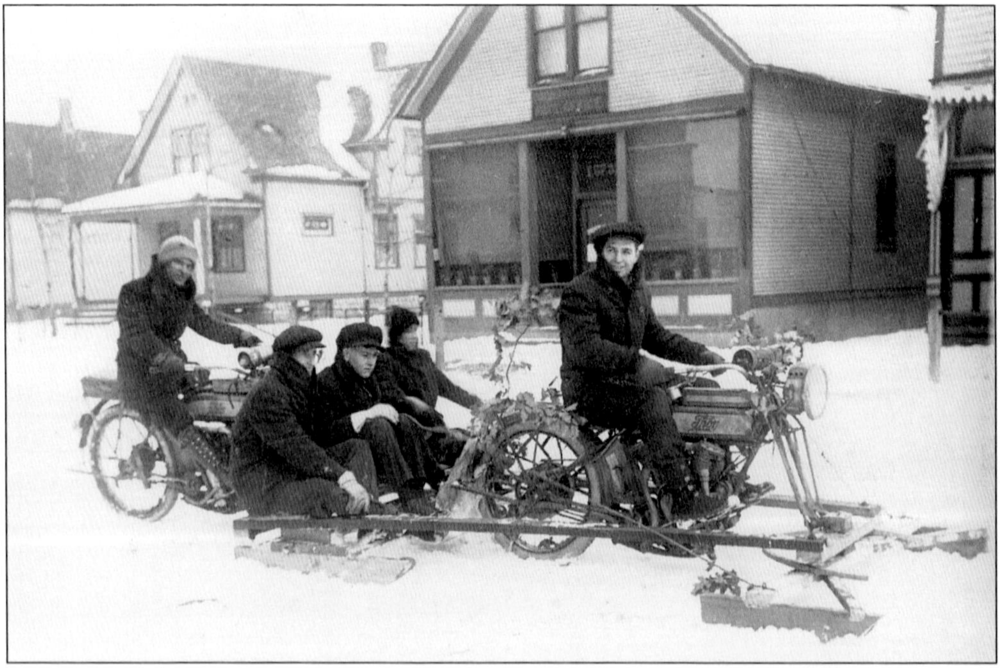

Some lads enjoy the winter weather by rigging up a home made snowmobile. On the front motorcycle is Russel Bales and on the rear motorcycle is Luke Van Drunen. Seated on the sled are Hank Van Drunen, Al Friesman, and Dick Van Dommelen. The snowmobile was made from a 15 horsepower Thor motorcycle by Russel Bales. (Photo courtesy of South Holland Historical Society from the collection of Dr. Carl Walvoord.)

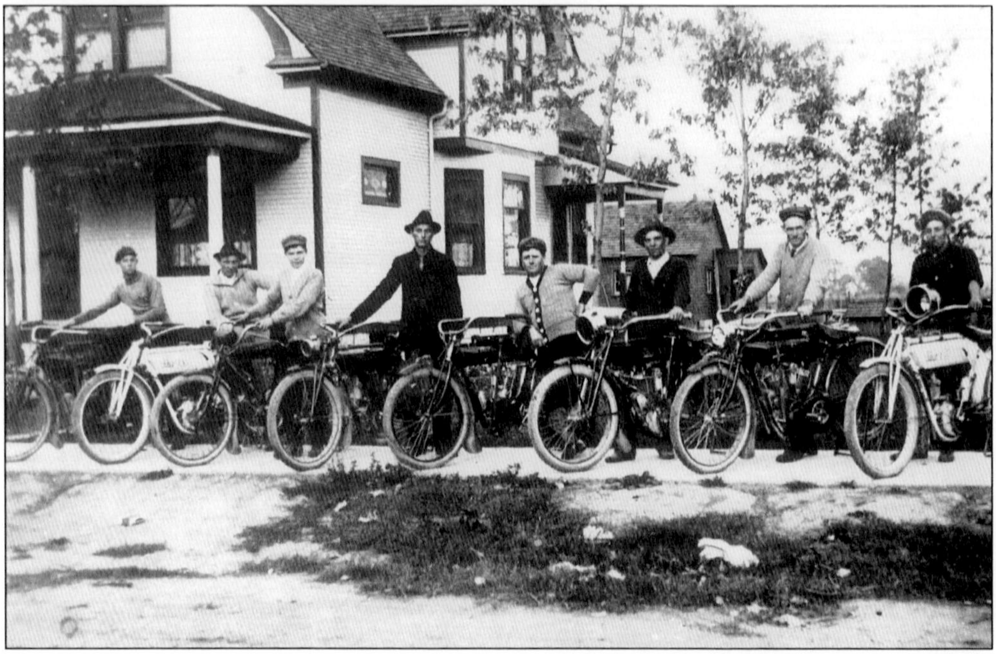

Motorcycles seemed to be a popular mode of transportation for young men in South Holland. (Photo courtesy of South Holland Historical Society from the collection of Dr. Carl Walvoord.)

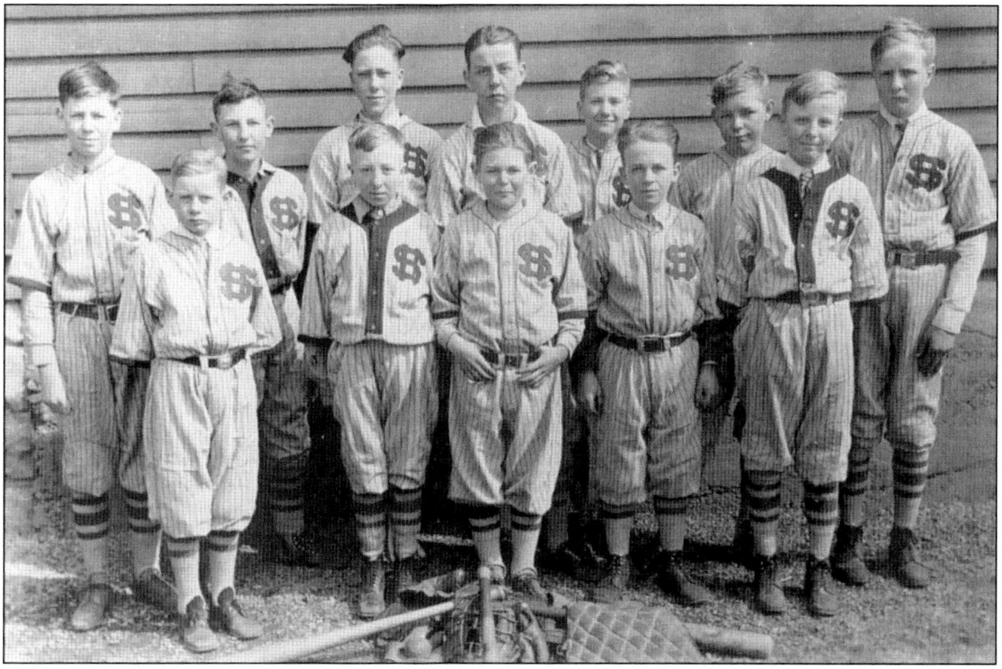

The 1930 baseball team at Roosevelt School. Pictured from left to right are: (front row) Henry Voss, Ray Vanderbilt, Richard Vanderbilt, Art Van Kley, and "Gabby" Kickert; (back row) Walter Dodson, Emery Hazelbrink, Cornelius De Graff, Henry Peerbolt, Henry Rinkema, Robert Van Vuren, and John "Spanky" Kickert. (Photo courtesy of South Holland Historical Society from the collection of Dr. Carl Walvoord.)

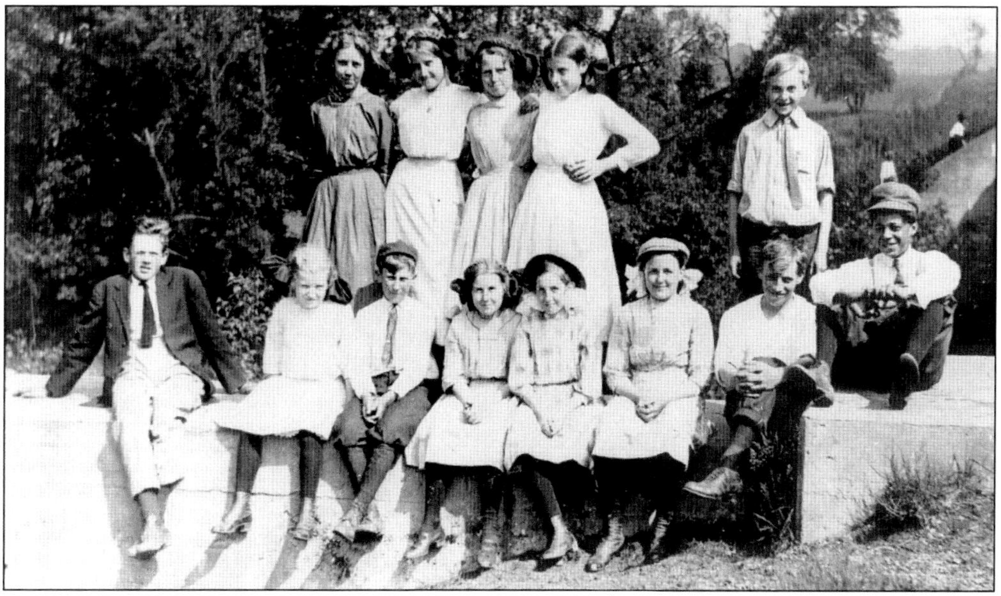

Pictured from left to right are: (front row) Henry Veld, Blanche Dalenberg, Seymour Rietveld, Mary Veld, Clara Koeslyher, Elizabeth Vyvernberg, Arnold Dalenberg, and Bill Rietveld; (standing) Minnie Rietveld, Cornelia Veld, Ribey Koeslyher, Annie Vinke, and John Dalenberg. (Photo courtesy of South Holland Historical Society from the collection of Dr. Carl Walvoord.)

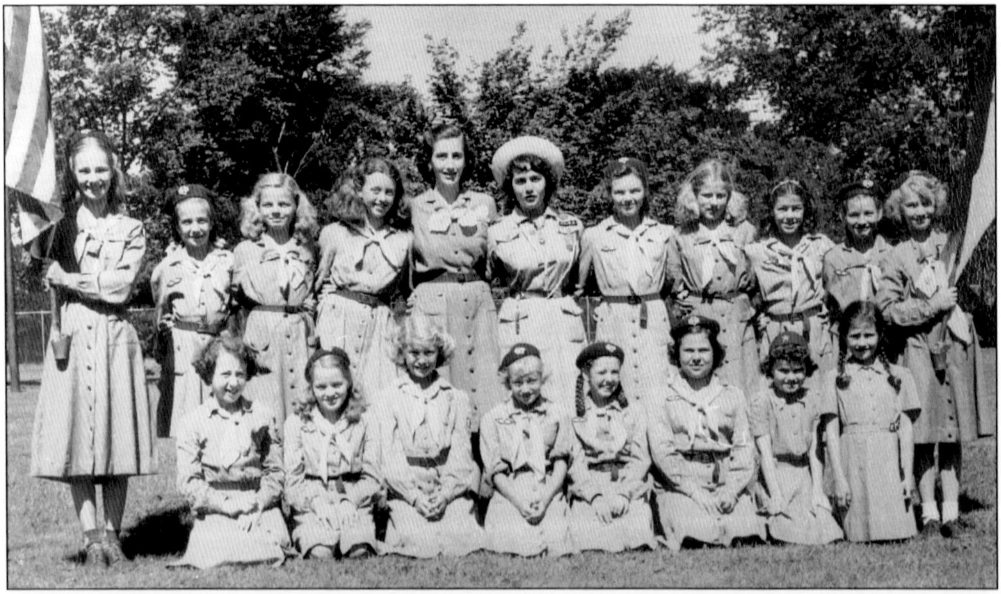

A group of South Holland Girl Scouts in the late 1940s. From left to right, they are: (front row) Ann Gordon, Nancy Gowens, Marlene Voss, Jeannine Hoekstra, Ruth De Young, Marion Wognum, Kathy De Young, and Kathy Wognum; (back row) Jane Gowens, Marlene Bardo, Ruth Tysee, Marilyn Kortenhoven, Maridell Braham, unidentified foreign exchange girl scout, Joan Koesma, Nancy Tysee, Cheryl Turngren, Gaye Van Duersen, and Donna Vander Wall. (Photo courtesy of South Holland Historical Society from the collection of Dr. Carl Walvoord.)

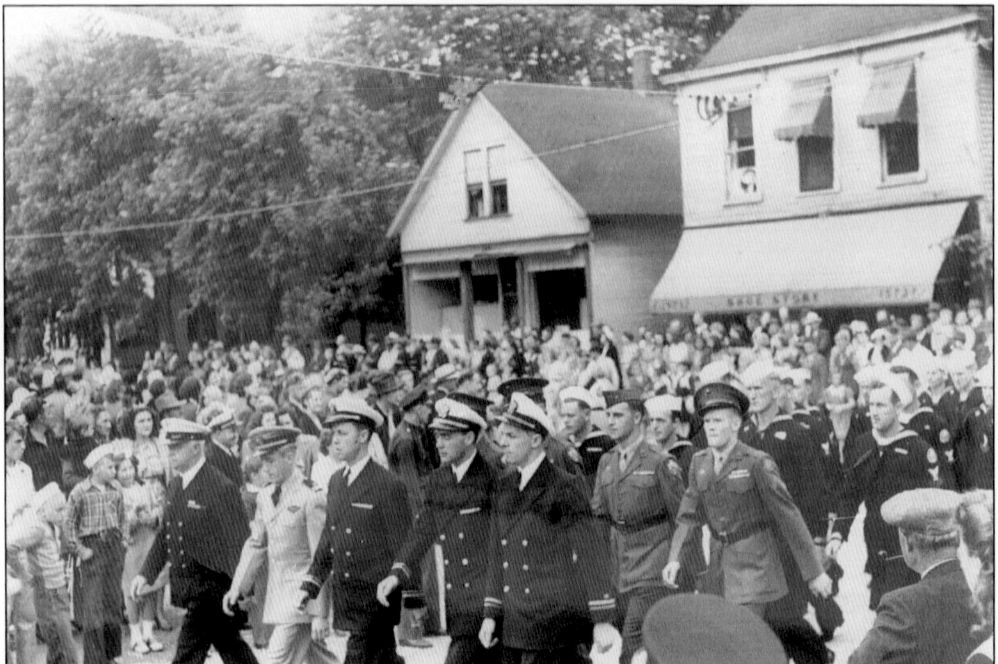

A World War II homecoming parade in June 1946. (Photo courtesy of South Holland Historical Society from the collection of Dr. Carl Walvoord.)

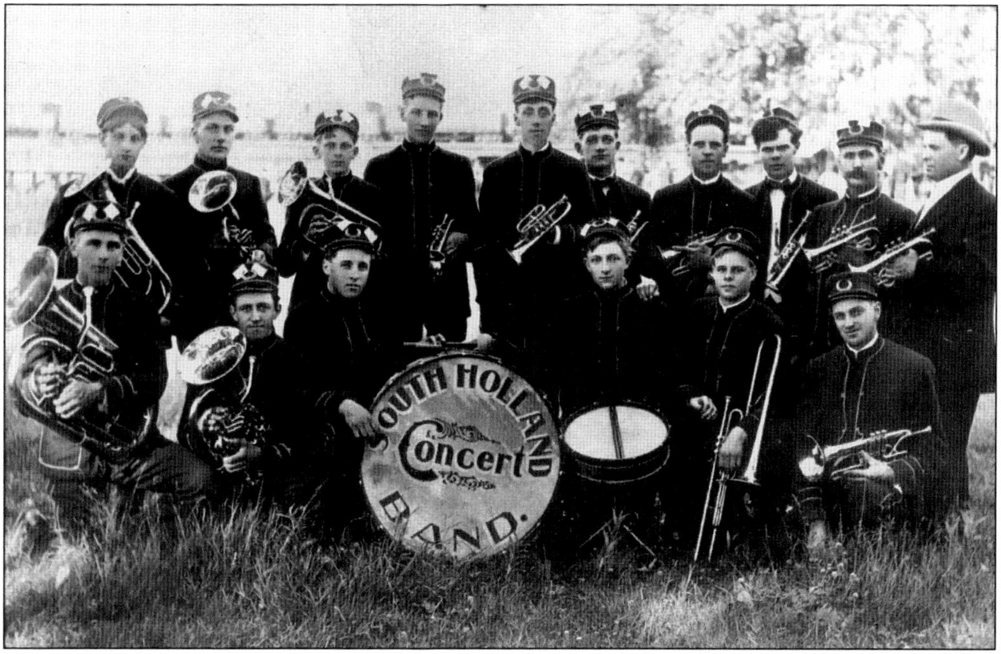

A photo of the South Holland Band prior to 1910. The band rehearsed in the old village hall. Pictured from left to right are: (front row) Tunis Verduin, John C. Rietveld, John Shilling, Estey Gouwens, John In Hout, and Peter T. Paarlberg; (back row) Peter Gouwens, Henry Versuin, Clarence Dalenberg, Tunis Gouwens, Harry Rietveld, Joe Fisher, Tunis Paarlberg, Ed Gouwens, Will Swets, and Director Robertson. (Photo courtesy of South Holland Historical Society from the collection of Dr. Carl Walvoord.)

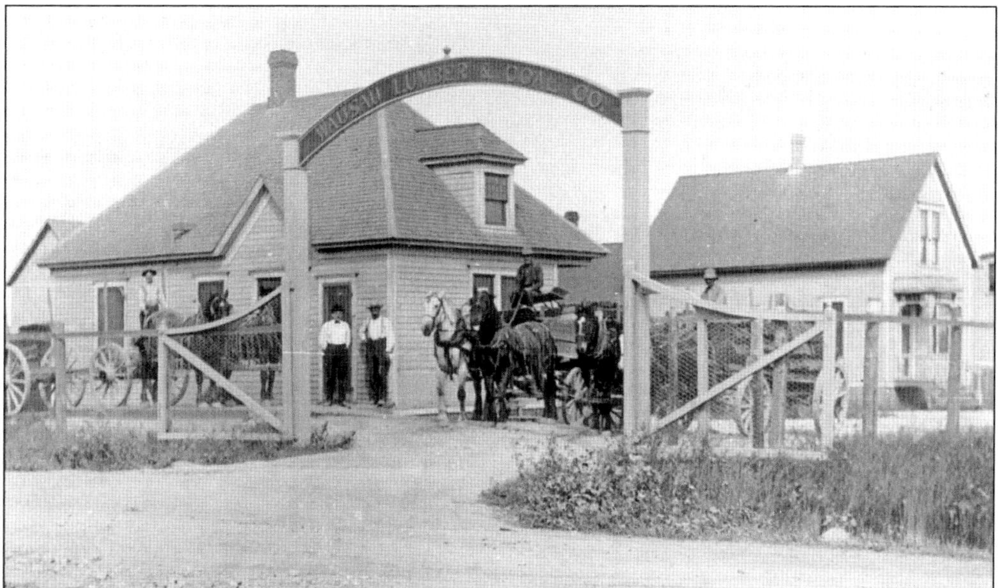

Wausau Lumber & Coal Co. was established around 1900. The front building was the office and the house behind it is was the residence of yard boss Mr. Santefort for many years. (Photo courtesy of South Holland Historical Society from the collection of Dr. Carl Walvoord.)

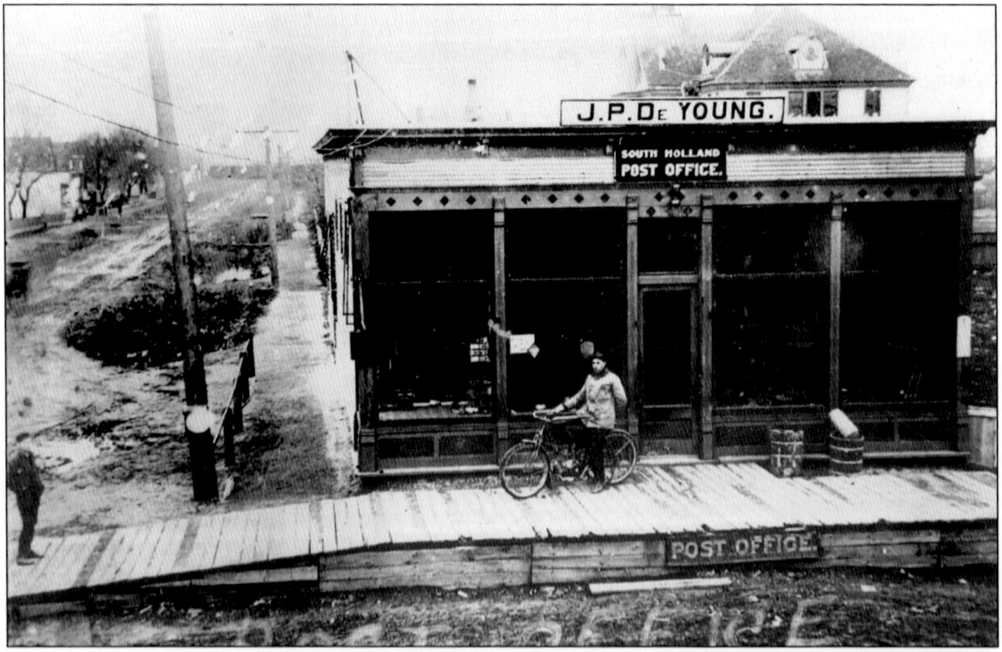

The J.P. De Young store served as the village's first post office. The South Holland Public School can be seen behind the building and the old horse hitching rail is to the left of the building. This was later Teddy Van Der Aa's store and ice cream parlor. (Photo courtesy of South Holland Historical Society from the collection of Dr. Carl Walvoord.)

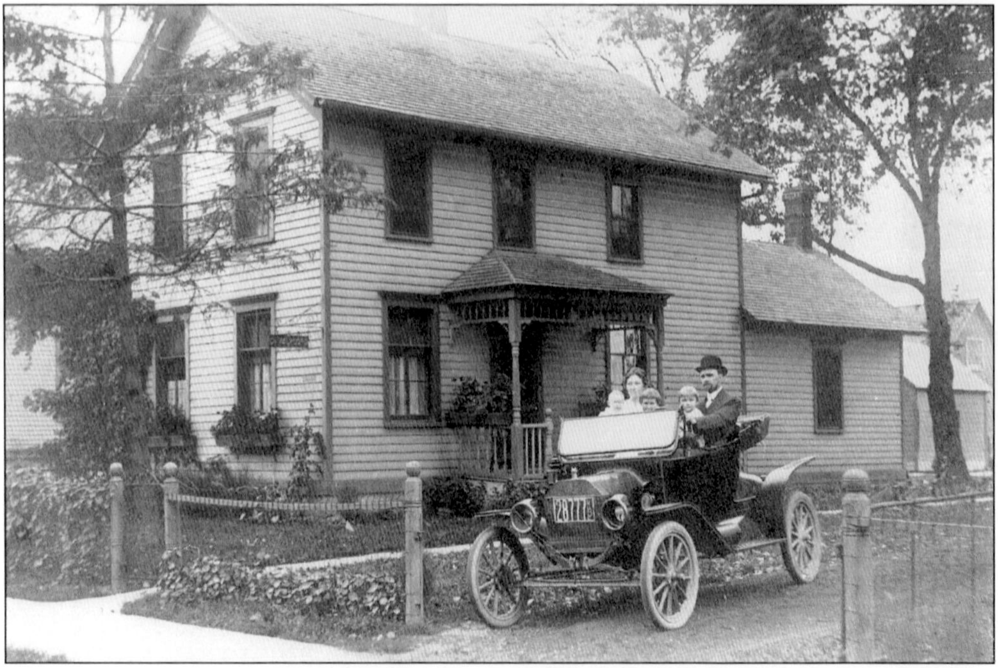

Dr. Gerrit W. Walvoord and his family are seated in the car in front of his home/office. His son, Carl, also became a doctor who practiced in South Holland. (Photo courtesy of South Holland Historical Society from the collection of Dr. Carl Walvoord.)

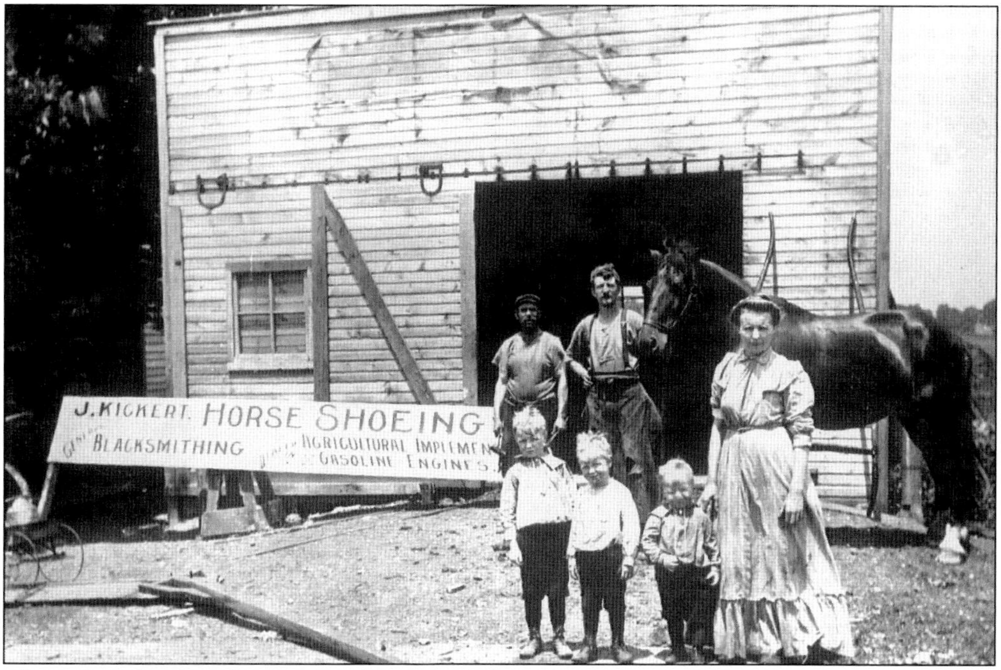

The Kickert family in front of their blacksmith shop. (Photo courtesy of South Holland Historical Society from the collection of Dr. Carl Walvoord.)

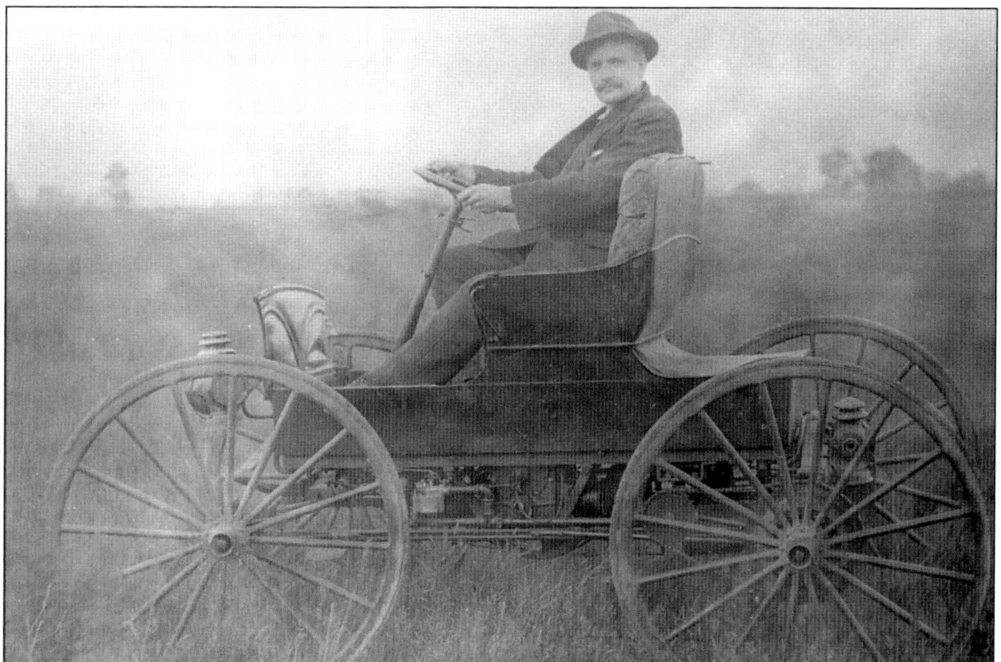

Joe Ravesloot was one of the first in the village to own an automobile. (Photo courtesy of South Holland Historical Society from the collection of Dr. Carl Walvoord.)

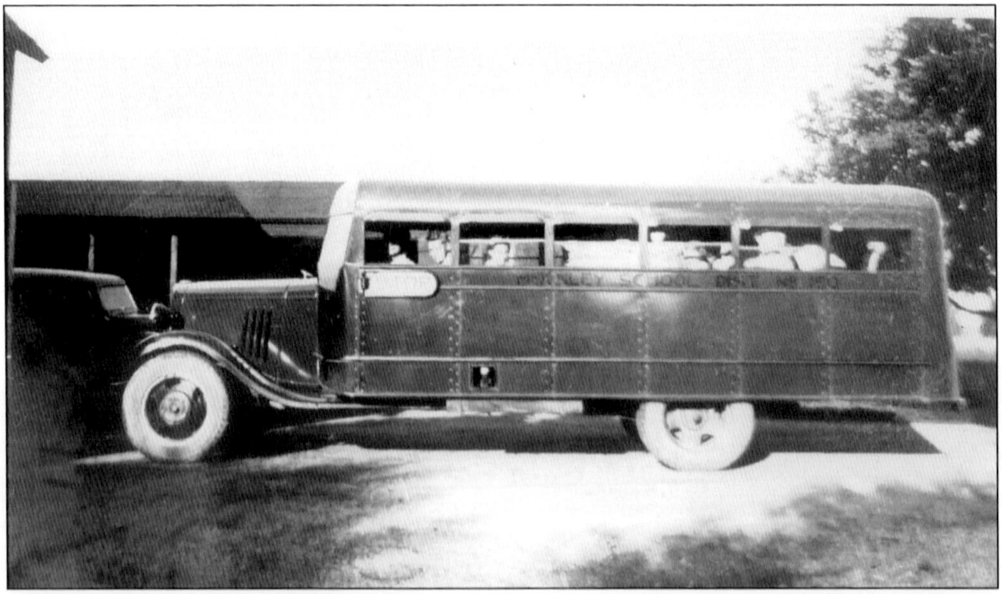

The first all-steel bus operated by the Van Der Aa's. The company is still in existence in South Holland today, now called VanCom Transportation. (Photo courtesy of South Holland Historical Society from the collection of Dr. Carl Walvoord.)

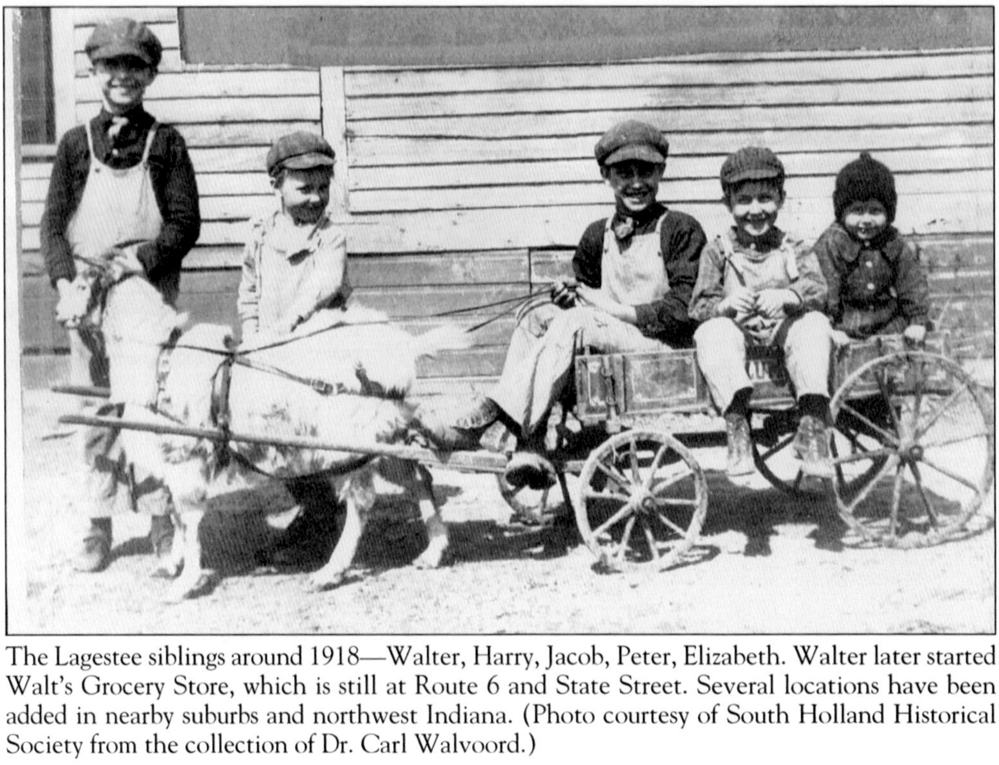

The Lagestee siblings around 1918—Walter, Harry, Jacob, Peter, Elizabeth. Walter later started Walt's Grocery Store, which is still at Route 6 and State Street. Several locations have been added in nearby suburbs and northwest Indiana. (Photo courtesy of South Holland Historical Society from the collection of Dr. Carl Walvoord.)

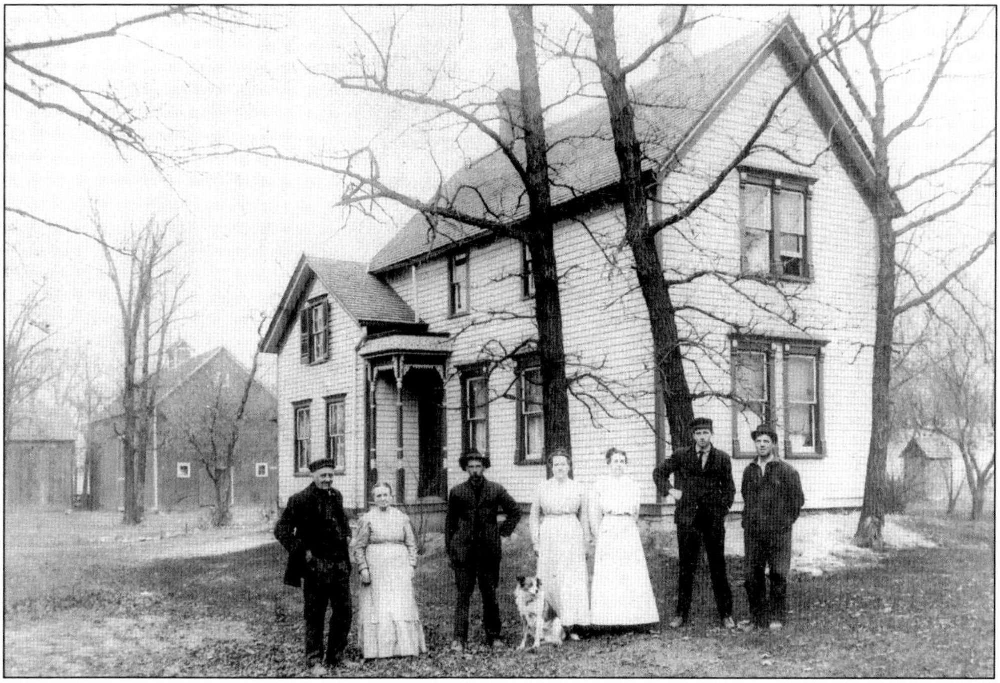

This home, built in the 1880s, still stands on land owned by the Paarlberg widow. It has been restored by the South Holland Historical Society and can be toured on weekends in summer months. (Photo courtesy of South Holland Historical Society from the collection of Dr. Carl Walvoord.)

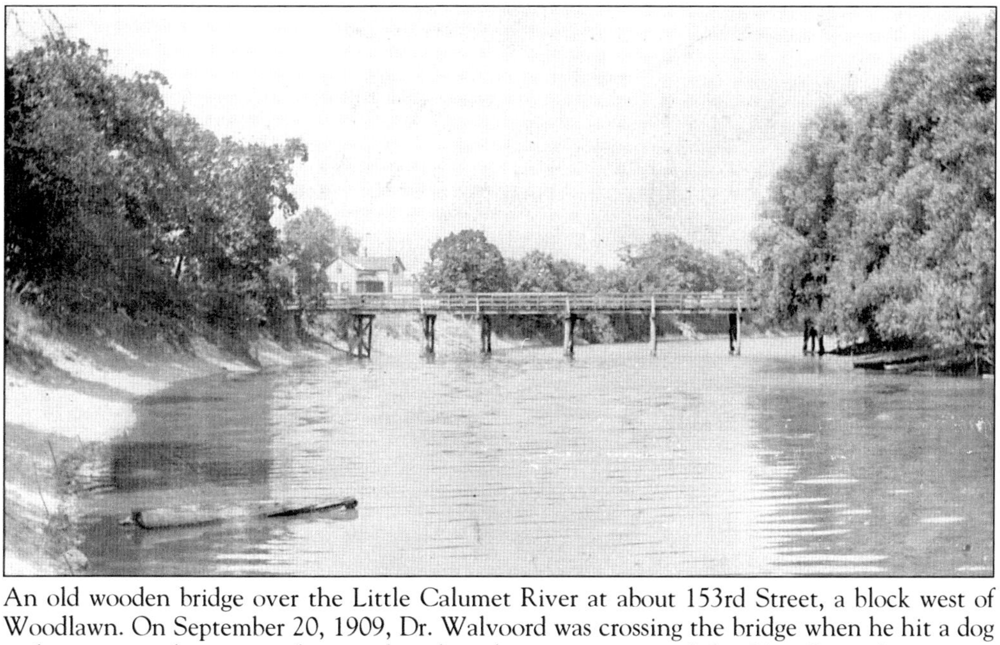

An old wooden bridge over the Little Calumet River at about 153rd Street, a block west of Woodlawn. On September 20, 1909, Dr. Walvoord was crossing the bridge when he hit a dog and went into the river in his car, knocking him unconscious. John Van Oostenbrugge was with him and pulled him out of the water, saving his life. (Photo courtesy of South Holland Historical Society from the collection of Dr. Carl Walvoord.)

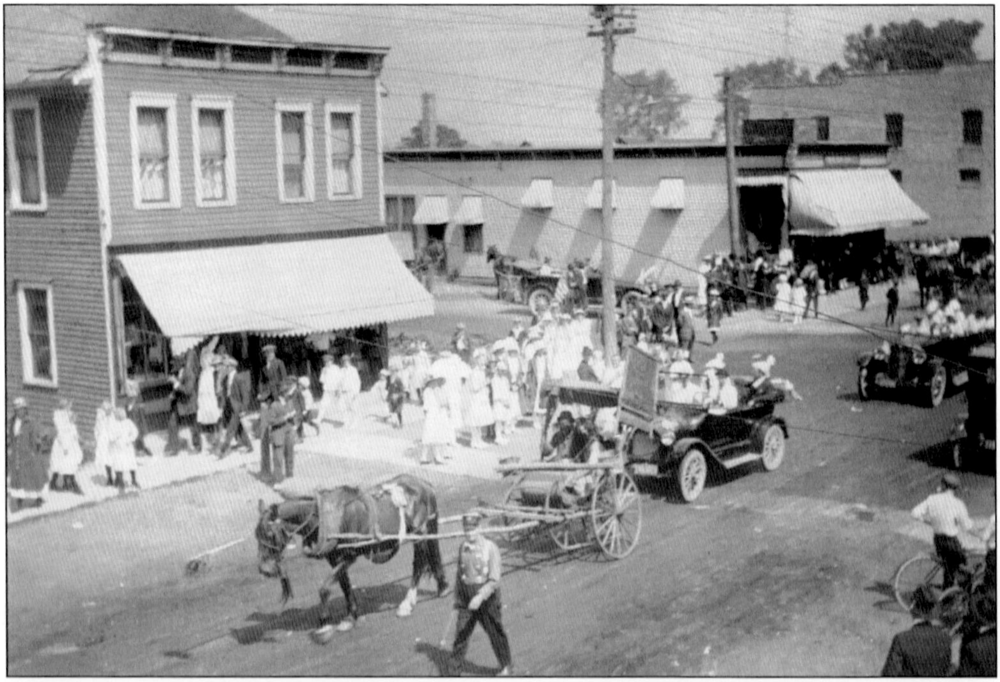

The fourth of July parade in 1915 on South Park Avenue (then Chicago Road). (Photo courtesy of South Holland Historical Society from the collection of Dr. Carl Walvoord.)

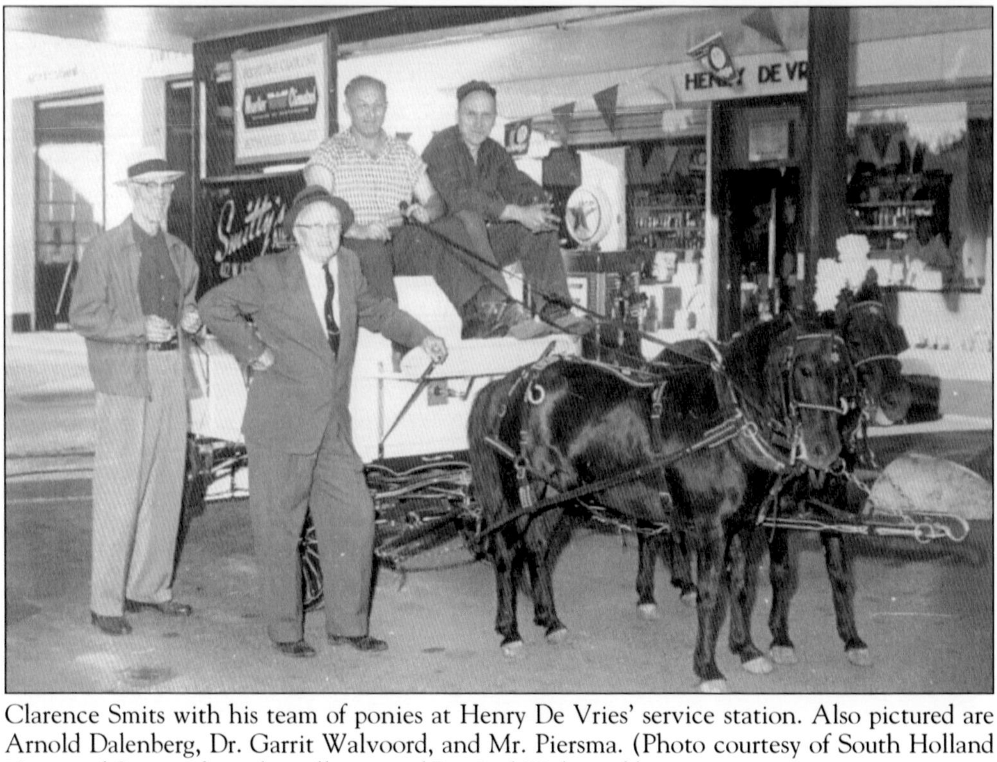

Clarence Smits with his team of ponies at Henry De Vries' service station. Also pictured are Arnold Dalenberg, Dr. Garrit Walvoord, and Mr. Piersma. (Photo courtesy of South Holland Historical Society from the collection of Dr. Carl Walvoord.)

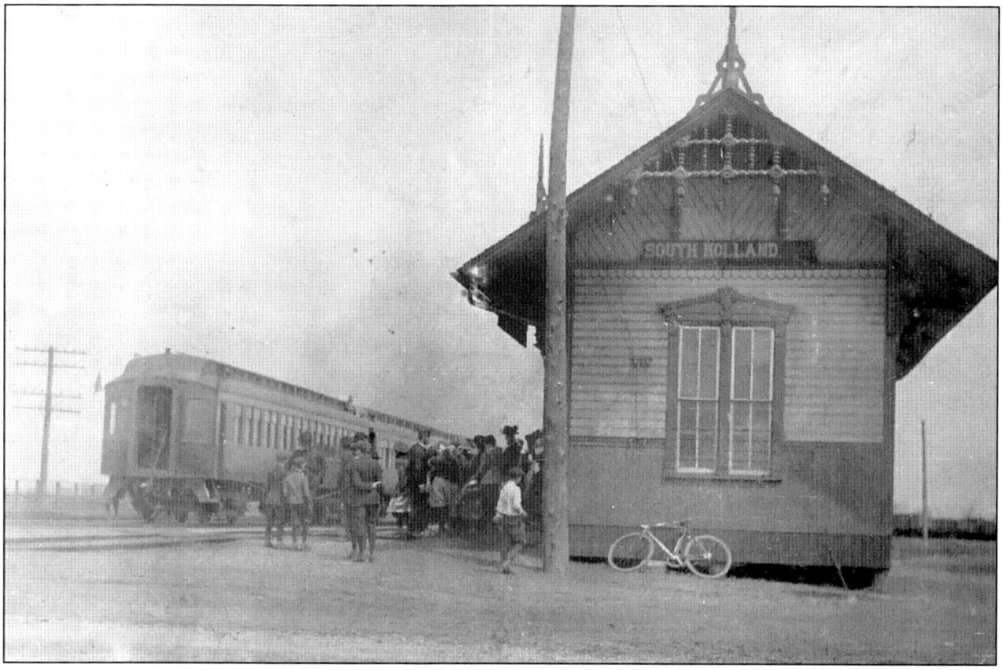

The old South Holland railroad station, seen here, burned in about 1910 or 1911. Jake Meeboer was the ticket agent. In this photo, the congregation of the First Reformed Church are bidding farewell to Rev. Harmiling. (Photo courtesy of South Holland Historical Society from the collection of Dr. Carl Walvoord.)

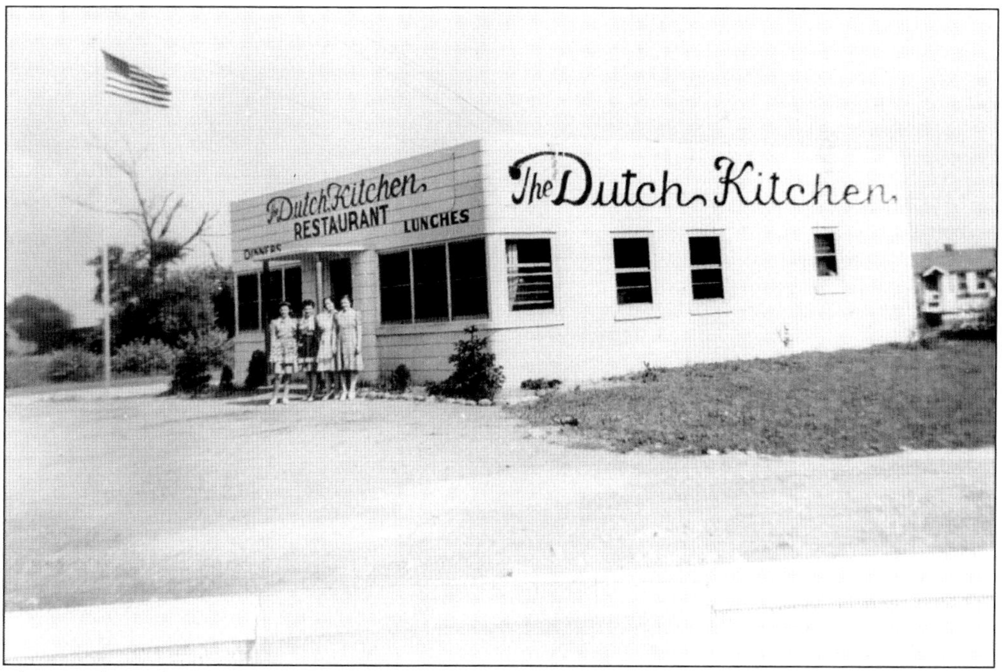

The Dutch Kitchen Restaurant opened in the fall of 1940, featuring the first neon sign on Route 6. (Photo courtesy of South Holland Historical Society from the collection of Dr. Carl Walvoord.)

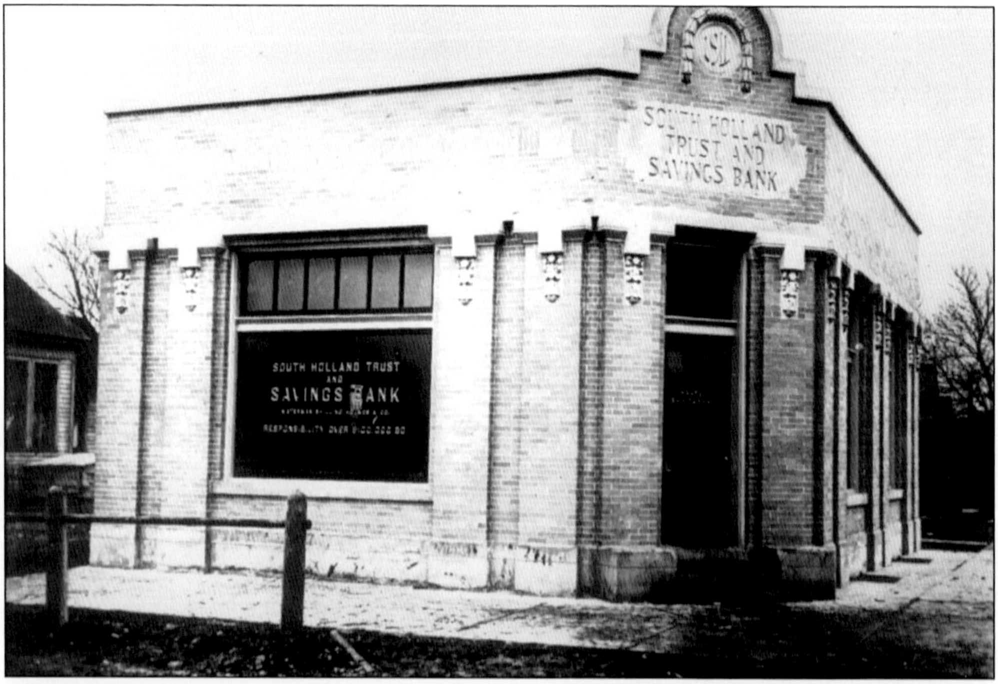

The South Holland Trust and Savings Bank was established in 1911. This is the first bank building that was located on the northeast corner of Route 6 and South Park Avenue. (Photo courtesy of South Holland Historical Society from the collection of Dr. Carl Walvoord.)

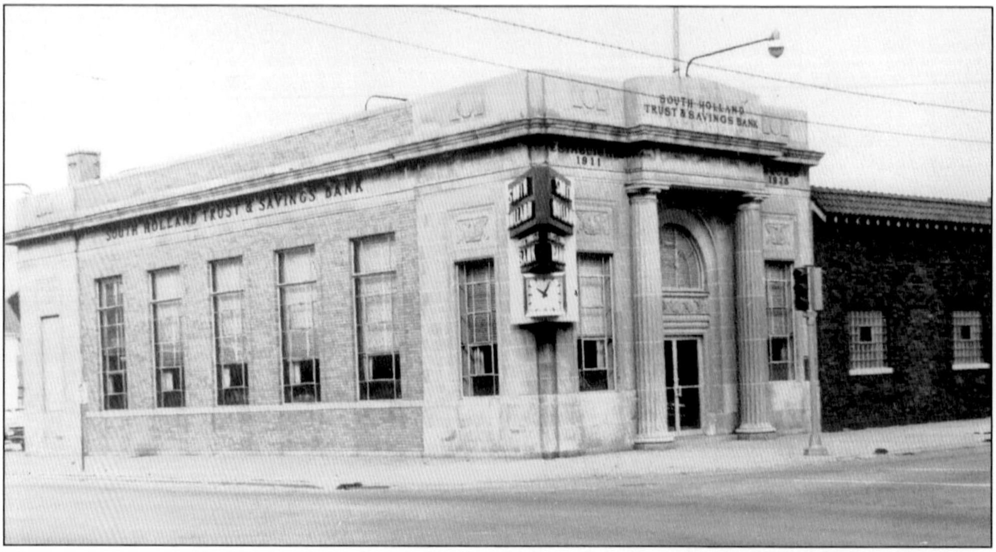

This is the second building of the South Holland Trust and Savings Bank, built in 1928 on the northwest corner of Route 6 and South Park Avenue. This picture was taken in 1955. This bank building saw four bank robberies during that year. A February 1934 bank robbery took the life of Peter De Young, who was filling in for his father, who was the regular watchman. In May of that year, a team of bank robbers returned to the bank, but the police and several citizens, including Mr. De Young, were waiting for them. The most recent bank robbery took place in 1950. (Photo courtesy of South Holland Historical Society from the collection of Dr. Carl Walvoord.)